LE, ILLINOIS————1922

BANK PRESIDENTS

E.M. West
1868-1887

W.R. Prickett
1887-1899

W.F.L. Hadley
1899-1901

Wm. H. Krome
1901-1917

George W. Meyer
1917-1933

Edward H. Stolze
1933-1942

W.L. Hadley
1942-1958

Leo W. Dustmann
1958-1974

John A. Hunter, Sr.
1974-1981

Robert A. Wetzel
1981-Present

TheBANK
of Edwardsville℠

Member FDIC

Main Office • *330 West Vandalia* • *Edwardsville, IL. 62025*
Phone 618/656-0057

On behalf of the directors, officers and staff of TheBANK of Edwardsville, we offer our sincere thanks to the people whose hard work, enthusiasm and love of history have preserved Edwardsville's heritage and traditions. We are pleased to present *Edwardsville: An Illustrated History.*

TheBANK is proud to have played a major role in the development of Edwardsville over the years. It is with this same pride we bring you this handsomely illustrated and well-documented volume. We are certain it will prove to be a valuable addition to your family library and a rare collector's item in the future.

Robert A. Wetzel
President & CEO
TheBANK of Edwardsville

TheBANK of Edwardsville was located on its original site, on the corner of Main and Purcell, for 104 years.

Edwardsville, Illinois:
An Illustrated History

by Ellen Nore and Dick Norrish

G. Bradley Publishing, Inc.
St. Louis, Missouri 63131

Edwardsville, Illinois:
An Illustrated History

BY ELLEN NORE AND DICK NORRISH

PUBLICATION STAFF:

Author:
> Ellen Nore
>
> Dick Norrish

Advisors:
> John Abbott
>
> Debbie Caulk
>
> Sue Dietrich
>
> Stephen Hughes
>
> Deanna Kohlburn
>
> Karen Mateyka
>
> Fern Stone
>
> Joe Weber

Cover Artist: Michael E. Bruner

Book Design: Diane Kramer

Photo Editor: Michael E. Bruner

Publisher: G. Bradley Publishing

Sponsor: TheBANK of Edwardsville

ISBN-0-943963-54-0
PRINTED IN THE UNITED STATES OF AMERICA

TABLE OF CONTENTS

Edwardsville's original public cemetery included additional land donated by John Lusk. It is located on Randle Street.

Introduction

A goal of the Edwardsville Historic Preservation Commission, founded in 1976, is to preserve and share the history of Edwardsville. The idea of compiling a book recording the history of Edwardsville came about as the Commission did research for various projects. As we researched, we realized there were many sources about the city's history, but nothing that was a comprehensive portrayal of the history of Edwardsville from the early 19th century to the present time. We have used a narrative form, enhanced by photographs, sketches, and first-hand recollections contributed by many Edwardsville residents to capture this history.

This book has been a labor of love and we hope that it will be enjoyed by the citizens of Edwardsville. The committee, comprised of members of the Friends of Leclaire, Goshen Preservation Alliance, and Edwardsville Historic Preservation Commission, is to be commended for its efforts. Many assisted in the extensive research necessary to make this first comprehensive history of Edwardsville as accurate as possible.

The Edwardsville Historic Preservation Commission and the book committee sincerely thank The Bank of Edwardsville for underwriting this history. Many thanks also to co-authors Ellen Nore and Dick Norrish for their expertise, persistence, and dedication.

We sincerely thank the Madison County Historical Museum for its cooperation and assistance. We appreciate the use of its many photographs and the extraordinary efforts of the research staff.

We now stand at the threshold of the next century and our beloved city is over 175 years old. To all present and future residents of Edwardsville, the Edwardsville Historic Preservation Commission presents Edwardsville: An Illustrated History. We hope you enjoy this book as much as we have enjoyed bringing it to you.

Edwardsville Historic Preservation Commission

Members: Karen Mateyka-Chairman, John Abbott, Debbie Caulk, Carol Fruit, Jamie Henderson, Kathryn Hopkins, Jean Hughes, Deanna Kohlburn, Steve Mudge, Meg Solon, Steve Stolte, Joe Weber, Jim Zupanci.

Publication Committee

Standing, left to right: Deanna Kohlburn, Fern Stone, Stephen Hughes, Debbie Caulk, Joe Weber, Sue Dietrich. Seated, Karen Mateyka. Absent from photo, John Abbott.

FOREWORD

On behalf of our residents, it is my pleasure as Mayor to present you an illustrated history of one of the oldest cities in the State of Illinois--Edwardsville. It is a city with a proud past and an exciting future; a city in which we take great pride and a city that we are blessed to call home.

As we embark upon our journey into the future, it is important to remember how we got to this point in time. From our origins in the Illinois Territory in the early 1800s, through statehood, the Civil War, the establishment of Leclaire, and into the twentieth century, the journey on which you are about to embark is a walk through our history.

The photographs show us the way we were, while the text introduces the people of Edwardsville--their accomplishments, their lifestyles, and the

roles they played in history. As you travel through the past, I hope you will, as I did, gain a new respect for where we came from and a keen understanding of how that affects where we are going as a community.

Edwardsville: An Illustrated History --
Let the journey begin.

Gary D. Niebur
Mayor
1996

EDWARDSVILLE CITY COUNCIL

Standing, left to right: Susan Donnelly, Winston Brown, Richard Madison, Janet Haroian, Richard Walker, Rosemary Bratten, Brent Bates, Joseph Simons. Seated: Nina Baird, city clerk, Gary Niebur, mayor, Diana McKaig, treasurer.

Thousands of years ago, families made a living from the land on which Edwardsville now sits. During the summer of 1992, archaeologists from the State of Illinois excavated a hunters' camp near Troy in Madison County that dates from before the end of the last ice age, 10,000 years ago.

By the year A.D. 800, the Mississippian city of Cahokia, whose population of many thousands rested on the production of corn, had begun expanding on the rich bottom lands southwest of the site of Edwardsville. This growing city needed enormous amounts of wood for fuel, for housing and for building and rebuilding a stockade wall perhaps two miles long around the central city. As the trees were chopped down around the site and on the bluffs to the east, less and less vegetation slowed the runoff, and the rains began washing more and more upland soil onto the bottom. Bottomland streams silted up, water flooded the cornfields, and the crops drowned. The great city declined, and its people, disgruntled and discouraged, dispersed.

In the immediate Edwardsville area, some prehistoric sites have been studied by archaeologists. Others---both contemporary with Cahokia and earlier---await discovery.

By the time Europeans arrived in the Illinois country, beginning in the 17th century, groups of people who spoke different but related Algonquian languages and who subsisted through a combination of growing corn, harvesting wild crops, such as hickory nuts and maple syrup, and hunting lived in many parts of Illinois. Marquette and Joliet, canoeing with their Kaskaskian guides down the Mississippi in 1673, surely glimpsed parts of Madison County. The place occupied by Edwardsville may have been the site of both summer agricultural villages and smaller winter camps. People who might have lived on the land now occupied by Edwardsville lived in buildings constructed of bent wood frames covered by large woven mats or big pieces of elm bark. They did not wear eagle feather headdresses. In the winter, they wore skin hats with the fur turned in, a style later picked up by Europeans. Many of the places occupied by the first white squatters along the creeks and in the flood plain of the Mississippi, known after 1783 as the American Bottoms, had been previously cleared by Indian men for fields of corn cultivated by women. No one saw buffalo in Madison County after 1800.

During the late 18th century and in the 19th century before 1830, Indian people were a common sight in the growing American towns in Illinois. Edwardsville, until 1824, was the site of an Indian Agency, which meant that peoples who had signed treaties with the United States came here to pick up annual payments, called annuities, for their ceded land. As long as they could, Indian peoples pursued their own ways of living in this land. Foreigners entering the Illinois country---Europeans, and Africans, who had first been brought here as captives by the French---exchanged material goods and ideas with the Indians. Eventually, however, the balance of power shifted to the invaders, who wanted to own Indian land.

The story is complex. In our area, part of what Richard White has called "the Middle Ground," many Indian villages during the 17th, 18th and early 19th centuries were multicultural. One could find families speaking different languages and practicing different cultural patterns living together. Between 1641 and 1701, the groups who spoke Algonquian languages and were lumped together as the Illini by whites [Kaskaskia, Cahokia, Tamaroa, Michigamea, Peoria, and some smaller groups] suffered defeat at the hands of Iroquoian invaders who tried to dominate all the peoples of the Great Lakes. The Iroquois' goal was to monopolize the fur trade and set the terms of exchange. Remnants of Illini groups shattered and crushed by these Iroquois Wars gathered together and formed what we today would call refugee villages. Several

Here comes trouble: Indian women do their best to frighten away a menacing flock of birds about to descend on their cornfield.

Maple syrup time came early every spring for natives of this area. The dome-shaped house, made of elm bark over a framework, had been in use for many years. But the Indians no doubt welcomed European trade goods like the axe, the barrel and the iron buckets shown here.

Tamaroa villages on the American Bottom near Kaskaskia in the 18th century were of this type.

Lethal germs unintentionally introduced by the Europeans significantly weakened native peoples' ability to hang on to their homes in the face of invasion. Indigenous populations, who had lived in the Americas for thousands of years in isolation, did not carry in their blood the antibodies possessed by African, Asian, and European peoples, who had been exchanging germs through centuries of trade and interaction. In 1600, a smallpox epidemic might wipe out one third of a European, African or Asian village, but a significant majority of persons would be left to carry on. In an American Indian village, such an epidemic usually killed more than ninety percent of the population. Measles, another foreign germ, could be equally devastating. Major epidemics swept the Illinois country in 1692, 1704, 1714, 1732, 1800, and 1828.

Finally, events conspired against Indian diplomatic strategy. When the European invaders of North America quarreled with each other, Indian diplomats sought secure survival by trying to keep the white enemies in balance with each other, keeping the role of go-between for themselves. After 1756, many groups sided with the French against the British, as the Europeans fought over North America. When the British defeated the French in the Great War for Empire, 1756-1763, the Indians' balance-of-power strategy was in trouble. During the American Revolution and the War of 1812, the British gained many Indian allies by promising to deliver desirable presents and to protect Indian lands in return for Indian assistance. But the British lost these wars. Afterwards, Indian peoples of the Northwest Territory often resisted the takeover by the United States and its agents of their fields and homes. But despite some significant victories in the early 1790s, they gradually lost the battle.

From a white viewpoint, Indian title to the lands of Madison County had been "extinguished," as they said, by the Treaty of Vincennes of August 13, 1803. Kaskaskias, Michigameas, Cahokias, and Tamaroas had yielded their claims. The survey of Madison County by John Messenger and others, the division of the County into townships and ranges, began in 1806. Because surveyed land could now be "legally" sold and titles granted to non-Indians by the Government of the United States, a federal land office opened in Edwardsville in 1816. However, Kickapoo peoples, who regarded the area around Edwardsville as part of their hunting grounds, continued to use it.

In the Treaty of Edwardsville in 1819, some representatives of the Prairie Band of Kickapoo agreed to future cession of their lands in Illinois. In the same year, by terms the Treaty of Fort Harrison, some of the Vermillion Band of Kickapoo also agreed to a cession. These negotiations, which resulted in the eventual removal of the Kickapoo from Illinois in 1833, represented a personal victory for Ninian Edwards, Territorial Governor of Illinois (1809-1818) and later Governor of the State (1826-1830). As a businessman with extensive real estate holdings, he regarded the Kickapoo as a men-

Here's a typical Kickapoo house and storage platform. The roofing is of bark; tightly woven mats of cattails or similar plants kept the weather at bay.

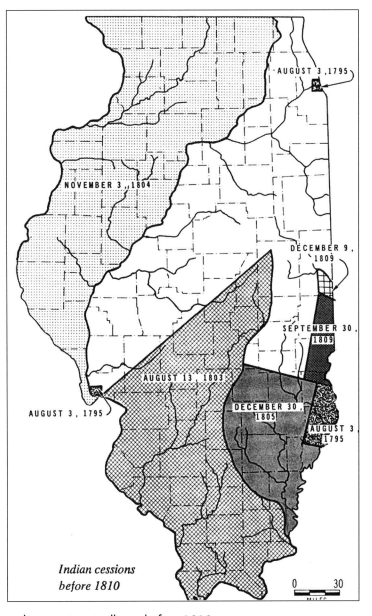

Indian cessions before 1810

Indian cessions in Illinois before 1810.

ace to sales. On December 24, 1814, the territorial legislature had passed an act offering a bounty to encourage whites to enter Kickapoo territory, that is lands which still belonged to the Kickapoo and not to the United States, and kill Kickapoo people. A sum of $100 was offered to any person entering "the Territory of any hostile indians" who killed "any indian warrior" or took "prisoner any squaw or child." Rangers going into Kickapoo land to kill or capture would get $50 per dead warrior or woman/child prisoner. (Rangers belonged to militia units mobilized for service by the United States.)

In contrast to the suggestion of a famous painting of the Treaty of Edwardsville, 1819, hanging in the Madison County Administration Building, Ninian Edwards was one of more than 30 witnesses to the signing of the treaty, which was negotiated by Benjamin Stephenson, who had the contract for the Indian Agency in Edwardsville, and by Auguste Chouteau, the other official representative of the United States Government.

THE EMERGENCE OF EDWARDSVILLE

Squatters came to the site of future Edwardsville, during the first decade of the 19th century, before the surveyors with their chains and compasses had marked the sections as Township 4, Range 8. After treaties with the Illinois Indians in 1803 and 1804, white and occasionally free black pioneers could risk squatting on land without fear of retaliation. Thomas Kirkpatrick, two of his brothers, and a large clan of Gillhams arrived from South Carolina on or near the site of our town in about 1805. Thomas had purchased from Pierre Lejoy, a Frenchman who had been enrolled in the U.S. Militia on August 1, 1790, a warrant for any 100 free acres. Congress had granted unspecified plots of land to these soldiers in an effort to recruit men at a time when Indian peoples in the Old Northwest were successfully defending their homes against the United States. Kirkpatrick brought the paper to a site on the Cahokia Creek and marked off 100 acres, later noted as Sec. 23, T4N, R8W,

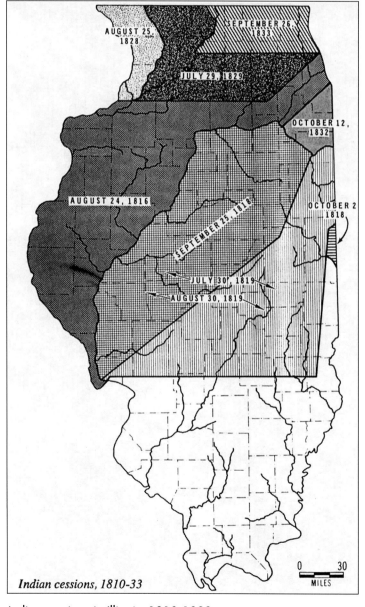

Indian cessions in Illinois, 1810-1833.

A Kickapoo woman holding a prayer stick.

A Kickapoo man adorned in feathers and beads.

and recognized as his by a U.S. Land Commission in 1809. The Commission also recognized "preemption" claims of five Gillhams and three Kirkpatricks, to eight adjoining bundles of 320 acres each, totalling 2560 acres, mostly situated on Cahokia Creek.

Of the Gillhams, we know much, since they persisted and became "Old Settlers" of Madison County. Their ancestor arrived in British America, probably in Philadelphia, from Protestant Ireland in 1730. Although we cannot verify this, the Kirkpatricks were probably part of the same world historic migration across the Atlantic Ocean in search of land, the greatest wealth for aspiring families in that culture. Gillhams and Kirkpatricks followed the Shenandoah Valley to Virginia and then continued to the western regions of South Carolina, where we find them at the time of the American Revolution. According to lore furnished by Gillhams to the author of Brink's *History of Madison County* (1882), the father of Thomas Kirkpatrick and his brothers had been shot and killed at the dinner table by angry Tory neighbors. Unlike most of the backcountry folk, who were staunch Tories, Thomas' father had fought with the American army during the Revolution. After James Gillham came to the Illinois Country in 1794, numerous Gillhams and the Kirkpatricks followed, taking up land in and around what was not yet Edwardsville.

Thomas Kirkpatrick combined public service with

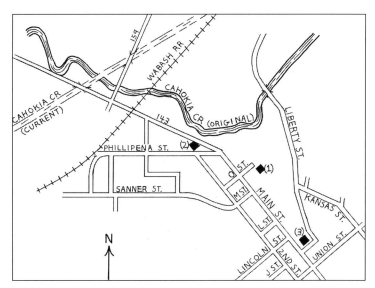

Cahokia Creek. This map shows the course of Cahokia Creek as it appeared before and after it was diverted and channelized around 1912. Originally, Main Street came to an abrupt end shortly past where it is currently intersected by Phillipena Street. From there the land sloped steeply down to the creek bed. To help control the flood prone creek, it was straightened and diverted around 1912 to flow directly into the Mississippi River to the west. To facilitate orientation, three well-known structures are indicated: (1) The site of Thomas Kirkpatrick's cabin near the present home at 100 East O Street; (2) The Klingel home at 1801 North Main Street; and (3) Lincoln School.

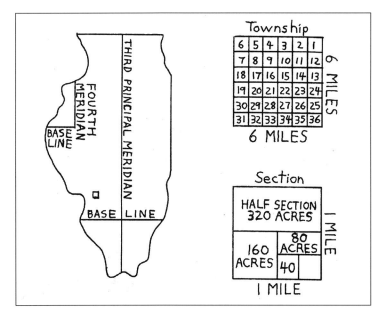

The Township-and-Range-System. The Land Ordinance of 1785 established the township-and-range system of parceling the land. The basic territorial unit is the six-mile-square township. These townships are laid out according to a system of north-south meridians and east-west baselines. Edwardsville Township, for example, is located as being 4 north of the baseline and 8 west of the third principal meridian. The townships themselves are divided into thirty-six sections numbered in sequence, beginning at the top right and ending at the bottom right. Each section is one-mile-square, containing 640 acres. The sections, too, may be further divided.

This water mill probably is much fancier than the flour mill Thomas Kirkpatrick built on Cahokia Creek almost 200 years ago. Few, if any, authentic drawings of the buildings built in Edwardsville's earliest days exist today.

profitable business enterprises. In 1805, the Papers of Indiana Territory reveal that he had been appointed to the St. Clair County Court of Common Pleas. Illinois was separated from Indiana Territory in 1809, and Ninian Edwards was appointed Governor. When Madison County was created in 1812, Governor Edwards designated Kirkpatrick's house as the County Seat. When the first session of the Court of Common Pleas was held, Thomas Kirkpatrick served as judge. In 1816, Edwards appointed him a County Judge.

Meanwhile, Kirkpatrick had built a water-powered flouring mill on Cahokia Creek and obtained both a merchant's license and a permit to keep a tavern. In 1814, he platted a town on his land and named it for his political patron. Documents of 1816 establishing a U.S. Land Office record the name, Edwardsville. The Madison County tax list of 1814 shows Thomas Kirkpatrick with one person in slavery and six horses.

After 1816, it is likely that Kirkpatrick moved on to Bond County. He disappears from the surviving traces of life in Edwardsville, and his name appears as judge in the Court of newly created Bond County. He also represented Bond County at the Constitutional Convention of 1818, which drew up the frame of government for the new State of Illinois. Although he appears in the Madison County Census of 1818, a notoriously corrupt count, taken for purposes of demonstrating that Illinois possessed the 40,000 population necessary for Statehood, Kirkpatrick also appears on the Bond County census of the same date.

Notable historian, Solon Justus Buck, wrote that only 18 households comprised of 166 people, can definitely be attributed to Edwardsville in the Census of 1818. He counted 74 "white" men and 71 "white" women and children grouped together. Seventeen persons, presumably African Americans, were slaves or servants, while four were free persons of color. Eight of the slaves belonged to Benjamin Stephenson, registrar of the land office whose house still stands on Troy Road, and four belonged to Ninian Edwards, who was counted a resident in this census. At least three and probably four of the households were taverns where more than half of the men boarded. A traveler passing through in 1819 spoke

A modern sketch shows what Kirkpatrick's home may have looked like. Starting in 1812, this building served as the first courthouse here.

These three pictures are of Edwardsville's oldest house, at 1712 North Main Street. The original log cabin (top left) was built in 1805, by Thomas Kirkpatrick, to accommodate workers who would build a larger home for Kirkpatrick nearby. Sometime in the 19th century, it was enlarged and sided over (top right), and by 1939, a front porch had been added. The house looks pretty much like this today.

of Edwardsville as "a small but flourishing little village."

After statehood, in May 1818, Hooper Warren began to publish the town's first newspaper, *The Spectator*, which lasted until 1826. Ever after, residents have enjoyed at least one newspaper. In 1817, Madison County officials had contracted for the building of the first of four official courthouses, this one a log structure long gone, which stood on the east side of present Main Street now occupied by the former Lincoln School building. In 1818, the State Legislature chartered a Bank of Edwardsville to receive payments from sales of the public lands. The presence of a flour mill assured a steady stream of business for the town outside of Court days. According to a local account written in 1864, "the big store" in Edwardsville during the early days of statehood was kept by Robert Pogue, who offered readers of *The Spectator* goods ranging from Prime Green Coffee to Bed Cords and Ink Powder.

Because of his many responsibilities as Territorial Governor (1809-1818) and dealer in real estate, Ninian Edwards must have spent much time in Edwardsville

before Illinois became a State in 1818. He lived with his family in Edwardsville during his terms as a United States Senator, 1818-1826. Local history places Edwards' home at the site of present-day St. Boniface Church. The home burned around 1823. Land records show Edwards owned the lot at the corner of Fillmore and E. Vandalia, a corner lot of St. Boniface property. Local newspapers carried his ad in July 1819 for building materials to be delivered to Edwardsville for a 2 story brick home, using his timber without charge. The Edwards family stayed with the Benjamin Stephenson family for some time after their home burned, and then lived in Belleville

Hooper Warren published *The Spectator*, the first newspaper here. Warren was a staunch opponent of slavery.

Print shop.

The Benjamin Stephenson house, on South Buchanan Street, dates from 1820 and is the oldest brick building in Edwardsville.

This building housed Robert Pogue's store, and the Indian Agency after 1819. Today, brick walls of this building survive within Rusty's Restaurant at 1201 North Main.

FOR SALE,

SEVERAL quarter sections of LAND, on Crooked creek, in town 1, N. range 1, west of the third principal meridian, including a first rate mill seat.

800 acres of Land, part well timbered, the balance rich prairie, on Shoal creek, near Mr. Barber's, and about three miles north of the road from Carlyle to St. Louis, including one of the best mill seats on Shoal creek.

800 acres first rate Land, with a suitable proportion of good timber and rich prairie, on Silver creek, adjoining or near to the town of Lebanon, on the road from Carlyle to St. Louis. This tract also includes a good mill seat.

160 acres of well timbered Land, on Cahokia creek, about six miles above Edwardsville, including a good mill seat.

About 490 acres, principally timbered Land, on Richland creek, about 2 miles above Belleville.

Three quarter sections of very rich prairie Land, about 2½ miles east of Belleville.

Several quarter sections of Land in Ogle's Prairie, directly between Belleville and Edwardsville.

Land, land, land by the hundreds of acres was advertised for sale by Ninian Edwards, for whom Edwardsville is named, in the *Edwardsville Spectator* on July 24, 1819.

A YOUNG ARTIST IN EARLY EDWARDSVILLE

On May 19, 1818, Anna Maria Von Phul, a young artist from Lexington, Kentucky, while visiting her brother Henry in St. Louis, traveled to Edwardsville in the Illinois Territory to visit her sister and brother-in-law, Sarah and John Mason. Maria traveled with her watercolors, pencils and sketch book and made a series of drawings and paintings of subjects she observed along the way. She painted keel boats and boatmen and several trees in and around Edwardsville. Because of this visit and several others in 1819, 1821 and 1823 to St. Louis and Edwardsville, there remains today a rare record of life in the early days of the Missouri and Illinois territories. Over 100 of her drawings and paintings reside in the collections of the Missouri Historical Society, St. Louis, Missouri.

During a visit to Edwardsville on July 23, 1823, she became ill and died at her sister's home. Her obituary appeared in the Edwardsville *Spectator* on August 2, 1823. She was 37 years old.

A sketch by Anna Maria Von Phul. Courtesy of the Missouri Historical Society

By Joe Weber, SIUE Department of Art and Design, 1996

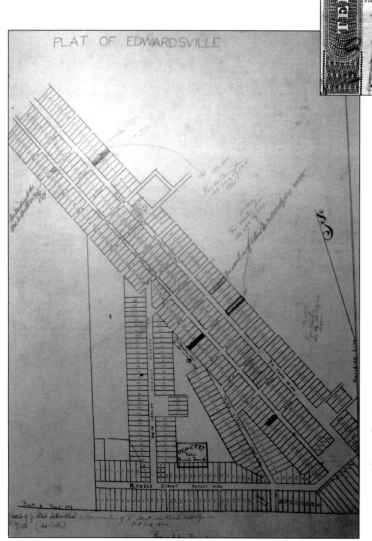

PLAT OF EDWARDSVILLE

A $10 note issued by the state-chartered Bank of Edwardsville after 1818. This bank, which failed, has nothing to do with the present-day The Bank of Edwardsville. It has been suggested that the scene on the bank note is an artist's conception of early Edwardsville.

Shown is one of the oldest plat maps of the town of Edwardsville, drawn in 1825 and redrawn in 1908. Notice the courthouse square.

where Edwards died in 1833.

Born to a wealthy family of tobacco farmers in Montgomery County, Maryland, Edwards had a good education at private schools and with tutors before he went to Kentucky at the age of 19 to study law. In Kentucky, he was Chief Justice of the Court of Appeals and a loyal Jeffersonian. President Madison appointed him Territorial Governor when the Territory of Illinois was created in 1809. Before building a family home in Edwardsville, Edwards probably boarded at one of the local taverns, perhaps that of his friend Thomas Kirkpatrick. During the War of 1812, it is likely that he lived at Fort Russell, which he ordered to be constructed soon after the United States declared war on England. Fort Russell, the location of which is now unknown, was a few miles northwest of the present Edwardsville. According to John Reynolds, later Governor and a young ranger at Fort Russell, Governor Edwards

made this frontier post his headquarters. . . . .This fort was not only the [seat] of military operations, but was also the resort of the talent and fashion of the country. The Governor opened his court here and presided with the character that genius and talent always bestow on the person possessing them. The cannon of Louis XIV. . .were taken from old Fort Chartres, and with them. . .Fort Russell blazed out . . . .

Fort Russell formed part of a number of local forts constructed in Illinois to protect American communities from attacks by Indian peoples allied with the British. There is no evidence that it witnessed any action during

the War, but from it, Edwards launched several expeditions against Indian villages near Lake Peoria.

When Illinois was admitted to the United States in 1818, he was elected a short-term Senator by the legislature and re-elected for the full six years in 1820. From 1826 to 1830, he served a term as Governor of Illinois. In 1832, he ran for a seat in the House of Representatives and lost. He died of cholera during an epidemic of 1833, which struck him down at his new home in Belleville.

As a businessman, Edwards made considerable money as a land speculator. He was a proprietor of Belleville, owning more than 100 lots there. He owned 100 acres, including a good mill seat on the St. Mary's River 10 miles below Kaskaskia. He bought for resale lots near Kaskaskia. In an early issue of the *Edwardsville Spectator* [June 19, 1819], he advertised land near Carlyle and Lebanon, on Ogle's Prairie between Edwardsville and Belleville, and six miles above Edwardsville on Cahokia Creek. Advertisements for the same parcels appear in the *Intelligencer* published at Kaskaskia. He well represents the entrepreneurial spirit that motivated many early capitalists of American towns in Illinois.

During the first two decades of the 19th century, Edwardsville gradually emerged as a town, a recognizable and named center of population. This was a process. It did not happen in a day, a week, a month or a year. Edwardsville appears gloriously on John Melish's "Map of Illinois," prepared for the General Land Office in 1818,

Ninian Edwards, political leader and wealthy dealer in real estate.

As a political and business center, Edwardsville attracted many people, like Ninian Edwards, who were here only long enough to conduct their business. While here, they probably boarded at a log tavern like this one.

Much about Fort Russell, intended to ward off attacks by Indians allied with the British, is veiled in mystery. Exactly where was the fort? What did it look like? This model in the Madison County Historical Museum is an educated guess.

This patriotic group gathered in 1912, during the county centennial, at what they believed to be the site of Fort Russell.

along with the older French towns, Kaskaskia, Prairie du Rocher, St. Philips, Cahokia, and newer American villages, some now extinct: Chicago, Belleville, Alton, Ripley, Perryville, Independence, Pope, Albion, Mt. Carmel, Shawneetown, Golconda, Massac, America, Cairo, Jonesburg, Carlisle.

Official recognition is not a reliable means of dating the existence of towns. The first place in Illinois incorporated by a government of the United States was Shawneetown, chartered by the territorial legislature December 8, 1814. The last territorial legislature, in January 1818, made Kaskaskia, a town since 1704, a city, and chartered the City of Cairo, which existed only on paper. In 1819, Illinois' first State Legislature granted charters to Belleville, Carmi, and Edwardsville. The Second General Assembly, in 1821, incorporated Alton and the new capital, Vandalia. Mt. Carmel received a charter in 1825. Before 1830, Illinois had nine officially recognized incorporated places but many more actual towns. Edwardsville's citizens take pride in their town's status as the fourth oldest officially recognized by the new state of Illinois, as determined by State records.

Between 1812, the first territorial census, which showed 12,282 persons, and the census of 1850, Illinois' population reached 851,470, ninety-two percent of whom were farmers. By 1850, Edwardsville was no longer a cen-

Thomas Ford, lawyer here, later governor.

Thomas Ford, Governor of Illinois, 1842-1846, who practiced law in Edwardsville from 1825 to 1829, described Ninian Edwards campaigning for Governor in 1826:

Edwards was a large, well-made man, with a noble, princely appearance, which was a circumstance greatly in his favor as governor over a rude people, of whom it may be said that the animal greatly predominated over the intellectual man. . . . [H]e never condescended to the common low arts of electioneering. Whenever he went out among the people he arrayed himself in the style of a gentleman of the olden times, dressed in fine broadcloth, with short breeches, long stockings, and high, fair-topped boots; was drawn in a fine carriage driven by a negro; and for success he relied upon his speeches, which were delivered with great pomp and in a style of diffuse and florid eloquence.

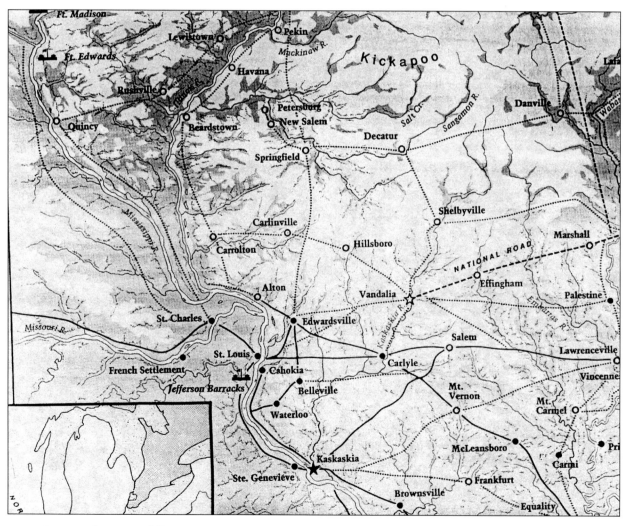

Map shows early towns of Illinois.

ter for the transfer of public lands. It had settled into its future role as agricultural market and county seat. In 1840, the population was 616. In 1850, 677.

LIFE IN THE REGION OF EARLY EDWARDSVILLE

John Reynolds, governor from 1838-1842, loved Southern Illinois. His family's journey to the Illinois country is fairly typical of the majority of emigrants before the 1840s, who came to Illinois from the Carolinas, Tennessee, and Kentucky. In Spring 1807, Joseph Reynolds, John's father, purchased a "plantation" in the Goshen settlement three or four miles southwest of Edwardsville. John Reynolds remembered that, as a young man of nineteen, he had thought it "the most beautiful country that I ever saw." His parents were both Irish-born Protestants. John, their first child, arrived after they had immigrated to Pennsylvania in 1788. When he was six months old, the family, including both sets of grandparents, had removed to Tennessee, near Knoxville. When John was five, they pushed on to "the interior" of Tennessee. In 1800, the Reynolds family, mother, father, six children, "a colored woman," three hired men, and eight horses pulling two wagons started for Illinois. Crossing the Ohio at what became Golconda, Illinois, they walked overland the 110 miles to Kaskaskia, taking four weeks because of spring rains and the necessity of fording many swollen waterways. After a few years of planting corn with the French families on the common field at Kaskaskia, the Reynolds group headed north to Goshen in 1807.

Because the public lands had not yet been surveyed in the region of Edwardsville, Reynolds notes that most of these pioneers were "squatters on government lands." Reynolds' father purchased a squatter's improvements. The Gillhams, Whitesides, and their "connections" were already occupying Goshen. John and his father came ahead of his mother and the rest of the children and "made a crop of corn."

In 1855, John Reynolds remembered his activities as a pioneer hunter, an activity essential to feeding the family. Deer still abounded, but the raccoon and muskrat, he wrote, "are measurably hunted out, until there are only a few of them in the State at this day." Even in 1807, he had seen few otter, beaver and elk. Flocks of swans, which he had observed on the Bottom in 1807, were no more in 1855. Though Reynolds did not comment on wolves, W. R. Brink, historian of Madison County, noted that Illinois territory paid a bounty of seventy-five cents for wolf scalps and that in 1816, wolf-scalp certificates showed a total of 121 for the county, with a number of payments to Gillhams and Whitesides, neighbors of the Reynolds family.

Starting to farm the prairie meant hours of hand labor. "At that day, the sickles, or reap-hooks, were the only implement used to cut the wheat. . . . Reaping with a sickle was a severe labor." In these "olden times," Reynolds remembered threshing and cleaning the wheat. "The Americans used horses at times to tread it out. About the hardest work I ever performed," said Reynolds, "was winnowing the wheat with a sheet."

Relief from such labor came through neighborly cooperation in house-raisings, with horse races, Fourth

John Reynolds: "The most beautiful country that I ever saw."

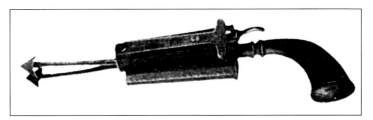

A bear trap, tool of the early hunter. The pistol was loaded, the barbs pushed together and baited with meat and the handle fastened to a tree or stake. When the bear pulled at the bait, both bullets were fired and the barbs spread out, catching the animal in the mouth or throat.

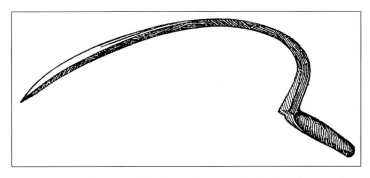

Frontier agriculture was hard work, most of it by hand, as with this sickle, used to cut wheat.

of July "frolics," and Protestant camp meetings, where families took food and stayed for several days to hear preaching and, perhaps, to feel the call of the Holy Spirit. Reynolds joined crowds in spring 1807, at the "first camp-meeting that was ever held in Illinois" on Mr. Good's farm, about three miles south of Edwardsville. Perhaps because he knew how to read and expressed his feelings in other ways, Reynolds took a distant view of

persons seized by "the jerks" during these religious services. "It seemed an involuntary exercise, and made the victims sometimes dance and leap until they were entirely exhausted, and would fall down helpless on the ground." As they gyrated, "the parties would generally shout and cry aloud on the Lord. . . . These jerks," Reynolds added, had "long since disappeared."

Letters of pioneer farmer Gershom Flagg furnish yet another perspective on country life around early Edwardsville. Flagg was a comparatively wealthy Yankee who purchased 1000 acres of surveyed land, mostly prairie, some for speculation, in section 3, township 5, range eight. Born in Vermont in 1792, Flagg had served as a drummer during the War of 1812 and studied surveying in Burlington, Vermont after the war. He left declining New England for Ohio in 1816. Stricken by "Illinois fever," he voyaged down the Ohio river to Cairo, walked to St. Louis in 1817 and worked there painting the first steamboat on the Mississippi. Early in 1818, he crossed the river and joined the ranks of men and women farming around Edwardsville. In 1827, he married Jane Rich, the widowed daughter of his Massachusetts-born neighbor Gaius Paddock (1758-1831). Gaining fame as a surveyor and agricultural innovator, he kept constantly in touch with a wide circle of family, ten brothers and sisters, and friends in St. Louis and the East. Gershom's letters, the many writings of Willard Flagg, Gershom and Jane's only child born in 1829, and the diary of Willard's wife, Sarah, form a valuable historical legacy.

These New Englanders were atypical innovators and

Washington C. Ballard, an early circuit-riding preacher.

Agricultural innovator Gershom Flagg taught others about the richness of the prairie soil.

experimenters. As Barbara Lawrence and Nedra Branz, historians of the Flagg family point out, they possessed the capital to buy new tools coming on the market and to hire tenants and other workers to do much of the hard labor. While the Reynolds family and many others farmed lands on the American Bottom, Gershom Flagg was among the first to break the prairie and display its richness. This challenged the wisdom of many pioneers from the South, who firmly believed that big trees signaled the richest land and thus made their first fields by clearing forested areas. During 1819 and 1820, Gershom ploughed about 100 acres of prairie land, "with the help of four yoke of Oxen and a man to drive them." Because the roots of prairie plants often penetrated to depths of ten feet, and because existing plows were made of wood with a cast iron tip, not polished steel, breaking the prairie sod before the late 1840s was expensive. The same year, Gershom fenced in 40 acres and built a log house for his tenant. (Before his marriage in 1827, he boarded with his future father-in-law, Gaius Paddock.) By 1845, when Gershom's farms ranked among the most valuable land in the county, another old settler recalled that "Mr. Flagg, a Green Mountain boy, but not a greenhorn, undertook to make a farm on the prairie in Madison County, and was told by the settlers in the thick woods that he was crazy to think of cultivating land that was so poor as not to bear timber." When he died in 1857, neighbors and friends also remembered Gershom's orchard of 300 seedlings, planted in the spring of 1822.

John Reynolds, Gershom Flagg, and other farmers of the area around early Edwardsville viewed themselves as agents of transformation. Willard Flagg, supplying information on the "Progress of Horticulture" for Brink's *Illustrated Encyclopedia* of 1876, located individual pear trees planted by early pioneers, including a "noted Lady apple" growing on a farm long since incorporated into the town and the 40 trees set out by Solomon Pruitt "grown from the seed of a yellow apple brought up from the French settlements." The only native evergreen, the "red cedar" fringing the bluffs and occasionally found growing in isolation "inland," had been joined by Norway Spruce, brought from the East in 1836 and by White Pine in 1838. Non-native crops, such as red clover, oats, winter wheat, and bluegrass made their appearance in the 1820s, but varieties of corn developed

---

A WEALTHY YOUNG FARMER IN 1825

I have 275 acres Land 60 acres fenced into 5 fields and under good cultivation an Orchard of 530 apple trees 100 Peach trees twelve Cherry trees & pear trees also a well and several log buildings. I rent all my farm except the orchard of 13 acres to a man who lives on the place and gives me 390 bushel[s] of Corn and 50 bushels wheat pr. annum. I board with a family half a mile from my farm at $1.25 per week including washing. I have four yoke of good oxen 4 Chains yokes & c good ploughs two wooden Carts two sleds one large Grindstone two axes 4 augers shovel, hoe, & c a Surveyors Compass and two Chains and Mathematical instruments worth 60 dollars. I purchased last June about 15 hundred acres of valuable land for the taxes which amounted to $103 dollar. . . I owe $56 dollars and have due me $110 from good men and have $34 in cash on hand I have twelve shirts six pair Pantaloons 6 vests ten cravats & handkerchiefs two roundabouts [short jackets] 4 pair stocking two pair shoes one Coat in Short I suppose my whole property to be worth about $1500 in cash and I do not wish any one to see this letter except yourself.

Gershom Flagg to his brother, Artemas
Edwardsville, August 16, 1825

Early prairie plows had wooden blades tipped with cast iron.

by Indians were still preferred. Gershom Flagg wrote his brother, Artemas, in 1820 that he had used seed "brot from the Mandan Nation of Indians who reside 12 hundred miles up the Missouri."

Until cheaper Southern cotton gradually made it uneconomical between 1836 and 1854, local families often grew cotton and sometimes flax for their own clothing. People wore cotton, woolens, and linens made by female family members' spinning thread and weaving cloth on their own looms. According to Brink (1873) women and children, often bare-footed, wore "moccasins (when they wore anything)". But "wedding shoes. . . were made of leather to order." Men wore leather shoes and often, buckskin pants.

Between 1818 and 1836, families' labor on the wheat harvest was lightened by the invention of the grain-cradle, attached to a large one-person scythe, which caught the wheat as it was cut and saved the back-breaking labor of gathering the cut stems from the ground. Threshing, that is, separating wheat grains from the stem before machines appeared to do this, was usually accomplished by hand with a flail or by having horses walk over the stalks. The resulting grain could be quite dirty. Separation of dirt and chaff from the seed, winnowing, done for centuries by tossing the grains into the air, was improved before 1836 by a hand-cranked fanning mill, which blew out the impurities. After 1850, wealthier farmers began to plow with steel, to reap with a mechanical reaper, and eventually, to use steam-powered threshing machines.

Remembering early crops in 1873, Willard Flagg pointed to another Vermonter, John Adams (b. 1796), who came to Edwardsville in the early 1820s. Adams first set up a wool-carding mill to which farm people brought wool washed and cleaned of burrs to be prepared for spinning by the women of the families. Then, beginning in 1825, Adams pressed castor oil from seeds of *Ricinus communis*, paying farmers between $1.25 and $1.50 per bushel or with bottles of the finished product. Castor

Heinrich Christian Gerke, a German citizen, visited his son who farmed near Marine and wrote:
I spent a most pleasant winter (1831-32) in Edwardsville. The town has but one street and unpaved at that. It is situated on a ridge alongside the Cahokia river, has a castor oil mill, a woolcarding machine, a flouring and saw-mill, on the Cahokia; four attornies' offices. . . ; one physician--- Dr. Edwards, brother of my friend, Ninian Edwards, . . .; a post-office. . . ; a real estate broker's office. . . ; a newspaper office . . . ; a United States land office; five stores of some magnitude. . . . and one tavern, with the sign, "Washington." During the winter of my stay we had six balls and two soirees. . . and every Saturday a meeting of the literary and debating society. On the twenty-second of February the militia was out on parade. . . inspected by the honorable [John] Reynolds, governor of the state, who remained four days occupying my room at the tavern. Thus I got acquainted with the American city or town life.

This early wagon, drawn by cattle in this picture, was made by hand.

oil, a bitter pale yellow fluid, was taken by spoonfuls as a laxative. Adams produced 14,000 gallons of the stuff in 1835, branching out with smaller mills in Alton and Brighton. Adams tried unsuccessfully to make Edwardsville into a center for sugar made from beets.

LAW AND JUSTICE IN THE EARLY TOWN

Frontier justice in Edwardsville, like justice of any age, any locale, presented moments of gripping drama. Here are two examples, one about the lack of African-American rights and a stable-owner's wife who showed great courage, and the other, about a killer, a reluctant judge and a famous Baptist preacher.

James D. Henry, from humble circumstances in Pennsylvania and Ohio, came to Edwardsville in 1822, and set up shop as a shoemaker. Regarded by townspeople as peculiar, Henry had little education, but a desire to learn and an enormous ambition to make something of himself in the militia. Henry was also prone to violent fits of temper. One day, according to Brink's *History of Madison County* (1882):

He fancied that a negro named Jarrett, who belonged to Joseph Conway, had insulted him, and he inflicted on the black man a terrible revenge. The negro had taken refuge in the stable of Rowland P. Allen, whence Henry dragged him forth. Stripping him of all his clothing, except his trousers, he fastened him to the end of the horse rack in the public street. He had procured five hickory withes as the instruments of punishment, and laying a sword and pistol on a block within three feet of his victim, with a dagger in one hand and whip in the other, he began to lash the poor negro unmercifully. When the negro drew back on the rope and begged for mercy Henry would draw the keen edge of his bowie knife over the negro's naked abdomen and threaten him with instant death unless he submitted quietly to the punishment. Court was in session, and a hundred men were in town, present and looking on, including the sheriff and other officers of the law, but none dared to interfere.

When he had used up his second, or third whip, the wife of Rowland P. Allen heard the [man's] cries and ran to his rescue. Appealing to the men present in vain, she went back to her kitchen, and procuring a formidable carving knife, rapidly approached and cut the rope by which the negro was bound. Henry stood still with astonishment, suspending his blow in the air, and as the woman led the negro away said threateningly that a woman might tie his hands but it would not have been well for any man to have done to oppose him.

Readers of this anecdote are left to wonder about both the fate of the battered man and the lone woman who displayed no fear of a bully and defied a hundred gawkers, including men of the law. We imagine her determination to do the right thing as she saw it.

James D. Henry left Edwardsville for Springfield in 1826, became sheriff of Sangamon County, and later led militia as a general in the brief Black Hawk War (May-August 2, 1832). This encounter pitted 7,000 Americans eager for military glory against a small band of no more than 500 Sauk and Mesquakie [called Sac and Fox by whites] warriors and their families. After starving during the winter of 1831-32, the Indians had returned from lands in Iowa to plant corn in the fields of their ancestral village, Saukenuk, near present-day Rock Island, which whites argued had been ceded to them.

A second story of justice in early Edwardsville concerns the hanging of Eliphalet Green, whose hot temper cooled dramatically at the end of a rope on February 12, 1824. Brink's chapter on the early law tells us that Green, who worked at a distillery on Wood River, quarreled one day with another employee, named William Wright. Green---said by local people to be "slow"---went to get a gun and then, in a fit of rage, shot Wright to death as Wright left the distillery. Green fled. But his conscience got the better of him and he surrendered in Edwardsville the next day. During Green's trial in the court of Judge John Reynolds, later fourth governor of Illinois (1830-34), there was some question as to the charge. Was it first-degree murder, premeditated? Or was the shooting the rash result of temporary insanity? The jury opted for the stronger charge because Green had taken the time to run and get his gun. The crime took place in December, the trial in January, and the hanging in February.

Eliphalet, according to the Second Book of Samuel, was one of the sons of David. His name means "God is deliverance." Whether or not Eliphalet Green knew this is unknown, but he did seek religion in his final days, summoning the noted Baptist circuit rider, John Mason Peck, to counsel him. Peck spent many hours with Green, who felt the rush of salvation. Villagers cut a hole in the February ice so that Peck could baptize him in the waters of Cahokia Creek. Peck stood with Green at the hanging. For 2000 spectators, Peck preached a sermon and read a memoir about Green, which Green had dictated. There were hymns, and onlookers sighed as Green's hands clasped in prayer came apart in death.

Judge Reynolds later presented himself as an opponent of capital punishment, who, forced to pronounce Eliphalet Green's death sentence, completed "the most painful duty I ever performed." Several sources noted Reynolds peculiar speech at Green's sentencing:

Well, Mr. Green, the jury in their verdict found you to be guilty of murder, and the law says you are to be hanged. Now I want you and your friends down on Wood River to understand that it is not I that condemns you but the jury and the law. Now I want to allow you all the time you wish to prepare, so the court wants to know at what time you prefer to be hanged.

Green is said to have replied that any time would suit him.

21

CHAPTER 2: GROWTH, REFORM, AND THE WAR OF THE REBELLION

EDWARDSVILLE AND NATIONAL TRENDS

As mid-century approached, Edwardsville remained a small town, but it reflected national trends. Like the nation in the nineteenth century, Edwardsville's population doubled about every 25 years. During the 1850s, the town reconfigured itself, and the physical outlines of Edwardsville as we know it today began to emerge. Log cabins huddled along the ridges around Cahokia Creek gave way to more substantial brick and sawed wood structures. As local agriculture thrived, so did the town. Edwardsvillians participated in the Age of Reform that preceded the Civil War. As communications improved, political activity, interest, and participation expanded. Highly organized parties, Republicans and "The Democracy," emerged to replace the "gentleman's politics" and the looser Whig and Democratic Parties of previous eras. People thought carefully about the question of slavery, the meaning of freedom, and the structure of economic opportunity. When political crisis became civil war, men and women of all persuasions pulled together to rescue their nation.

A GROWING TOWN

In 1834, according to John Mason Peck's *Gazetteer of Illinois,* only 70 families, about 350 people, resided in the town. A vote taken in 1837 on the issue of incorporation under a law of 1831, showed 57 white male voters in favor and seven against. Alton had absorbed some of the trade that had gone to Edwardsville in the 1820s. But during the 1840s, the population reached between 700 and 800, and by 1860, almost 2,000. In 1853, Edwardsville was again incorporated, this time by a special act of the legislature under the new Illinois Constitution of 1848.

During the 1840s, Edwardsville's hold on the county seat was threatened by vigorous Alton, which already claimed 2,340 people in 1840, three times more than Edwardsville. As W. R. Brink put it, certain Altonians "kept up a constant agitation with the view of obtaining the public buildings." The names of Madison County towns that had died---Milton, Augusta, Fitz-James, Mount Auburn, Chippewa, Gibraltar---might have stirred anxiety in Edwardsvillians' minds.

But the prize was saved by Edward M. West, delegate to the Convention which produced the new Constitution of 1848. West, a Virginian who had moved to Edwardsville in 1833, ran a general store from 1835 to 1854, and subsequently became a respected banker. He drafted Article VII, Sec. 5, of the 1848 Constitution, which, by requiring a majority of voters to approve changes in the location of the county seat, made Alton's dreams of dominance impossible. West probably reasoned, correctly, that Edwardsville's central location would keep a majority of the county's voters in its camp.

Changes in the courthouse symbolized growth, security, and development of the town. The first courthouse, a simple log structure, had been sold to Isaac Prickett, a town merchant, for $15.50 in 1826. A second courthouse, this time of brick, was built on land which became the original town square and with materials partially furnished by a group of wealthy citizens in 1826. Thus, it was quickly nicknamed "the donation courthouse." According to the evangelist Lorenzo Dow, who was invited to preach in it after completion and refused, "it was only fit for a hog pen." There were no floors, except a narrow platform for the

EDWARDSVILLE'S POPULATION, 1840-1910	
1840 -	616
1850 -	677
1860 -	1,965
1870 -	2,193
1880 -	2,887
1890 -	3,561
1900 -	4,157
1910 -	5,014

Edward M. West: His shrewdness kept county government in Edwardsville.

West's Home, seen here about 1873, stands today as Pletcher Funeral Home, 627 St. Louis St. The building dates from 1858 and has elegant Italianate and Greek Revival details.

court and bar, and no stairs to reach the upper floor. As W. R. Brink wrote, "It was painful to see old men serving as jurors, climb up a steep and fragile ladder." Between 1831 and 1835, "the donation" was finished off at public expense by raiding the school fund to furnish a paneled desk for the judge, four jury boxes, five seats for lawyers, plaintiffs and defendants, doors, floors, venetian window blinds, and plaster for the walls.

The charming neo-classical third Madison County courthouse, with its luxurious Corinthian columns, balcony, spacious windows, and many chimneys was erected between 1853 and 1857, nearly a mile from the old town square, in an area then called Upper Edwardsville. By mid-century, the public lands of Illinois had been sold. The closing of the Federal Land Office in 1857, marked the closing of an era. After 1857, businesses followed the courthouse and moved away from the original townsite to cluster around the new town square.

AGRICULTURAL INNOVATION

Farms in the surrounding countryside became more and more productive, thereby supporting the growth of Edwardsville. Between 1836 and 1854, German immigrants had launched "a very beneficial influence upon our customs of field culture," according to Willard Flagg, writing in 1873. The steel plow began to cut the prairies in record time, and a few local farmers began to use Cyrus McCormick's mechanical reaper. After 1854, wheat was planted with drills instead of sown by hand.

Some farmers, among them Edward Coles, Abraham Prickett, and George Churchill, had started an Agricultural Society in 1822, which had died by 1825. Permanent agricultural organizations appeared in the 1850s. Building on an English tradition of such groups, these farmers sought to encourage use of better breeds of livestock, new technology, craftsmanship, and diversity in crops.

In 1854, the Madison County Agricultural Society, led

Edwardsville was a real newspaper town in the 1800s. Here are the nameplates of two weeklies.

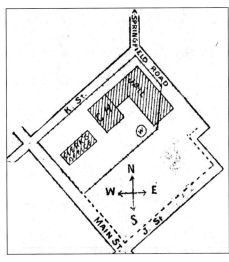

A plat of the original town square, date unknown.

The "donation courthouse," the county's second courthouse, was built of brick, with land and some materials donated by wealthy citizens. The courthouse, whose construction dragged on for a decade, is probably the middle building in this view, published in 1882.

The third courthouse with Renaissance and Romanesque styling, was built between 1853 and 1857 on today's courthouse square.

With county government growing, more space was needed and an addition to the courthouse was opened in 1890 (inset). Its style was compatible with that of the main building, but it was of brick, with simpler details.

by Thomas Judy, Jacob J. Barnsback, John A Prickett, and William T. Brown, purchased 10 acres of ground, later 15, located one mile west of the Court House. Fairgrounds Road later became Fair Avenue and finally, St. Louis Street. Members sold shares in the Society, enclosed the grounds, and put up two 50 foot sheds, with stalls and pens, all in time for the first Madison County Fair, held for three days in September, 1855. Entries totaled 360 and prizes $800. By 1869, the fair had become institutionalized and the grounds, representing an initial investment of $1,472.82, were valued at $10,000. After the Civil War, people played lawn tennis on the grounds inside the racetrack.

ROADS TO A MARKET TOWN

Although Illinois had 2,790 miles of railroads by 1860, none of them touched Edwardsville until after the Civil War. Yet, the town's success as a market center was assured during this period by several important plank roads constructed in 1849 and 1850. To the private company that built the road to Venice in 1849, the County granted a right of way 22 feet off of the right hand side of the road free of charge. The company could sell this valuable land along the road to raise capital for investors or for maintenance. Another new wooden road ran along what is now Highway 157 to Collinsville. Edwardsville's inns, after

Built during the early 1850s, the Gaertner Three-Mile House, about three miles north of Edwardsville, was one of the stopping places on the old St. Louis-Springfield stagecoach route. It was torn down in the 1980s.

AMERICAN BOTTOM PLANK ROAD, JULY 1850, MADISON COUNTY

We learn from Col Buckmaster, who came up from the Ferry yesterday, that the grading of this Road has been contracted for with Messrs. Bennett and Conran, of St. Louis, who have had from forty to fifty men at work for the last twenty days. Contracts have been made for lumber nearly sufficient to complete the route, and arrangements for placing it on the road. A considerable quantity of lumber is daily expected by the river, and the remainder is now cutting at the St. Croix Mills, to be delivered in August next.

Madison Record, July 11, 1850

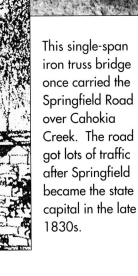

This single-span iron truss bridge once carried the Springfield Road over Cahokia Creek. The road got lots of traffic after Springfield became the state capital in the late 1830s.

Here an unidentified local farmer uses a John Deere steel plow, which broke the prairie much faster than older cast iron plows.

1832, hosted guests taking four-horse coaches between St. Louis and Springfield on the Springfield road, now north Highway 159. Between 1853 and 1857, the county spent $3,150 on what W. R. Brink called "a substantial bridge" across Cahokia Creek on the Springfield Road near lower Edwardsville. Some local roads, for example, Fruit Road, retain the names of local pioneers who were required to work on them as a form of labor tax. Today, Fruit Road passes near the former homestead in Pin Oak Township of Edmund Fruit, a native of North Carolina who came to Madison County in 1818.

Unpaved streets, with their dust and mud, angered local folks just as potholes do today. This is North Main Street, east side, unpaved, but with stone gutters and brick sidewalks, just north of the Hillsboro intersection in 1892. The "wagonette" belonged to the St. James Hotel and probably was used to transport guests from the depot and back.

INTEREST IN PUBLIC EDUCATION

Figures for the School Census not only registered Edwardsville's increasing population, but also the community's interest in providing basic education. In 1850, 472 potential students were counted; in 1860, the numbers reached 1,150. If they were in school before 1864, these children attended a variety of institutions. In the early days, Illinois law did not require communities to establish free public schools. There was no system. Many people thought that "subscription schools" were good enough because the families with children paid for them and others were not taxed. Even the new Constitution of 1848 did not provide for a statewide, tax-supported system. Finally, in 1855, the legislature passed "An Act to Establish and Maintain a System of Free Schools," which required communities to implement property taxes to finance tuition-free education. Edwardsville's first free, tax-supported school building was completed in 1864. A more effective state network of schools, partly financed by a state fund, awaited the Constitution of 1870.

Early schools in and around Edwardsville reflected the hodgepodge permitted by law. In 1809, a log "subscription school" was established by a group of families about 2 and 1/2 miles south of town. For cash or goods, early unknown teachers sharpened goose quills and assisted scholars with spelling, arithmetic, reading, and penmanship. Passers-by could recognize a local "loud school" by the chorus of reciting voices issuing from cracks and paneless windows. The first recorded teacher associated directly with the town is Joshua Atwater, a transplanted New Englander, who probably began to teach some students in a "subscription school" near Edwardsville in 1807. Beginning in 1825, John Barber, a man who knew Latin and Greek, attracted many pupils from Edwardsville at his log school three miles south of lower Main Street in the middle of what is now Troy Road (Highway 159). According to a pioneer informant, Mr. Barber "was an erudite man. He occasionally preached, but not often enough to harm his own powers. . . .He taught school, lived upon his farm, and died with

BUILDING A LOG SCHOOL BY AN OLD SETTLER

A number of the old settlers met together. . . to erect a schoolhouse. They cut down and trimmed a number of trees that would average six inches in diameter. Of these they made a pen about 12x16 feet in size. Having built it eight feet high, they covered it with rough clap boards which they weighed down with heavier timber, next, a door was cut through on one side and the 'temple of learning' was ready. . . . To this chinkless, floorless, chimneyless structure flocked such children as could be spared from farm labor for two miles around. The same building was chinked, daubed, floored, with rough hewed timbers, provided with a stick chimney, a board extending the entire length of the cabin, attached to the wall to serve the purpose of a writing desk, and an aristocratic window of greased paper in readiness for winter scholars. The old puncheon bench. . . made by splitting logs and putting in wooden legs as supports was generally too high to enable the smaller urchins to rest their feet upon the floor. So there they were compelled to sit six or eight hours a day, legs dangling in air.

Pupils sat on puncheon benches made of a split log supported on wooden legs.

Schooling in the early days often took place in plain, log buildings like this one.

a larger stock of information and underdeveloped brain power than can be cited in any other instance in Madison County."

Most of the early schools were taught by men, who were thought more capable than women of handling rambunctious young males, but town lore places a Miss Hastings in front of subscription students in 1820. According to G. C. Lusk, who attended Edwardsville

ACCOUNT OF BROKEN DOWN TEACHER BY EARLY EDWARDSVILLE STUDENT

Schools in Edwardsville by G. C. Lusk, early student, who attended Edwardsville schools before 1839:

. . . . none of these schools were free schools, but were common schools to which any one could go, and tuition was paid by the parents or guardians of the pupils. The attendance varied from 40 to 80 persons.

John Gibson was a presbyterian minister, was well-educated and could read latin and Greek like English. Yet, he was partially broken down---at any rate, he had no congregation, and concluded to accept a school. . . .Matters went on very well with him and with the school , until he contracted a taste for opium, the use of which rendered him cross or stupid, according to supply and appetite.

schools, beginning in 1829, a capable Mrs. Stearnes, a sister of Joshua Atwood, opened a school in town sometime in the early 1830s and taught for many years. Stearnes "had spelling schools two or three evenings a month to which all other schools, and persons desiring to join in the exercises were cordially invited." A series of such schools are recorded in town in various temporary buildings and homes on lower Main Street during the years before the Civil War. Ebenezer Campground, southeast of Edwardsville, also housed a school during the decade before the Civil War.

Completely private schools also were established to meet a demand. The Edwardsville *Spectator* of October 10, 1820, reported the opening of an Academy of Science, taught by a Madame Jerome, who offered instruction in "French, geography, history, drawing, arithmetic, embroidery, plain needlework for young ladies, and the English language." Should parents doubt her qualifications, she offered to be examined. By 1830, this school was gone, but Peck's *Gazetteer* of 1834 and other sources mention a short-lived Edwardsville Female Academy located in a frame building on Third Street. Tuition ranged from $2.50 to $3.50 per quarter. Later in the century, the building was moved---a relatively easy task, given that in those days buildings possessed no plumbing--- to the corner of Third and Purcell and recy-

Three-story M. G. Dale School was judged too big for Edwardsville when it was opened in 1864 on North Kansas Street between College and High. But new buildings were added to the site in 1886 and 1896. Dale School was torn down to make way for a new high school in 1909-10. This later building stands today, along with the 1886-96 building, as Columbus Elementary School. Children at Dale School are pictured in the photo below.

cled as a grocery store.

There were church-related schools, too, that helped bring learning to the frontier. John Mason Peck and other early literate Protestant circuit riders worked during the 1820s to organize Sunday Schools, which taught more than Bible verses to eager students.

By 1851, Edwardsville was one of four places in Madison County that had a school library. Inspired by the public school law of 1855---which also encouraged professionalism in teaching---teachers of Madison County met in January, 1858, at the Methodist Church on Main Street to organize an Association. Five of the nine officers were Edwardsvillians, all men: Edward M. West, W. J. Elam, H. K. Eaton, Joseph H. Sloss, and Michael G. Dale.

Dale, a well-educated lawyer from a prominent Pennsylvania family, had come to Illinois in 1838 and lived in Greenville until 1853, when he came to Edwardsville to close out the United States Land Office as its last Registrar, 1853-1857. He was remembered as a leader in school reform. In 1864, the community built, at a cost of $13,500, a single building for all white children in the town, the M. G. Dale School, which stood on North Kansas at the site of the later high school and present Columbus School. Dale School could hold 350 pupils taught by five teachers. After the Civil War, in 1869, a public school for black children was first established in the brick county clerk's office, which had been built on the original public square in 1833.

Starting in 1869, black elementary students in Edwardsville went to Lincoln School, in the 1833 county clerk's building on the old town square in Lower Town. Students and teachers posed for this picture in 1910, shortly before the building was razed. A new, larger Lincoln School was built in its place.

County Court Judge Michael G. Dale, leader in school reform.

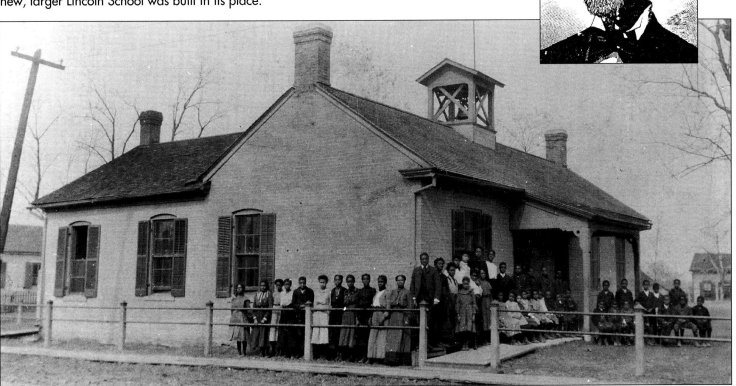

A SAMPLING OF RURAL SCHOOLS

Center Grove School building was built in 1869 and first used as a Methodist Church. It served as a school from 1894 until the early 1950s. The building, which later burned down, was west of Route 157 opposite the end of today's Center Grove Road.

Loos School, Pin Oak Township.

Bohm School, Edwardsville Township

Silvan School, Pin Oak Township.

Goshen School, Edwardsville Township.

Progress School, Fort Russell Township.

AN AGE OF REFORM

Edwardsville, because it housed the county court, also witnessed reform in the areas of crime and punishment, care of poor dependent persons, and temperance. For many years after the county court was established in 1812, public whipping in the courthouse square was the punishment prescribed for less serious crimes. In May 1834, Daniel Piper, tried and convicted of petty larceny and sentenced to 15 lashes, was the last to receive corporal punishment of this kind in Madison County. But the law was not through with Daniel Piper. In the same term, he became the first convict from Madison County to go to the new penitentiary in Alton, "thus blending," wrote W. R. Brink, "the age of pillory and lash with that of modern modes of punishment." The name of the new penal institution, "penitentiary," reflected the optimism of the age. Reformers believed that, in the right institutional setting, repentance would occur.

As the population of the county grew, the old system of caring for the needy ended. This system, grounded in English law, required appointed overseers of the poor in each township and paid the bills presented by individuals who took dependent elders without relatives or the occasional sick poor person into their homes. Beginning on January 1, 1844, one house in Edwardsville was designated in the county commissioners' report as "an asylum" for the county's dependent persons, "a temporary abode" with a salaried "agent." James Ruggles received the appointment for 1844-45 with a yearly salary of $250 and the privilege of billing the county for expenses of keeping the poor. In the spirit of an earlier age, George Barnsback, according to W. R. Brink "a number one farmer," donated his $150 legislator's salary to the county for poor relief in 1844, the year of a tremendous flood in the Bottoms, but he stood as an exception.

Beginning in 1850, the supervisor received a fixed amount from the county for paying himself and caring for the poor. Robert Stewart, in 1850, got $624 for "keeping, feeding, clothing, and nursing the inmates." If the average number of poor needing care exceeded six, then the agent would get an additional $2 per week per person. In 1846, and again in 1852, the county bought land with the intention of establishing a "poor farm" with a county-owned building, but each time, the land was sold,

MADISON COUNTY POOR, 1844-48, COMPILED BY COUNTY BOARD			
NATIONALITY	SEX	AGE	DEATHS
Americans - 72	Female - 43	Under 10 - 15	Pneumonia - 2
Germans - 19	Male - 83	10 to 20 - 24	Congestion - 2
Irish - 14		20 to 30 - 26	Dropsy - 2
English - 12		30 to 40 - 19	Diarrhea - 2
Norwegians - 4		40 to 50 - 25	Fever - 2
Africans - 3		50 to 60 - 12	Syphilis - 1
Swiss - 1		Over 60 - 5	Scrofula - 1
Italian - 1			Cancer of Stomach - 1
			Convulsions - 1
			Paralysis - 1

As Edwardsville grew south, Upper Town, the new part, became distinct from Lower Town.

The Madison County Poor Farm, as depicted in 1873, stands today, largely intact, on South Main Street. Its structure has been much modernized, along with its name, Madison County Sheltered Care Home.

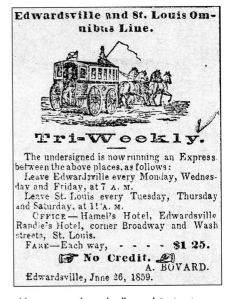

Travel between Edwardsville and St. Louis was easy in the 1850s via this coach-and-four express.

and a poor farm was not developed until the mid-1860s.

Temperance emerged as the most popular reform cause of the 19th century. Petitions for the "suppression of grog shops" were presented to Madison County Commissioners as early as 1832. A strong branch of the Madison County Temperance Society existed in Fort Russell Township, beginning in March 1833. Among the active members were many young, single women.

Since the County Commissioners in this period fixed the price of a drink, along with rates for lodging and meals at local establishments, they responded to reformers' pressure by doubling the price of a half-pint of whiskey in 1836 from 12 1/2 cents to 25 cents. Local option, community choice on whether or not to permit the sale of hard liquor at all, existed in Illinois after 1838. In Fall 1850, the cost of a license to "keep groceries" (sell liquor and wine in quantities less than a quart) in Madison County was raised from its historic level of $5 to $8 to $100 after a grand jury reported to the county court that they had found "a number of those who [became] inmates of the jail and the poor house

addicted to the use of ardent spirits, and in consequence [became] charges to the county."

The legislature in 1851, passed a "quart law" outlawing sales of less than a quart, but was an unpopular law and there were widespread violations. It was repealed in 1853. Voters in Madison County rejected a statewide total prohibition law in 1855. Edwardsville, with a population of 1,965 in 1860, contained at least six places where liquor could be bought by the drink, plus one distillery.

ILLINOIS LAW: PERSISTENCE OF SLAVERY AND DISCRIMINATION

Antislavery, the other major reform cause of the pre-Civil War era, had been a hot issue since the town's founding before statehood. The issue was complex. First, for many decades after statehood, slavery persisted here. The Constitution of 1818 stated that "neither slavery or involuntary servitude shall hereafter be introduced into this state." But some whites attempted to keep slaves through a variety of subterfuges. Nearly perpetual servitude in the form of indenture, beginning in the territori-

Edwardsville Division, No. 72,
SONS OF TEMPERANCE,
MEETS every Friday evening at their hall, at 7 1-2 o'clock. By order of the W. P.
J. H. WEIR, R. S.

The handsome, Federal Style home of Dr. John Weir, 715 N. Main Street., has been the Madison County Historical Museum since 1964.

The Klingel House, 1801 N. Main St.reet, once housed Edwardsville's only brewery. The house was built in 1858 by George, Henry and Phillip Ritter. Tunnels led northeast to cool, bricked caves in the Cahokia Creek bluff, nearby, where the beer was stored for aging. The brewery closed in 1870.

al period, 1809-1819, remained legal until 1841.

Although the Northwest Ordinance of 1787 had prohibited slavery in the Northwest Territory, French settlers, here before Americans, claimed a "right" through treaties in 1763 and 1783, to hold persons in slavery who had been slaves before 1787 and to keep their children as slaves. In 1845, the Illinois Supreme Court ruled in *Jarrot vs. Jarrot* that the Northwest Ordinance's promise of freedom applied to all people born in Illinois since 1787. But some whites continued to bring captives to Illinois for farm labor on a "temporary" basis from neighboring slave states. In 1847, the Supreme Court finally outlawed this form of bondage in Illinois. The census of 1850 was the first to show no enslaved people in the state.

But state law denied to free African-Americans important privileges of citizenship. Participation in elections, jury duty, the militia, and public education was specifically for whites only. Black Edwardsvillians' freedom from intimidation and their protection against criminals was severely limited by laws forbidding their testimony in court cases involving whites. Free African Americans moving to Illinois had to present certification of their status and to post bond of $1000, conditions imposed on no other group of emigrants.

All of these so-called Black Laws were in place by 1819. After he became Governor in 1822, Edward Coles created great turmoil among whites by calling for repeal of these statutes. But they were popular. In 1853, free blacks were forbidden to move to Illinois. These restrictions on African Americans' freedom and rights, the Black Laws, remained on the books until the closing days of the Civil War in 1865. After the war, although discrimination was theoretically outlawed by the Constitution of 1870, segregated schools emerged and discrimination persisted in many Illinois communities, including Edwardsville.

Coming behind these issues was the question of slavery in the future of the United States. Some people favored abolition of slavery everywhere, either immediately or gradually. Others thought that the Constitution of 1789 guaranteed slavery where it already existed but granted power to Congress to prevent slavery in the territories. Some wanted the issue left to a popular vote of people living in the territories. Some favored expansion of slavery everywhere in the country.

INDENTURE CONTRACT FROM MADISON COUNTY COURT RECORDS

Be it remembered that on this Day [April 11, 1816] personally came James Reynolds of Madison County & Territory of Illinois before me Josias Randle, Clerk of the Court for the County of Madison, and Black Woman by the name of Aggy, 22 years of age, lately brought to the said territory by said Reynolds, the said black woman Aggy Agreeing To and with her said master James Reynolds to serve him faithful [sic] during the term of sixty years from this date. . . .

FAMILY IN BONDAGE TO BENJAMIN STEPHENSON

Be is known that on the 15th day of January in the year of our Lord 1817 personally came Benjamin Stephenson late of Randolph county Illinois Territory. But now of Madison County and Illinois Territory and entered of Record as the Law Directs the following negroes towit: Hark and Winn, whom he the said Benjamin Stephenson say was Indentured in the said County of Randolph. Also Debb, aged 9 years and Morian aged 6 years, and Caroline aged 4 years and Louisia aged 2 years. And Barksley, aged 42 days at the present Date.

AFRICAN-AMERICANS' COMMUNITY IN EDWARDSVILLE

African-Americans formed part of the Edwardsville community from its earliest days. A free black man, whose name we do not know, was with Thomas Kirkpatrick and the Gillhams among the early squatters whose improvements and claims were recognized by the United States Land Commission in 1809. From the Madison County Court's Register of Slaves, Indentured Servants & Free Persons of Colour, the names of free people and of people held in various forms of bondage by some of the early white families are recorded. We do not have a written African-American voice describing life in and around Edwardsville during this time. But, as we read the names and descriptions written in surviving records and listen to oral tradition, we can imagine black men, women, and children who also worked to build a life in a new country.

A nucleus of free black people formed after 1819, when the Virginian, later Governor, Edward Coles (1786-1868), came to Edwardsville accompanied by 10 former slaves whom he had inherited in 1807 from his father, John Coles, one of Virginia's most prosperous planters. County documents recorded the names of Robert Crawford, age 25, and his sister, Polly Crawford, age 16, their elder relative, Ralph Crawford, age 46, and his wife, Kate Crawford, age 43, and their children: Betsy, age 16, Thomas, age 13, who had a weak right arm and leg, Mary, a girl of 11 or 12, and William, a boy of 8 or 9. Another man, Thomas Cobb, nearly 40, and a woman, Nancy Gains, age 16 or 17, arrived with Coles in 1819. In April of that year, as the group floated together down the Ohio River, Coles had informed them that they were free. He had given them a choice of going on to Edwardsville with him or leaving immediately. Those who came to Edwardsville had evidently chosen to try freedom here.

At the log courthouse, on the Fourth of July, 1819, before Justice of the Peace Hail Mason, and with a local farmer, Jacob Linder, as witness, Edward Coles legally recorded that the Crawfords, Thomas Cobb, and Nancy Gains possessed "that unalienable liberty of which they have been deprived." In each person's freedom paper, Coles included the following statement of his philosophy: ". . .I do not believe that man can have of right a property in his fellow man, but on the contrary that all mankind were endowed by nature with equal rights."

Soon after the group reached Edwardsville, Coles fulfilled an intention he had announced on the way: "That in consideration of this delay [the time between 1807, when he inherited the Crawfords, Todd, and Gains, and 1819], & as a reward for their past services. . .I should give to each head of a Family a quarter Section containing one hundred & sixty acres of land." From lands belonging to the U. S. Government, he selected good prairie acres, watered by Silver Creek, Sections 14, 15, and 16 in Pin Oak Township, three to four miles east of Edwardsville. Since Coles had not furnished capital for improvements, these families must have worked very hard on the land. Some of the land, according to Reverend Warren Wider, belonged to previous homesteaders. The Census of 1820 shows that Robert Crawford had been joined by other free black pioneers: Michael Lee, Samuel Vanderberg, Henry Daugherty, and Thomas Sexton. More arrived over the decades.

The African-American settlement at Pin Oak, according to W. T. Norton's history of the County (1912), at one time numbered 300. Among these was Henry Blair, a freedman from Tennessee, who homesteaded in Section 9 and came to own more than 500 acres before the Civil War. Later in the century, the black community in Pin Oak hosted a "milk dump" at Kuhn Station, where the train stopped to pick up milk and cheese from local farmers. A black-owned general store supplied the community with basic items, and a grain elevator stored corn and wheat for storage. Before the Civil War, the community also had a "subscription school."

Young Robert Crawford of the Coles group, known as "Uncle Bobby," made a name for himself among both blacks and whites as an able preacher of the gospel. We have no likeness of him, except the Court's notation that, at 5'7", he was considered tall for the times. Captain A. L. Brown, an old settler, remembered in 1912: "In the days of camp-meetings at Silver Creek, on the Edwardsville Marine road, Uncle Bobby was a foremost figure thereof. Days when it was announced that he would preach, scores of white people were there from neighboring towns."

Among the forgotten traditions from early camp meetings is the fact that African-American circuit riders regularly

Gov. Edward Coles: "I do not believe that man can have of right a property in his fellow man. . . "

preached and were often highly respected. Edward M. West, Edwardsville banker and Methodist historian, recalled in 1882, a Methodist camp meeting of 1829 at the Ebenezer grounds. Ebeneezer grounds, school, and cemetery were on four acres in the southeast corner of the southwest quarter of Sec. 10. To reach that one would follow present Hwy. 157, up what some still call Tanyard Hill, where hides were made into leather before 1850. At the top, where the road flattens, the Ebeneezer gounds could be seen on the north or right side of the road. A dispute, over the qualifications of a young white aspirant to the ministry, was settled by "Immanuel Wilkinson, a colored local preacher...a member of the Quarterly Conference," who "was acquainted with young Ames [the candidate] and voted to recommend him. It was the vote that elected him."

GOVERNOR EDWARD COLES, AN UNUSUAL VIRGINIAN

Edward Coles' own career as an antislavery activist and politician in Edwardsville generated both positive excitement and menacing hostility. What made him different from his four brothers and five sisters, none of whom were associated with antislavery, we may never know. According to an autobiographical statement penned in 1844, Coles had decided before his father's death in 1807 to free any slaves he might inherit. He dated the beginning of his questioning of slavery to reading and discussion of "the rights of man," while completing his education at the College of William and Mary. When his father died, he informed his family of his plans to free the twenty people whom he had inherited. Fearing discontent among their own enslaved people, the family talked Edward into keeping his plans a secret as long as he resided in Virginia. He conceived the notion of taking those people whom he owned to the Northwest Territory, where the Ordinance of 1787 had forbidden slavery. He put up his Virginia farm for sale, but his appointment in 1809, as President Madison's secretary and a trip to Russia as an American negotiator during 1816, delayed his planned exit from Virginia.

Meanwhile, he tells us that he needled President Madison on the subject of slavery and sadly concluded that "from the force of early impressions, the influence of habit & association, & a certain train of reasoning, which lulled

> ### G. C. LUSK, WHO LEFT EDWARDSVILLE IN 1839, REMEMBERS EBENEZER CAMPGROUND IN THE 20TH CENTURY.
>
> *Ebenezer, during the early settlement. . . of Edwardsville township, was the great centre of Agricultural, political, social and religious intercourse. . . . A portion of the grounds was set apart for burial purposes. . . . The Methodist was the leading church of the times. Itinerant ministers and regular circuit riders preached in the old log cabin or under the forest trees surrounding it, and people from all parts of the country went and sat 'under the drippings of the sanctuary.' But the place has been desolated and desecrated. . . .The old tabernacle has been demolished, the forests have been felled, the tombstones and monuments have been broken and removed, the plow and harrow have leveled the sacred hillocks with the ground and but a few years more will pass away when the inquiry will be heard---where was Ebenezer?*

in some degree his conscience, without convincing his judgment (for he never justified or approved of it) he continued to hold Slaves." In 1814, he tried to talk Thomas Jefferson into supporting general emancipation. Assuring the young Coles of his "great friendship and respect," Jefferson replied, "This enterprise is for the young, for those who can follow it up and bear it through to its consummation. It shall have all my prayers, and these are the only weapons of an old man. . . ."

In 1815, before he went on the mission to Russia, Coles and Robert Crawford, then a slave, whom Coles appears to have respected and even trusted with his business on many occasions, journeyed from Virginia to Ohio, Indiana, Illinois and St. Louis. From St. Louis, Coles traveled down the Mississippi to visit New Orleans and then sailed on to Virginia. Robert Crawford took one of the horses and returned alone to Virginia by land. During the excursion to Russia the next year, Coles compared slavery and serfdom and decided that serfdom was "an essentially different form of servitude to that of our Negroes, & infinitely of a milder & less oppressive character." Proud of the new United States, he lamented "that solitary defect, that blot of Slavery on its otherwise enchanting escutcheon. . . ." In 1818, Coles made another trip to look at land in Illinois. Then, he pulled up his stakes in Virginia and, with Robert Crawford in charge again, headed West in the spring of 1819.

Through the patronage of his fellow Virginian and former neighbor, President Monroe, Coles first served as Registrar of the Federal Land Office. Because of his prominent family and national political connections, he quickly gained a following. In the context of the national debate over slavery precipitated by the Missouri Crisis and the Compromise of 1820, Coles appealed as a champion of free soil. Hooper Warren, the Vermonter, had already launched the Edwardsville *Spectator* as an antislavery voice during the Missouri Crisis. He and Coles formed a natural alliance. In a contest against two strongly pro-slavery men, whose total vote outweighed his, Coles became Illinois' second Governor in 1822 with a plurality of about a third of the votes cast. Coles was judged a worthy leader because of his social position. This was a time of "gentleman's politics." Political parties as we know them did not exist. Family connections and social position often determined who achieved office.

Coles' inaugural address asked French Illinoisans to free the people whom they were still keeping as slaves and called for elimination of the Black Codes. But the proslavery majority of the legislature in Vandalia and the Lieutenant-Governor decided to plunge ahead with an effort to make Illinois an out-and-out slave state by amending the Constitution of 1818. During 1823, these leaders secured passage of a call for a referendum at the election of 1824 on the issue of a constitutional convention. Coles, Hooper Warren, Morris Birkbeck, an English developer of eastern Illinois, and John Mason Peck, another New Englander and Baptist missionary, organized antislavery

societies in 15 counties. Nicholas Biddle, soon to be President of the Bank of the United States in Philadelphia, joined the battle by writing pamphlets showing the ways in which slavery made non-slaveowning whites, the majority, poorer. In Edwardsville, a proslavery newspaper, the *Illinois Republican,* was started by Theophilius Smith, a New Yorker, one of the benefactors who would later make possible the "donation courthouse" and a future Justice of the Illinois Supreme Court. U. S. Senator Jesse B. Thomas, another Edwardsvillian, also supported the proslavery forces. Coles and his allies defeated the convention, 6,640 votes to 4,972. Writing in 1855, when the discussion over slavery was tearing the nation apart and giving birth to the Republican Party, Governor John Reynolds remembered this election as "the most important and excited. . .ever witnessed in the State."

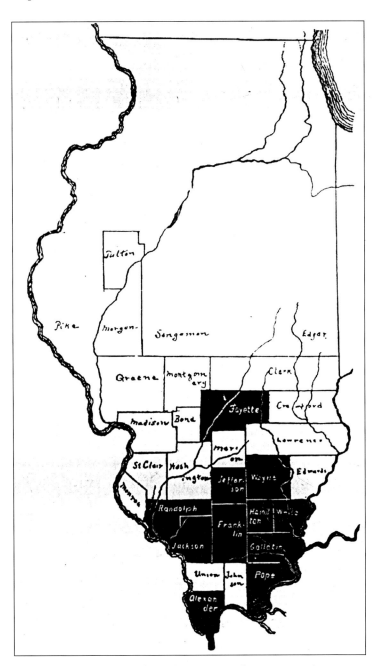

Map shows results of referendum on pro-slavery amendment to the Illinois Constitution in 1824. White counties voted for freedom, black for slavery.

Yet, after the referendum, what Robert Howard, noted historian of Illinois, called "pseudoslavery" continued. White Illinoisans' will to fight against that practice and the racist Black Laws was lacking. Even Coles was not free of a prejudicial wish to discourage African American migration to Illinois. In his inaugural address, he said, "I should not be for encouragement for the emigration of free negroes to the state, as they are a kind of population not to be desired." Thus, Coles defined the strengths and limits of radical antislavery among whites in Illinois. Coles would have abolished slavery in Illinois and repealed the Black Laws, while discouraging black migration. A majority, not so generous, wanted to exclude slavery and African-Americans and to keep the Black Laws. Arguments heard in 1824 against slavery being introduced to free soil echoed again in the 1850s.

Coles' political success ended after 1824. Meanwhile, his enemies harassed him continually. Joseph Gillespie noted in 1882 that Coles faced lawsuits because he had not posted $1,000 bond, as required by Illinois law, for each person he freed and that "he was threatened with death [and] his property was destroyed by fire." In 1833, Coles married a wealthy woman from Philadelphia, moved to that city, and lived comfortably from the revenues of his investments in St. Louis real estate.

POLITICS BEFORE THE CIVIL WAR

Edwardsville history before the Civil War records no active abolitionist society. No club or organization demanded an end to slavery in the states where it already existed. Individual members of the community may have favored abolition of slavery in the United States before the Civil War, but they did not expose their views on public

platforms. We know, however, that literature by famous abolitionists, such as Frederick Douglass, did circulate within the Edwardsville community. On March 30, 1856, Sarah Smith Flagg, newly wed to Willard, son of pioneer Gershom Flagg, and living in the Flagg homestead, confided to her diary that the family was reading aloud Douglass' *My Bondage & Freedom,* "which," she wrote, "gives me a new insight into the horrors of slavery."

Gaps in the surviving Edwardsville newspapers, from 1827 to 1862, hamper research into local politics in that era. After 1854, the Republican Party formed and based its central appeal on leaving slavery alone where it already existed, while preventing its spread to territories. Republicans, however, did not gain majorities in Edwardsville until after the Civil War. Stephen A. Douglas, the leading Democrat of the age, favored popular sovereignty, letting voters in the territories decide whether or not they would permit slavery. Republicans viewed human slavery as a moral evil, not as just another public policy.

The Democratic Party won elections regularly in Edwardsville throughout this period. But no one here ever openly advocated the "Southern Rights" position on slavery: that it should be allowed everywhere in the United States. Edwardsville did produce a famous Illinois Republican leader, Joseph Gillespie, a lawyer and friend of Abraham Lincoln, who campaigned with him in the famous Lincoln-Douglas contest of 1858 for members of the legislature to elect a U. S. Senator. Gillespie was himself defeated in his bid for the State Senate in 1858 by Democrat Samuel Buckmaster of Alton.

LINCOLN AND DOUGLAS IN EDWARDSVILLE

Abraham Lincoln and Stephen A. Douglas both came to Edwardsville on the same day, September 11, 1858. They did not meet. Lincoln was an unknown here, while Douglas was famous and adored. In these times, Lincoln often timed his appearances to follow those of Douglas in order to get his ideas out to the crowds Douglas attracted. In a few days, they would clash at Jonesboro in one of the famous debates. Before noon, Douglas and a large crowd walked up Main Street to the steps of the new courthouse. Douglas spoke in his dynamic way, attacking the "Black Republican Party" and counting on the racism of the crowd to support his argument that the Republicans were abolitionists in disguise who wanted to do away with Illinois' popular Black Laws. Enthusiasm reigned.

Lincoln arrived in the early afternoon and attended a reception at the home of Joseph Gillespie's brother and partner, Matthew. (He could not go to Joseph's house because of the impropriety of being greeted by a very pregnant Mary Gillespie, Joseph's wife.) Then, Lincoln was taken to dine at Haskett's Tavern, later Wabash Hotel, on the second floor of a wooden part of the structure which long ago burned down. In 1928, Mrs. Mary Rollins, age 81, who, as a little girl of ten had

Stephen A. Douglas, a leading Democrat, favored popular sovereignty.

Joseph Gillespie, of Edwardsville, was a close friend of Abraham Lincoln. They were born in the same year, 1809; both were self-taught, both served in the Black Hawk War, and both were "honest Whigs," serving one term together in the General Assembly (1834-35).

helped in the kitchen at this dinner, remembered two long tables and lots of flags and people eating there until after two o'clock in the afternoon.

A handwritten account in the Joseph Gillespie papers at the Illinois State Historical Library notes that, after this dinner, the Gillespies had arranged for a band to escort Lincoln up Main Street to the courthouse. "It was a poor showing for a political meeting," said a resident interviewed by Josephine Prickett in 1912, "with only Joseph Gillespie and the distinguished guest the only ones following the band up the street to the place of the meeting." People apparently distanced themselves from this effort to stage a Republican parade. The crowd at the courthouse was respectable, but, in the words of Paul Nygard, a Gillespie biographer, "the overall atmosphere of the gathering was one of caution and concern, with the majority of the voters displaying a reluctance to commit themselves too strongly to the antislavery party." Lincoln pounded home the differences between the new Republican party and the Democrats on the question of slavery. "The Republicans," he affirmed, "hold that this government was instituted to secure the blessings of freedom, and that slavery is an unqualified evil to the negro, to the white man, to the soil and to the State. . . . they will do nothing . . . to those who hold slaves by legal sanction, but they will use every constitutional method to prevent the evil from becoming larger an involving more negroes, more white men, more soil and more States in its deplorable consequences."

As Lincoln was scheduled to speak the next day in Greenville, he and Gillespie set off late in the afternoon toward Highland, where Lincoln was indeed welcomed warmly. Joseph Gillespie noted that "the bare sight of the man threw them into ecstasies. I here got the first inkling of the amazing popularity of Mr. Lincoln among the Germans." After Lincoln's death, admiration for him developed as strongly in Edwardsville. Today, as we walk down Main Street from the Wabash Hotel to the courthouse, we might imagine a tall, thoughtful figure walking ahead of us in the August heat and dust, following a band, savoring the Gillespie hospitality, hoping for an audience.

Mary Rollins, photographed at age 81, was a girl of ten when she helped in the kitchen at Haskett's Tavern, part of what later came to be known as the Wabash Hotel, when Lincoln was wined and dined there in 1858. Mrs. Rollins recalled two long tables of diners and a lot of flags.

Home of Matthew Gillespie, brother of Joseph, was the site of a reception for Lincoln in 1858. The home still stands, at 606 N. Main Street

The Wabash Hotel dates from 1840, when it was built as the Edwardsville Hotel. Just a block from the original town square, the brick, Federal Style building was a center of social activity. The dinner for Lincoln took place in a wooden addition to the rear, now long gone. The building stands today, minus the porch, at 1101 N. Main Street, as apartments, the brick having been covered with siding.

CIVIL WAR

Because leaders in the South would not accept the legitimate election of Abraham Lincoln as President in 1860, the fragile nation broke down, and Civil War came. In the histories of Madison County written in the late 19th and early 20th centuries, the term of choice for what happened was "The War of the Rebellion." Madison County sent 4,221 men to battle for the stars and stripes. Volunteers served in 69 different regiments during the war. A breakdown of service by town of origin has not been done, but Edwardsville names appear frequently among the ranks in Edwin G. Gerling's study of one famous unit, the 117th Illinois Infantry Volunteers, which included his Edwardsville great-grandfather, Private Henry Head. In July, 1862, when President Lincoln issued a call for 300,000 men from Illinois, Captain Jacob Kinder, a 53-year-old farmer, gathered 100 men in Edwardsville. The men, later Company F of the 117th, marched all the way, 120 miles, from Edwardsville to Springfield. Writing in 1882, when memories could be freshened with rhetoric, W. R. Brink noted that "[t]he lawyer left his office, the artisan his shop, the physician his practice, the minister his sacred desk, the farmer the plow, and marched away. . .in defense of the grand principle of nationality."

The war divided and then ended one well-known team of Edwardsville lawyers, Joseph H. Sloss and Friend S. Rutherford. Both had come to Edwardsville in the late 1840s. During the political turmoil of the 1850s, they took different paths. In 1858, at the Lincoln-Douglas Debate in Alton, Joe Sloss made the preliminary speech for Stephen A. Douglas, while his partner, Rutherford, warmed up the crowd for Abraham Lincoln. In April, 1861, when President Lincoln called for troops to defend the United States, Sloss went South to volunteer for the Confederate Army. After the war, he stayed in Alabama and represented his district during two terms in the United States Congress. Rutherford rose to the rank of Brigadier General in the Union Army and died in battle.

The career of Joel Waters, a carpenter who came to Edwardsville in 1858, and enlisted in the 10th Illinois illustrates the prosperity of the town and the forces expanding its population in the 1850s. Waters had left his native Indiana farm in 1856, at the age of 23, to seek his fortune in construction farther west. He worked around in new towns connected to the new Illinois Central Railroad---Olney, Centralia, Mound City, Cairo--- and even tried life farther south in Mississippi before coming north again. The nation's economy had taken a sharp dive in 1857, and Waters noted that in St. Louis "there were three thousand idle carpenters." Taking the boat to Alton, he "got no work" there, but Edwardsville proved a different story: "I got work at $1.75 per day," he wrote his brother on May 30, 1858. "I expect to stop here all summer and mabe longer. Times is harder this year for mechanicks than I have ever seen them since I been at the business. . . ."

This portrait of Lincoln was painted by Alban Jasper Conant (1857-1915) about two months before the election in 1860. When it was finished Mrs. Lincoln exclaimed, "Oh, that is excellent! That's the way he looks when he has his friends about him. I hope he will look like that after the first of November." It is owned by Southern Illinois University at Edwardsville.

LINCOLN'S SPEECH AT EDWARDSVILLE, SEPTEMBER 11, 1858

Question to Lincoln: "What is the difference between the Democrats and the Republicans?"

Mr. Lincoln replied: "The difference between the Republican and the Democratic parties on the leading issues of this contest, as I understand it, is that the former consider slavery a moral, social, and political wrong, while the latter do not consider it either a moral, a social, or a political wrong. . . .I will not affirm that the Democratic party consider slavery morally, socially, and politically right, though their tendency to that view has, in my opinion, been constant and unmistakable for the past five years. I prefer to take as the accepted maxim of the party, the idea put forth by Judge Douglas, that he don't care whether slavery is voted down or voted up....Every measure of the Democratic party of late years, bearing directly or indirectly on the slavery question, has corresponded with this notion of utter indifference, whether slavery or freedom shall outrun in the race of empire across to the Pacific."

A year later, he wrote, "I like this place better the longer I sta here maybe it is because there is so many good looking gals here." In November 1860, Waters in partnership with two other men, leased 80 acres of prairie land ten miles from Edwardsville. Still single ---"I am like a balky horse some times I am in a notion sometimes I aint about being harnessed."---Waters had developed an interest in politics. "I was glad," he wrote his brother, "to hear that your head was sound on the political question you went for a sound man when you went for old Abe. I saw him and he looks like an honest old Abe. The batle waxed hot in elinoy [Illinois] but old Abe won the day the democrats was hurted bad. . . ."

In October 1861, Waters notified his brother that he was now "in the service of the U.S.A. for three years" and camped above Cairo with the 10th Illinois Volunteers. "[W]e are stationed here to watch the gun boats building here to keep the secessions from taking them." Waters originally thought the "war would soon end." After his first three-month enlistment, he hurried home and planted 45 acres of corn, which he left "standing in the field" when he answered the call to serve again. During 1862, the 10th fought in southern Missouri. Being an artilleryman gave Waters a special vantage point on the war. He never felt discouraged. "The great union ball is rolling on to victory," he wrote in March 1862, "and it will sweep cecesh wherever it goes. . . .My gun has got a raised sight that is marked 900 yards and it wont be very safe for cecesh to stand on fair ground that distance. . . . Excuse my bad spelling for I am siting in the woods writing on our grub box."

Later, the 10th fought in Mississippi, Alabama, and Georgia. From Camp Chattahoosie, Georgia, he wrote in August, 1864, that he "remained safe from the perils of war that surounds me altho many of my comrades has fell on all sides. . . Deserters is coming in every day. I think after we take Atlanta what we dont kill and capture will desert. The casualties in our regiment has been near 100 since the campain commenced." The majority of the men, he thought, were "sadisfied with Lincons nomination" for the Presidency in 1864. "They think he will soon crush the confed to atoms." After the war, Joel Waters returned to Edwardsville, picked up his carpenter's tools from a friend who had kept them, sold his share in the farm, married and moved to town. He drops from history, but several of the lovely wooden frame houses in town bear the stamp of his craftsmanship.

Edwardsville soldiers represented both native men and foreign-born. Thomas H. Kennedy, for example, was born a fifth child in Rosscommon County in impoverished northwest central Ireland in 1837. As a young man of 21, he left his family on their small farm and came to New York City, one of thousands of Irish seeking a better future, in 1858. For a while, he did common labor in New York, saved his money, and then headed West, first

This ad for Waters and Son appeared in the 1894 Edwardsville City Directory.

Simon Kellerman, Sr's. home, built by Joel Waters, at 416 N. Fillmore in 1884, still stands as a display of his skillful carpentry.

PVT. JOEL WATTERS, STANDING GUARD AT MOUND CITY, NOVEMBER 3, 1861

I have to stand guard onc a week for 24 hours 2 on and 4 off there is 10 men detailed out of each Co per day to s[it] and guard to kep the boys in camp if they get out in town some of them gets tite on cecesh whiskey and want to clean out every thing they come to some of the boys gets in the guard house and has to wear a big canon ball to their leg for 8 or 10 days and live on bread and water. The officers has to be strict for ther is some tolerable hard caces to deal with.

SUFFERING IN THE SOUTH. PVT. JOEL WATTERS

Letter June 20, 1862

When the rebels left Corinth [Mississippi], they took every thing from the people in the country and left them in a starving condition. They even took the milch cows and the calves was so hungry they had to lean against the fence to ball as we passed by. I saw men and women with carts going around camps we left picking up scraps of provision. They come into our camps every day beging.

PREJUDICE AGAINST BLACK TROOPS: PVT. JOEL WATTERS February 20, 1863

There is considerable excitement here amongst the souldiers on account of the niger question. There is a great many opposed to old Abes policy but I think it will blow over without any evil consiquences. I dont think they will arm the darkeys and put them to fight with us. If they do it will be a good way to get rid of them for wat the rebs dont shoot we will if they put them with us to fight....I go in for using the darks to work on our forts while the war lasts but not to fight in the ranks with us. After the was is over sell them to the highest bider to help pay expenses. They had beter be inslavery than turned loose in the north which will cause trouble if they are. . . .

A DIFFERENT VIEW OF BLACK TROOPS: PVT. JOEL WATTERS JULY 8, 1863

Our Colored Brigade marched out like regulars with a black Col mounted on a fine horse sash on and a sword like a sythe blade swung to his side. A band. . .at the head of their colums playing Hail Columbia hapy land hail ye heroes of the colered brig and they marched around through the City and the way the cleared the streets of vehicles and every thing that opposed them. The sun was in a partial eclips for bout 2 hours finaly they went to the government yards sout of town. A such and an othe fume was raised with their fidling and dancing.

to Edwardsville and then down river to New Orleans, where we find him in 1861 when the war exploded. Kennedy must have expressed sympathy for his new flag and country because he was made to feel unwelcome in the South. According to his biographer, the "gallant young Irishman" addressed "the fiery Southrons" thus: "Mark ye! I go; *but to return!*" Reaching Edwardsville in April of 1861 just as President Lincoln issued his call for 75,000 men to defend the Union, the Irishman immediately signed up as a private with Company K of the 9th Regiment. Since the original enlistment lasted only three months, he came back to Edwardsville that summer and joined Company K of the 10th Illinois Volunteers. The men elected him a sergeant. Rising through the ranks, he was elected lieutenant, then captain by the men of his Company. He marched with General William T. Sherman from Atlanta to the Sea during 1864 and was mustered out on July 4, 1865.

Thomas Newsham's career also illustrates the love of country felt by new Americans. Born in Lancashire, England in 1832, Newsham came to the United States with his parents in 1840. They farmed in Monroe County, and both were dead by 1845. Young Thomas became a carpenter's apprentice in St. Louis. After he turned 18, he migrated to Edwardsville and during the booming 1850s gained a reputation as a skillful builder and bass singer in the town's first barbershop quartet. Brink noted in 1882, that Newsham had "been identified with every temperance movement started in Edwardsville

since 1850." Like Kennedy, he answered the call for 75,000 troops in April, 1861. The men elected him first lieutenant of Company I, 9th Illinois.

Within a month, Newsham had been commissioned Adjutant of the 9th Illinois Regiment. The 9th guarded a battery which had command of the Ohio above Cairo. When his three months expired, Newsham re-enlisted for three years and was again commissioned adjutant of the 9th. When an expeditionary force moved to capture Paducah, Kentucky, Newsham was detached from the regiment and moved on to the staff of General C. F. Smith with the rank of Captain. He fought at Fort Donelson and Shiloh. Illness forced his resignation in April 1862, but when President Lincoln's summer call for 600,000 came, he assisted in raising the 117th regiment and was elected a major by the staff officers and commissioned. In December, 1862, he was detached again from the regiment and placed in command of Fort Pickering, Tennessee, where he served with distinction until sickness again forced his resignation in April, 1864.

The County History reprints a letter from General William T. Sherman saying that Newsham was "held in high esteem." But Edwin Gerling notes that at the end of January, 1864, all but three of the commissioned officers of the regiment signed a request for Newsham's dismissal. Newsham had married a native Edwardsvillian, Mary Jane Eaton, in 1858, and left several young children when he marched to war. Soon after the Party was organized in 1855-56, Newsham had joined the Republicans. He must

Capt. Thomas H. Kennedy returned to Edwardsville after the Civil War, married, and became a regular Democratic Party politician. In the 1870s, he was elected county assessor and treasurer.

Civil War veterans and members of Edwardsville Post 461 of the Grand Army of the Republic (G.A.R.), posed for this portrait in 1912, on the steps of the public library. Seated at left front is Post Commander Dr. H.T. Wharff. The others are, seated in first row, left to right, Edwin Wood, Charles Lenz, Henry Brensing, Ernst Schomberg, Henry Schmidt, Louis Bode, W.H. Shaffer; second row, John Daniels, C.W. Arbuthnot, James Ryan, Max Tabor, C.G. Lynch; back row, S.O. Bonner, Joel Waters, George Shaffer, Ed Naehr, Sam McDaid, Simon Bradley, James Fahnestock, Winfield Hall, Dan Lynch.

have numbered among Lincoln's listeners in 1858. After the War, Newsham led in organizing the Chapter 461 of the Grand Army of the Republic in 1884.

At least 1,811 black Illinoisans served in the Union Army, mostly in the 29th U.S. Colored Infantry. Three of them, Simon Bradley, Levi Scott, and George W. Smith were from Edwardsville and belonged after the war to the Grand Army of the Republic, Lodge 461. After the war, according to Edward E. Williams, an historian of African-Americans in this area, Simon Bradley became the first hoisting engineer in Madison County and "worked for all the leading coal mines here at different times." Levi Scott hailed from a family of farmers at the Ridge Prairie settlement in Pin Oak Township. George Smith, partly due to his name, remains elusive. He does not appear in any town records and may have moved

here after the war.

Twenty-one-year-old Corporal Adolphus P. Wolf and his brother, Private Otto Wolf, a drummer and, at 15, the youngest member of Company F, volunteered in 1862. Both were born in the Benjamin Stephenson House, when the lands along Troy Road were still fields and orchards, to German immigrant farmer parents. In later life, Adolphus, called Dolph by friends, rose to the top of Edwardsville society as assistant cashier and Vice-President of the Bank of Edwardsville, where he kept office hours until the age of 92. Adolphus guarded the regimental colors of Company F, 117th at the battles of Fort Ripley, Pleasant Hill, Tupelo, Nashville, and Mobile. This job ranked among the most dangerous of the war, and being selected to do it represented a high honor. Enemies aimed their fire at the men in the center in

Exploits of the 117th are proudly listed on this post-war poster.

This is the flag of the 117th Illinois Infantry Regiment, which included many local men. The official guardian of the colors was Adolphus P. Wolf, of Edwardsville, who survived the war despite the serious danger of carrying the flag into battle, and who lived well into his 90s.

Albina Kinder Wolf, wife of Adolphus P. Wolf, is seen in a formal sidesaddle portrait.

The Wolf brothers, Adolphus on the right, Otto in the center, and an unidentified elder brother on the left.

Adolphus and Albina Wolf with rustic-looking studio props.

order to capture the flag. The flag of the 117th never fell. Adolphus Wolf's license plate always bore the number, 117. At his death in 1935, Madison County lost its last Civil War veteran. Adolphus and Otto wrote letters which describe in detail the often tedious life in camp.

Like the Wolf brothers, other veterans played important roles in the post-war community. Dr. Joseph Pogue (1835-1919), who was still practicing in 1912, came to Edwardsville in 1858 from Pennsylvania, where he had attended Pennsylvania Medical College. During the war, Major Pogue served as Chief Surgeon of the Western Sharpshooters (14th Missouri Volunteers). After the war, his experience in surgery and his willingness to travel to patients, gained him a large practice. In the days before automobiles and telephones, he kept a stable of six or more horses so that he could come "on call." He was also retained as a physician by all three of Edwardsville's railroads and by one of the streetcar companies. His tools and medical library on Commercial Street were lost in a fire in 1911.

Major William R. Prickett, born in 1836, served with the 150th Illinois Infantry in the Army of the Cumberland. A son of one of Edwardsville's earliest merchants, he later became one of Edwardsville's leading bankers and Democratic Party politicians. He entered the banking business through marriage to the daughter of successful banker Edward M. West. Banks with which he was associated withstood both the panics of 1873 and 1896. Presiding over the founding of the Bank of Edwardsville in 1896, he was its first president until he retired in 1899. He also served two terms in the Illinois General Assembly, during one of which he chaired the powerful Committee on Banks and Banking. In a Republican year, 1885, he ran in the legislature, which still selected the U. S. Senators, against the powerful Southern Illinois Republican, General John A. Logan. As a Delegate to the Democratic National Convention of 1892, he cast his vote for Grover Cleveland. At the Madison County Centennial of 1912, he was honored as the oldest living native of Edwardsville.

William R. Prickett, shown in the photo below, was a major in the Civil War, and returned home to become a leading banker and a Democratic Party politician.

The government provided rations for enlisted men, like the Wolf brothers. But the men had to split themselves up into "messes" and cook the food themselves. *I am getting so I can cook most anything,* Adolphus wrote home from camp near Memphis in April, 1863. *That is, anything in our Bill of Fare such as tea, coffee, beefsteaks, roastbeef, soup, cornbread, biscuits . . . flapjacks, mush (without milk), hominy beans & pork & pork & beans.*

Otto Wolf penned this comment about Memphis nights in May, 1863: *The mosquitoes are getting mighty thick here now. The way we keep them from eating us up is when we go to bed we take some gun powder and light it in the tent and that drives them out.*

Adolphus Wolf to parents on Republican Party success, November 22, 1863: *. . .the Union ticket has been elected in our old country and the Copperheads badly defeated. That is right. We can whip the Rebels in front if you can tend to the traitors in the rear.*

Otto Wolf to family. March 11, 1865. *Now about 100 miles from Shrevesport [Louisiana] where I guess we'll have a hard fight and God knows how many of us will never see the Mississippi again, but we hope for the best and if we must die we have one consolation and that is we died for our country.*

The crafting of quilts with elaborate designs was a popular activity for women in the 1850s—and remains popular today.

In the center photo is young soldier John Amschler in his Union Army uniform.

Amschler later in life, with medals. In 1879, he became the first sexton, or groundskeeper, hired by the new Woodlawn Cemetery, established in 1871.

NO CIVIL WAR MONUMENT

Unlike many of the overwhelmingly Republican towns farther north, Edwardsville never put up a specific monument commemorating the Civil War or Abraham Lincoln. Unlike many towns to the South, Edwardsville sent few volunteers to the Confederacy and hosted no openly pro-Confederate organizations. Parties were closely balanced. Some prominent community leaders, such as banker Edward M. West, whose family roots were in Virginia, switched from Whig to Democrat in the 1850s and stuck with their choice, while others, such as Willard Flagg, of New England stock and also once a Whig, became staunchly Republicans.

The Democratic party, very critical of Lincoln's leadership, remained powerful in Edwardsville during the war. Lincoln had carried Madison County by a plurality in 1860; he lost Madison County in 1864. In the election of 1868, Republicans Willard Flagg and Julius Barnsback, both prominent farmers, along with lawyers Daniel Kerr and A.W. Metcalf, vigorously "waved the Bloody Shirt" as the practice was called, reminding voters that every Confederate soldier had been a Democrat. Grant won in Madison County but only by 539 votes (a bit less than 7%) of 7,845 cast. In 1876, Madison County voters chose Democratic candidate Samuel Tilden in an equally close vote. The lack of a monument reflected the nearly even balance of deeply felt party loyalties within the town.

This remarkable photomontage of Edwardsville citizens from the Civil War era was the work of Harry Rundle, one of the town's earliest professional photographers and, evidently, a very patient man.

BLOODY SHIRT WAVES IN EDWARDSVILLE
TO THE UNION VOTERS OF MADISON COUNTY

The Southern Democracy defeated in the Presidential election of 1860, levied war on the United States with intent to overthrow the Union, destroy the Constitution, and disgrace our Flag. The war thus inaugurated cost the Nation Four Billion Dollars in Money, and Three Hundred Thousand precious lives. . . . Those of you who bore arms achieved greater results under GRANT and the other heroes. . .than have been hitherto recorded in the history of war. In every step of your progress you were met by enemies; infamous in their purposes, crafty in their measures, and. . .cruel in war. Those enemies, whatever names they may then have assumed. . .were, nevertheless, only parts of the Democratic party---the same organization that with [Horatio] Seymour and [Montgomery] Blair for its leaders is marshaling its forces, composed of all the dangerous elements that have cursed the nation, to endeavor to secure its control.

Edwardsville, October 1, 1868, Daniel Kerr, Chairman W.C. Flagg, J.A. Barnsback, A.W. Metcalf, Isaac C. Moore

Dr. Pogue's tombstone, one of the most imposing in Woodlawn Cemetery, was purchased by his friends after his death in 1919.

Dr. Joseph Pogue, a surgeon during the Civil War, was a prominent physician here, with a stable full of horses to take him to patients whenever the need arose.

A VILLAGE AFTER THE CIVIL WAR

Before 1868, Edwardsville was, in some ways, a very rural village. The railroad had not arrived. Most of the streets were unpaved, without sidewalks, and in wet weather became rivers of sticky slop. One rainy day in 1866, classes at the new Dale Public School were cancelled because students were arriving at school covered with mud.

The courthouse constructed in 1857 functioned in these times as both a legal and a social center for the town. During the fall of 1866, the Edwardsville Sewing Society held an oyster supper at the courthouse to raise money for a new fence around the Methodist Episcopal Church lot. The Friends of Irish Freedom met at the courthouse. Professor W. C. Lyman of St. Louis entertained all comers with renditions of Shakespeare. Ladies of St. Boniface Altar Society held a "fair" in the court-house on December 11 to 13, raising money for the new church, which still stands at the corner of Vandalia and Buchanan, a splendid example of German brickwork.

Remembering the 1857 courthouse and the sleepy town of his childhood, Attorney Leland Buckley recalled in 1964, that the Courthouse was surrounded by trees, grass, and benches. "There was a well on the north side where we'd go when we got thirsty. I don't know if there were sanitary cups or not—-I'm sure there weren't—-so many times I drank out of a bucket." In those days, Court met four times a year, instead of every day as it does now. Buckley noted that there had been "only one deputy in the circuit clerk's office and he went around swatting flies on the horses. When farmers came to town on Saturdays, they'd line the horses up along the courthouse and it was a big day in Edwardsville."

An unpaved North Main Street is lined with crisscrossing buggy tracks in this 1894 view looking northwest from about Vandalia Street. Trees on the left mark the courthouse square.

Members of Edwardsville's German-Catholic community bought their own brickyard to make bricks for St. Boniface Church built in 1869-73. It is still standing today at Buchanan and Vandalia streets, one of the busiest intersections in town.

A CHANGING LANDSCAPE REFLECTS MODERNIZATION

By 1912, when Madison County celebrated 100 years of existence, the town's landscape had changed dramatically and the population had reached 5000. The courthouse had been replaced by other centers of social activity. Many streets were paved and lined by cement sidewalks. Forests of telephone poles sprouted like weeds along thoroughfares. Some homes and streets were lighted by electricity, and a number of families enjoyed indoor plumbing made possible by connection to new city sewer lines. After 1904, townspeople could ride an intercity tram, the "Yellow Hammer," to St. Louis, Springfield and a number of regional centers.

Edwardsville's first railroad, the Madison County, an eight-mile spur connecting the town with the St. Louis, Alton & Terre Haute, was built in 1868. Telegraph wires arrived simultaneously. Edwardsville's business community understood the possibilities opened for their city through rail connections. There had been two decades of discussion on getting a rail link, with time out for the Civil War. During 1866 and 1867, $30,000 in stock was sold and $50,000 worth of bonds were issued by the town after voters approved the issue in a special election.

Later, the town issued $8,000 more in bonds when the Madison needed a new engine and threatened to go out of existence. When the Decatur & East St. Louis asked for $25,000 in bonds paying eight per cent interest as the price for coming through Edwardsville in 1868, voters supported the issue.

Both the Madison and the Decatur & East St. Louis became part of the Wabash system in the 1890s. Meanwhile, two more railroads touched the town between 1881 and 1891: the Toledo, St. Louis & Kansas City, called the Clover Leaf, and the Chicago, Peoria & St. Louis. The Clover Leaf Trestle near town appeared as a stupendous achievement of human engineering. The railroads sliced through the land like no previous human enterprise.

When the Madison County Railroad became the Litchfield & Madison, the company chose to locate its repair yards here, on Brown Street between Schwarz and East Vandalia streets. In recent years, this yard was a site for repairing historic railroad cars. According to Herbert Brockmier, who worked in the L & M office, this company employed about 100 people.

Railroads brought goods and numerous temporary workers to town on a regular basis. In 1895, Edwardsville traffic supported ten hotels and rooming houses.

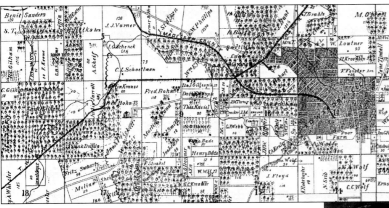

Edwardsville's first railroad, the Madison County Railroad, is shown on 1873 map, snaking into town from the upper left. The other tracks belong to the Toledo, Wabash and Western Railway Company, commonly known as the Wabash.

Woman, child and pet dog give scale to this railroad trestle over Cahokia Creek, in 1903. The tracks are probably those of the Wabash.

Crossing of the Wabash and the Madison County Railroad, left to right in foreground, was known as Bluff Junction. This 1903 view looks southeast across the former city sewage lagoon, now the Watershed Nature Center. The downtown water tower, behind City Hall at North Main and High streets is on the horizon, just right of the utility pole.

The Wabash tracks score the landscape in the north end of town.

Edwardsville Population Growth to 1920	
1850:	677
1860:	1,965
1870:	2,193
1880:	2,887
1890:	3,561
1900:	4,157
1910:	5,014
1920:	5,336

Luxury service was touted in the golden years of rail passenger service, as in this newspaper ad from 1900.

The Clover Leaf/Nickel Plate depot, off Wolf Street, shown in 1978, dates from the 1880s and was just across the tracks from the N.O. Nelson Manufacturing Company. The depot has since been acquired and moved off this site by the Goshen Preservation Alliance.

On September 3, 1901, at 10:00 a.m., the first electric railroad car arrived in Edwardsville after a 45 minute trip from Collinsville. Factory whistles joined in salute. Construction of tracks in the city had begun in late August 1899. In 1906, city officials made the first trip from Granite City to Edwardsville. By October 1910, Edwardsvillians could get on the electric car at the station on Hillsboro, near Main, and ride all the way to

St. Louis, via the new McKinley Bridge at Venice, named for William Brown McKinley, who consolidated a number of companies into a great interurban rail system.

The "interurban" or Illinois Traction System connected Edwardsville with many surrounding towns, as well as Peoria in the north, and Springfield and Decatur to the east. Ball clubs traveled to the next town to play. Churches organized "excursions" to nearby attractions,

The original Wabash depot, with its elegant ornamental touches, is seen in 1899. It was replaced by other buildings as passenger service continued into the 1960s, though in decline. Passenger service ended in Edwardsville when Amtrak, the passenger railroad backed by the federal government, took over in 1971.

Here's what the notorious Cahokia Creek flood of August 1915 did to an Illinois Terminal Railroad bridge. The surging waters attacked concrete abutments, shoving and cracking them, then washed out the beams supporting the roadbed. The tracks and their ties were left high and dry.

The Dinkey, steam engine No. 201, shown in 1895, kept the rail spur humming between the main line Wabash depot at the north end of town and this uptown depot for more than 40 years—1870-1913. The depot stood on St. Louis Street just east of the Vandalia Street angle. The six men, left to right, are Engineer Dalton, Fireman Clawson, Brakeman Thomas Dailey, Station Clerks William Berleman and George Hanser, and Telegrapher W. R. Kearney.

such as the park at Center Grove siding near present Route 159. Older residents of Edwardsville remember Saturdays in St. Louis, made possible by the electric trains. Between 1910 and 1940, sleeping cars accommodated passengers on longer trips. Before 1923, the cars were green. After 1923, the color was tangerine-orange, and people here remember the train as the "Yellow Hammer." In 1948, cars were painted blue.

As motorized vehicles appeared in greater numbers after World War I and "good roads" were built, use of street cars declined. After 1925, intercity buses challenged the trains. The last electric car rumbled out of Edwardsville in 1937 and tracks within the town were ripped up. Until 1955, passengers could still catch the Springfield to St. Louis electric train, which used the freight lines around the outskirts of the city, at a brick station on Troy Road.

The Illinois Traction System's electric interurban cars speeded travelers around central Illinois.

Sehnert's Hotel, later the Liebler Hotel, stood at South Fillmore and Wolf streets, near the N.O. Nelson factory and the Clover Leaf/Nickel Plate station. In recent years the building housed the popular Corner Tavern. It burned down in the late 1980s.

A GHOST OF EDWARDSVILLE PAST: REMEMBERING THE IT

People sitting on porches of the houses along Hillsboro waved to the train, and the conductor waved back. . . . The interurban slowed as it crossed Commercial Street near the passenger station. Passengers on board could smell the aroma coming from the restaurant beside the station. . . . The train traveled north [down Main Street] briefly, then went down Purcell Street. . . .The conductor stood on the steps and eyeballed the 90-degree turn south onto Second Street near Mr. Jones' Shoe Repair Shop. . . .The train curved to the right onto St. Louis Street, past St. John's Church, across the Wabash tracks near Dippold Brothers Grain and Feed Store, then slowed. . . .Perhaps the motorman was remembering the day several years before when a two-car passenger train came down [sic.] the Benton Street hill too quickly and couldn't make the 90-degree turn onto St. Louis Street. . . . the train curved onto Benton Street. . . .slowly climbed the hill and wheeled out of town.

A two-car interurban of the McKinley Lines (Illinois Traction System) turns west from North Main Street onto St. Louis Street at the Madison County Courthouse. The picture was taken from high on the Bank of Edwardsville building, probably soon after its construction in 1917.

Electric train crossing bridge over valley near Edwardsville. Note steam engine under bridge, far right, on 90-degree trackage.

Center Grove Park and its lake were popular with folks from St. Louis and other neighboring cities, who got there on the street car.

This natty-looking street-car was part of the East St. Louis & Suburban Electric Railroad, which ran south through Collinsville, and then westward. The photo was taken in the 200 block of North Main Street. The old county jail was at far right.

As a result of the development of railroads and heavy industry after the Civil War, the mining of bituminous coal emerged as an important activity, not only in Edwardsville, but also throughout Southern Illinois. For a long time, people had mined a little coal here and there. The French explorer LaSalle burned coal to keep warm in the 17th century, and many early gazetteers noted Illinois' rich deposits. A story about the local discovery of coal says that blacksmiths employed by Trappist Monks, who lived at Cahokia in the early 1800s, noted that a tree on the bluffs a mile away, struck by lightning, continued to burn. Digging around the roots, they unearthed a vein of coal. In Edwardsville, shafts were sunk as early as 1855, but the first successful mines were opened in 1875 and 1879.

By 1912, Edwardsville included two large "shipping mines," which sent their coal right out on cars to industrial customers. In 1879, the Wolf brothers, Adolph, Otto, and Fred opened a mine which they sold to The Madison Coal Company in 1891. From this time until the mine was sold in 1905, Madison Number 3 was the largest and most modern mine in Edwardsville. Around 150 men worked here in 1893; there were 350 by 1895. After the Madison Coal Company sold it in 1905, the mine experienced several reorganizations under various owners. In 1911, during a time of unemployment, the miners proposed to run the mine on a cooperative basis, but the Illinois state officers of the United Mine Workers did not approve. The mine was abandoned about 1929. In 1932, the buildings were torn down and the machinery sold to a local junk dealer. This mine was on Troy Road where the railroad tracks cross it. In recent years, a strip mall and a fruit and vegetable business occupy the site.

Another large mine, known locally as the "Henrietta," after Henrietta Voge, daughter of owner Henry Voge, opened in 1898. At its peak, the Henrietta Mine employed 120 men. It operated off and on under six different owners before it was permanently closed in 1934. Voge Park, the site of this mine, was later made possible by a federal grant, which paid for filling the shaft and making the grounds into ballfields.

Edwardsville's largest mine was Madison No. 3, located just west of Troy Road near the north end of Leclaire.

Henrietta (Voge) Mine was in the northeast section of town.

Smaller mines, sometimes located away from the rails, supplied the local market. The East Side Coal Company, which opened in 1910 and employed between 20 and 30 men and three mules, was located at the railroad overpass, now gone, on present Route 143, Marine Road, at the foot of the Vandalia Street hill. After 1934, it was the only mine still producing coal in Edwardsville. It closed about 1940.

What was it like to work in one of the smaller coal mines? Joe Gregor, who worked at the East Side Coal Company during the 1930s, remembered that the seams of coal averaged between five and seven feet in thickness and, at East Side, were 135 feet below ground. Wearing carbide lamps, miners in this mine used regular hand drills to make holes as big as a teacup five feet into the seam of coal. Filling each hole with blasting powder, well-tamped and with a fuse, they undercut the holes. Then, they lighted "the shot" at the end of the day. The explosion knocked down the coal. The next day, the miners broke up the larger chunks and loaded them into coal cars pulled on a track by mules to the hoist. The mules stayed in a stable down in the mine during months of the year when it was open.

Each car, about 4 by 5 feet, held about a ton of coal. Cars were initialed by each miner and were weighed before being hoisted to the surface. Miners were paid by the ton. Joe Gregor earned between $155 and $160 a month. He entered the mine between 7 and 8 in the morning and came up at 4 or 5 in the afternoon. Mining was seasonal. He did not work in the summer, when demand for coal used for heating dropped.

At the top of this smaller mine, the coal was dumped on a "shaker screen," which sorted it into three sizes: fine pieces, used in stokers by local businesses such as Woodlawn Gardens, "neat coal," baseball sized lumps used in heating stoves, and "lump coal," bowling-ball-sized pieces consumed in furnaces. Every load of coal that came up was called a "mine run." (Some readers will recall Vanzo's "mine run university.") Regular truckers and farmers with mules came to pick up coal at this mine. Weighed before sale, the coal brought between $3 and $5 a ton.

A mule is hoisted out of the Home Trade Coal Mine on St. Louis Road during a fire that destroyed the mine buildings. Mules were used at the bottom of a mine to haul rail cars filled with coal from the seam to the hoist.

The abandoned East Side Mine, on East Vandalia Street, was just a skeleton in 1948, not long after it closed around 1940. It was the last coal mine in Edwardsville.

Every mine had two shafts: one for hoisting men and coal and one for ventilation. After 1911, all shafts and surface buildings were supposed to be fireproof and supplied with adequate hoses, pipes and water for putting out fires. According to Norton's Centennial History of 1912, most of the accidents in Madison County resulted from coal and slate falling on the men from a high seam. Edwardsville mines were never the scene of major disasters.

According to Joe Gregor, many of the miners in Edwardsville were foreign-born, either Czech or German, and they mostly lived in a part of town called "Mt. Nebo" by local people. This area lies along East Union Street and includes the neighborhoods along Klein and Highland Streets.

GEORGE "SQUIRE" BARRACLOUGH: AN ENGLISH IMMIGRANT'S STORY

Imagine a teen-age Edwardsville boy, graduating from middle school at age 15, and leaving home to find a new life in Australia. That's basically what George Barraclough did in 1848. Having graduated from his academy in Yorkshire, England, young George took ship for America. He stayed for a while in New Orleans, until the cholera got too bad. In 1849, he came upriver to St. Louis and then to Edwardsville, where he settled. For whatever reason, he decided against joining the California Gold Rush of '49.

Barraclough became a coal miner in the Edwardsville area. He worked other people's mines—in places like Marine and Bethalto, in addition to Edwardsville—and sank a few of his own. He helped dig the Schmidt Mine, in the north end of town, near the Klingel House, and the very profitable Wonderley Mine, off West Union Street near the Wabash spur. In 1869 he prospected near the Banner Clay Works, but abandoned the effort after 60 feet of very tough digging through shale. He evidently gave up too soon; the Home Trade Mine, later sunk nearby to 90 feet, yielded much coal.

George "Squire" Barraclough

George Barraclough was a man of many interests. Not only did he know enough engineering to sink a decent mine, but he kept up with state legislation and learned enough law on his own to get elected police magistrate in 1879. In those days, and for the next 80 years or so, until the statewide judi-

cial reforms of the 1960s, police magistrates judged minor infractions of the law such as traffic cases. They did not need to be lawyers. Their duties involved minor cases arising within the towns. Their jurisdiction was separate from that of Justices of the Peace, who handled minor cases in groups of surrounding rural townships.

Barraclough served every term but one as police magistrate from 1879 until his death at age 80 in 1914. Sometime during his tenure he was given the epithet "Squire." A granddaughter and family historian, Gladys Hayter, writing in 1957, recalled a comment from an Edwardsville lawyer who served on the Illinois Supreme Court: "A few years ago Chief Justice Jesse L. Simpson told me that as a young attorney he tried many cases before Grandfather and found no fairer judge in the county."

Squire Barraclough also studied medical books owned by his good friend, Dr. Joseph Pogue, and learned enough about medicine to be able to assist the doctor in emergencies.

He and his wife, Martha, a native of Switzerland, had 10 children, six boys and four girls. Still, the fine Yorkshire name of Barraclough died out here, thanks to various circumstances: premature deaths, childlessness and female children who did not carry the surname.

by Dick Norrish, Barraclough descendent, 1996

Between 1915 and 1925, Madison Mine Number 3 brought one more change to Edwardsville's landscape, a large pile of smoldering slag, created by a new process for washing coal. It was visible from many parts of the city, an artificial smoking hill which remained until it was demolished in 1965.

A latterday remnant of Madison No. 3 Mine was this slag pile which smoldered spontaneously for years until it was demolished in 1965 as a public nuisance.

N. O. NELSON AND LECLAIRE: THOUGHTFUL INDUSTRIAL DEVELOPMENT by Steven Hughes

On Feb. 12, 1890, the proprietor of one of the largest plumbing goods manufacturers in the United States visited Edwardsville, to the excitement of local promoters. The N. O. Nelson Manufacturing Company of St. Louis was searching the suburbs for a place to locate its plants and establish a village. At an impromptu meeting that afternoon, businessmen formed a five-man committee for the purpose of luring the plant to Edwardsville. Building on their experience with railroads, they decided to offer an incentive in the form of a donation of land. Nelson turned down the first offer, a forty-six acre tract located within the town. He wanted a cheaper piece of land outside the city. A subcommittee including State Senator William F. L. Hadley, Mayor E. B. Glass and Charles Boeschenstein, editor of the *Intelligencer* worked out a new proposal. Nelson would pick out the property he wanted and the committee would negotiate the sale.

Nelson chose a tract of about 150 acres of "rich, high, gently rolling land" just to the south of town. The Clover Leaf Railroad abutted the property. A switch connected it to the Wabash line. The Wolf Brothers' Coal Mine lay just to the west. A pond suitable for recreational use as well as a water supply for the plant's boilers was located halfway along the eastern boundary.

Three hundred and twenty-seven contributors raised $22,900.20 to buy the land. The list of donors represented many groups in town's population. Business and professional people contributed roughly one-third of the funds, while local men, women and even a group of school children made up the rest. Nelson paid the balance, $3,384.50, required to make the purchase. On March 22, 1890, an agreement between Edwardsville and Nelson was signed.

Nelson promised the citizens of Edwardsville a return on their investment. They were guaranteed jobs and a payroll of up to $250,000. Wages would be spent in Edwardsville. Construction money would also flow to the city. On April 29, 1890, Nelson acquired the first parcel, 27.5 acres. The remaining acres were conveyed in increments as Nelson met certain conditions:

1. Twenty-five acres would be conveyed once 25 people had been continuously employed for one month in manufacturing for the company;

2. Five or more acres would be conveyed for every five additional people continuously employed for four months.

Ground was broken for the factory buildings on Monday, May 12, 1890. On June 21, Nelson, along with about 400 employees and their guests, took an excursion train of eight coaches from St. Louis to view the foundation of the factories and clubhouse. When Mayor E. B. Glass, a welcoming committee, and a brass band greeted the visitors, the fertile lands were still high with corn and wheat.

Leclaire was not to be an ordinary factory town. It was in fact a true experiment in cooperative management based on Nelson's belief in living by the "Golden Rule." His business principles had been shaped by the social and economic unrest of the quarter century in which he had founded his company in St. Louis. He entered business in 1876 "primarily to make money and to become a prosperous business man," but he wanted more from life for himself and others. He intended "to incorporate into the business as much of the social and liberal and broad-gauged elements as it would bear." He wished also to "cultivate close friendships with employees."

FROM EDWARDSVILLE *INTELLIGENCER*, MARCH 5, 1890

When the excitement was at its height, the boys in the public schools discussed the topic as earnestly as their elders in the streets. Ed Hagnauer, Willie Krome and Edgar Gerke were the chief boomers. They drew up a subscription paper and put it into circulation. The result of their efforts is the following:

To the N.O. Nelson Manufacturing Company Committee:
We, the boys of the Edwardsville public school, desiring to find employment at home when we grow up, and not be compelled to go west to make a living, hereby contribute the amount of fifteen dollars, collected by us here at school, for the purpose of securing the location of the N.O. Nelson Manufacturing Co. in our city:

Edward Hagnauer	...50	Louis Bishoff	25
Harry Turnau	25	George Pierson	5
W.J.Krome	50	Thomas Bodincek	50
Fred Fahnestock	25	Orrie Finch	25
N.W. Hagnauer.	50	J.H.Martin	25
W.E.Gerke	50	George Martin	25
J.Waters	50	George Klingel	25
F.T. Kendall.	25	Rudolph Wolf	25
W. McKee.	25	Emil Wolf	25
T.A. Desmond	25	Willie Wolf	25
Louis Mick	25	Ernst Schroeder.	5
Charles Nix.	25	Ben Woods.	25
Amos Gusewelle	25	Ben Hernins	25
H.Kirkpatrick	50	Charles Spilman	25
Chas.Fahnestock	25	Ben Klingel	25
Charles Crane.	25	Harry Graves	25
F.E.Sebastian	25	Edward Fredricks.	25
Frank Hoerner	25	John Hess	25
George B.Taylor	50	Joe Hlad	10
Samuel Dale.	20	Breese Glass	25
Lester Hadley	25	A.Gerber	50
Frank Ritter	25	J.Whitbread	25
C.Hoffmann	50	Louis Hartung	25
John Stokes	25	Paul Jones.	25
Henry Bischoff	10	Ed Suppiger	10
Joe Steis.	25	Ernst Bradshaw	25
W.Schotthoefer	10	Chas.Herder	25
		Total	...................$14.95

In 1886, Nelson had been one of three men called upon by a committee representing both business and labor interests of St. Louis to act as a mediator in a violent strike against the Gould Railroad System. Railroad management had refused mediation. This experience, combined with the wreckage of railroad property caused by the strike, had convinced Nelson that ingrained in capitalism was an "irresistible conflict" between owners and laborers. He thus began to look for a means of reconciling the differences between the two.

About this time, Nelson read a book on profit sharing by a reformer named Sedley Taylor. Taylor described two French capitalists who had taken their employees into partnership through profit sharing and cooperative ownership. In 1842, Edme-Jean Leclaire, a Parisian house painter had initiated

N.O. Nelson

profit sharing, dividing his previous year's profits among his workers. Nelson tried out this principle in March, 1886. A slip enclosed in his St. Louis workers' pay envelopes announced the N. O. Nelson profit sharing plan. The company would take seven percent of the actual capital invested. Ten percent of the profits would be set aside for a reserve fund to meet losses in bad years. Another ten percent went into a fund to care for the sick, the disabled, and the families of deceased work-

ers. Five percent was reserved for a free library accessible to all employees. The remainder was divided equally among employer and employees. An employee's share was determined by the amount of wages paid to him for one year.

That same year, Nelson visited Europe with his family to see how existing profit sharing systems were working. He toured the model community established by iron founder Jean Godin at Guise, France. He saw "[w]ell built and well-kept living quarters, day nursery, kindergarten, school, park, pension for old age and sickness, and growing ownership in the works." With this in mind, Nelson began to feel that "homes and social facilities were more important than dividends and stock." He submitted the idea of establishing a model community to a vote of his workers in St. Louis. They approved, and Nelson began his search that led him to Edwardsville. In his dedication speech, Nelson named the future village Leclaire, in honor of the French profit sharing pioneer, Edme-Jean Leclaire.

Nelson established Leclaire as an alternative to overcrowded and unhealthy cities like St. Louis. A better life was to be achieved by stressing six principles which Nelson believed essential for "rational living": work, edu-

Ivied walls gave a bucolic touch to Nelson factory buildings.

cation, recreation, beauty, homes and freedom. Leclaire's factory buildings, designed by notable St. Louis architect A. E. Cameron, were well-lit and well-ventilated one-story brick structures. Each was equipped with fire sprinklers, steam heat, electric fans and electric lights. Large semi-circular windows opened to allow fresh air and natural light to flow in. Visiting Leclaire in 1894, Nellie Bly, the famous reporter for the *New York World*, described the factories as "ideal perfection of buildings for man to labor in."

N.O. Nelson products are seen in planing mill show-room: medicine cabinets, mirror frames, mantels, bathtubs with claw feet, and toilet seats.

Nelson's brass foundry shipping room employed women, in center.

Men working in Nelson brass foundry.

A company-supported school system followed Nelson's belief that "The hand, the head, and the heart must be educated together." Education began with a kindergarten, followed by regular courses supplemented by vocational training. At age twelve, boys did light work for one hour each day in the factory or on the company farm, work for which they were paid. Their work hours gradually increased and study time decreased until they graduated at eighteen and were fully employed by the company. Curriculum for girls focused on home-making.

The Leclaire Academy, built in 1895, still stands. It measures 40 by 50 feet with four rooms and a central hall. Sliding partitions could be moved to create a single hall for lectures, meetings and family gatherings. The school's public library held over 1,400 volumes. Long-time residents of Edwardsville, such as Mrs. Mary Blixen, share fond memories of going to the Leclaire kindergarten and riding bikes to Leclaire Lake.

Leclairites enjoyed free access to a number of recreational facilities: baseball and football fields, tennis courts, and a building which housed a bowling alley and a billiard room. A literary society provided winter entertainments. Among lecturers who spoke at Leclaire were

Four-room Leclaire Academy, built in 1895, doubled as a community center.

Leclaire kindergartners try their hand at a Maypole dance.

the Reverend Edward Everett Hale, Jane Addams of Hull House, and Nellie Bly. A 23-member band, furnished by the company, gave concerts during the summer and on special occasions. The Leclaire Blues baseball team played regional clubs throughout the summer. An existing pond was developed into today's Leclaire Lake, where families rented rowboats, swam, fished and skated.

Julius Pitzman, one of the architects of Forest Park in St. Louis, designed the residential district. Large, 15,000 square foot lots were set on tree-lined, curvilinear streets that once merged into a single road leading to the factory complex. The factories were set apart from the residential area by a hedge of Osage orange trees. A steam heated greenhouse run by the company provided residents with free plants and flowers for their yards.

Nelson believed that possession of a comfortable home contributed greatly to the contentment and welfare of a working man. Buyers could purchase a one-third acre lot with improvements for between $200 and $250, or on installments. An employee could have his home built either by the company or someone else. If the company built the home, the owner was charged the cost of materials and labor plus the average profit made by the manufacturing company. Since the factory owned most of the means of production, the cost of a home was held considerably lower than the average price elsewhere. Monthly payments varied from $12 to $20. Leclaire is said to have had at one time the highest percentage of home ownership in the country.

In 1911, after visiting slums in New Orleans, Nelson

Leclaire Field then, as now, was the scene of many a baseball game.

Leclaire Lake in 1915 made a dandy swimmin' hole. The house in the background stands today at Lake Street and Madison Avenue.

57

launched a food cooperative there. He financed this venture by writing checks on his stock in the N. O. Nelson Company in St. Louis. Company leadership, particularly his son-in-law, Louis D. Lawnin, disapproved of Nelson's actions. The main bone of contention was Nelson's refusal to seek a profit. He sold merchandise in New Orleans only at cost. The venture collapsed in 1918, and Nelson was forced to cash in all his stock in the company to pay his debts. He was forced to resign as president, and his wife of fifty years, Almeria, died. Alone and disillusioned, he retired on his company pension to Los Angeles, California and died there on October 5, 1922, at the age of 78.

The Company continued profit sharing and survived the depression of the 1930s by closing some of its branches. By 1934 Leclaire faced the expensive problem of replacing the water and sewer system. Company officials decided the time had come for annexation to Edwardsville. The City of Edwardsville assumed responsibility for Leclaire Park, and the Edwardsville School Board took ownership of the kindergarten. The last of the Leclaire factories closed in 1948, and the property was sold.

A typical Leclaire home, with a big yard and a picket fence; note wooden sidewalks.

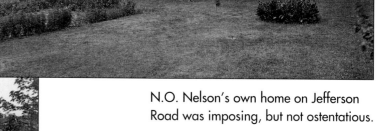

N.O. Nelson's own home on Jefferson Road was imposing, but not ostentatious.

A smaller two-story home with a variety of fruit trees.

These two homes have similar designs, different detailing.

OTHER MANUFACTURING AND BUSINESSES

Between 1870 and 1920, Edwardsville housed a variety of other manufacturing establishments. In the winter of 1912, the Illinois Factory Inspector looked at 186 places in Edwardsville. Statistics revealed 722 employees in the town, 634 men over 16, 76 women over 16, and 12 children under 16.

Richards Brick Company, founded in 1890 by Ben H. Richards and Thomas W. Springer, remains important today at its historic location on Springer Avenue. Richards Brick furnished all of the building bricks used in the construction of the N. O. Nelson Plants after 1890.

By 1912, the company used an electric tramway to haul clay and coal, employed 50 people, and produced 10 million building bricks per year. Another company, the Banner Clay Works, for which Banner Street is named, specialized in paving bricks, for use in streets. They were much harder than building bricks.

As chewing tobacco and spitting out the juice became an unacceptable public practice for gentlemen, many men took up cigars. Four enterprises made them in Edwardsville. Established in 1867, Fred Begemann employed 8 to 10 men making "Life Spring," "Golden Crown," and "Bouquet," which could perfume the air for

Richards Brick Company, founded in 1890, is still in business, but its smoke-stack is long gone. The stack, built in 1912, was enlarged in 1921 to 175 feet, second tallest in Southern Illinois.

Residence of Ben H. Richards, on St. Louis Street at Myrtle.

five cents, and "Begemann's Cervantes," which sold for ten cents. Another cigar factory, owned by Henry Yeager and Joseph Hotz, made "Rico de Fumar," "Modern Woodman," "Talk of Town," "Young American," and "No Match," all in the five cent category, while "The Hub" and "Henry Clay" brought ten. By 1912, Yeager was in business for himself in a little shop across from the McKinley Street Car Depot, which was on the north side of Hillsboro, near Main.

Until the Great Depression of the 1930s, Edwardsville harbored a garment industry. Downtown, the Jack Diamond Shirt Factory employed 20 women at machines making mostly men's work shirts, which were sold in a fifty-mile radius, for fifty cents apiece. Beginning in 1909, the company occupied the second floor of various buildings on Main Street and was still operating in the 1920s. A larger shirt factory, Elder, opened in June, 1917, in a new building heavily subsidized by a citizens committee in the way that N. O. Nelson had been underwritten. The building, on College Street, cost $30,000, of which Edwardsvillians raised $20,000. After Elder Manufacturing paid $250,000 in wages, they received the structure free and clear. Until 1933, this company employed between 80 and 100 people.

Workers stack bricks for firing at the Richards Brick Company.

August Selzer proudly proclaimed his name and the year his new East Vandalia Street building and cigar business opened; the building was in the 100 block, on the north side of the street, near the alley.

At one time Edwardsville had several cigar manufacturers and tobacco shops. This one was on Hillsboro, across the street from the street car depot, now the site of a parking lot.

Near the intersection of Brown Street and East Vandalia, presently occupied by RP Lumber, U.S. Radiator Corporation built a plant employing several dozen men after 1910. This was a foundry which cast molten metal to make these "modern" components of a new-style heating system.

Several Edwardsvillians patented devices and then manufactured them here. Springer Brothers' Manufacturing Company, founded in 1870 by Henry J. Springer, invented several parts of a superior buggy, which they made in their shop. Fred J. Springer patented an "easy riding spring," and he and his brother, Otto, registered the "Springer Adjustable Buggy Pole" in 1886, while Henry Springer patented an improved "coupling" for buggies in the same year. During the 1870s and early 1880s, their shop on the south side of Vandalia one block south of the City Park, occupied a two-story brick building, where 50 carriages a year were built by eight employees. A four horse power steam engine drove the machinery. In an attached two-story frame building, the buggies were painted, trimmed, and displayed to customers. By the 1890s, the Springer brothers were concentrating on manufacturing the hickory and iron buggy poles, which were sold all over the country. In 1904, they started manufacturing a steel potato planter, patented by Henry Springer, which planted two rows at a time. The company closed sometime after World War I, and the site was wrecked in 1927.

Throughout its history, Edwardsville had been a milling center for local farmers. In 1818, Josias Randle, for whom Randle Street was named, established the first flour mill that remained in operation for more than just a few years. Grinding wheat into flour by ox power, it lasted until 1830. After 1830, mills were powered by steam. Although fire posed a constant hazard, local bankers and businessmen repeatedly invested in steam-driven flour mills. They attracted trade and supported other small-scale industry, such as cooper shops. A steam mill, first opened in 1840, and owned at different times by George W. Phillips and John S. Wheeler, burned in

U.S. Radiator Corporation plant on East Vandalia Street made cast-iron steam radiators for distribution of heat in modern buildings.

The specialty of the Springer brothers was inventing and making improved buggy components, in addition to selling buggies. Their own buggy pole was sold all over the country.

1876. John T. Lusk built a steam mill in 1855, which was bought and enlarged by banker John A. Prickett and which burned in 1873. Fire also destroyed the Kehlor mill, which existed from 1885 to 1888, and the Farmers' Mill, which operated from 1889 until 1903.

The town's last big flour mill, the Hunter Brothers Mill Company, created in 1905 by local bankers and St. Louis investors, became Edwardsville Milling Company in 1911, and then Blake Mill Company in 1914. It sent Edwardsville flour in bags bearing the labels "Alma," "Good as Gold," and "Orchid" to distant markets in Europe and the West Indies. Thirty to thirty-five townspeople were employed at this mill along the Wabash Railroad spur on West High Street behind Second Street. On the site of the Madison County parking lot bounded by Second Street and West High Street a large mill pond existed. Blake Mill Company burned in 1926 and was not rebuilt.

Ad for John Lusk's flour mill, dated 1857.

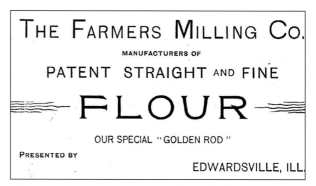

Then, as now, business cards played a big role in sales.

Farmers' Mill, shown shortly after it was built in 1889, produced two brands of flour, Edwardsville Best and Golden Rod. It was probably in the swale along North Second Street near downtown, along with a number of other mills. Note the mill pond, in foreground, and the railroad spur.

Hunter Brothers Milling Company, at West High and North Second, produced Alma brand flour. View looks southwest, with High at bottom right; site now is a parking lot.

Building at 207 W. High Street is all that remains today of Hunter Brothers Milling. It was renovated and opened in 1988 as a doll craftshop.

63

During the days of horses and buggies, livery stables were an important town business. The 1914 City Directory indicates change by listing the Edwardsville Garage under "Auto Liveries."

Blacksmiths, who shoed horses and mules and repaired farm machinery, were numerous before use of horses and mules decreased. Thomas Tandy, a black man, had a shop in the 100 block of Main Street for many years. The smithy's shop served as a social center. While waiting for work to be done, men gathered around the pot-bellied stove to exchange news and gossip. Hot tea was available in winter and lemonade in summer.

Edwardsville's last blacksmith was Al Gerling, whose shop was open at 110 East Vandalia, near the present location of Kriege Hardware. Apprenticed as a teenager in 1905 to Peter Bernhart, whose shop was at 115 E. Park, Gerling opened his own shop in 1913, which operated continuously except for a time when Gerling went to Newark, New Jersey to work as a riveter in a shipyard during World War I. The shop closed when he died in 1956.

Livery stables like this one, at 132 North Main Street, across from the courthouse, kept transportation moving on Edwardsville streets. Note the Springer Brothers' buggy, locally made, on the right.

Thomas Tandy's blacksmith shop is seen around 1910 in a sketch done from childhood memory by Edwardsville Architect Edward A. Kane, Sr. Next door is the Berleman House (circa 1865), still standing today.

Steam-powered threshing machine gets plenty of admiration during a downtown showoff in front of the Madison County Jail at right, behind the trees.

Al Gerling, the last blacksmith here, worked up until he died in 1956.

This picture of men threshing in a field near Edwardsville was taken in the late 19th century.

The Desmond Machine Shop, located on St. Louis Avenue at the Wabash tracks in downtown Edwardsville, was built in 1882 by Michael Desmond, who employed eight men in a shop with steam-driven, and later electric, lathes, planes and drills for building and repairing engines and turning out all sorts of iron and brass work. In 1908, Desmond built 100 cars of steel, including their roller bearings, for use on tracks at the Banner Clay Works. The plant had some U.S. Government contracts during World War I and continued in operation until the mid-1920s.

In 1890, J. F. Ammann started a greenhouse and florist business at the west end of St. Louis Street across from Woodlawn Gardens. Using seven acres, he produced flowers during the entire year and sold to retailers in Edwardsville, East St. Louis, Alton, Collinsville, and Staunton. A member of Eden Church, Ammann involved himself in many civic enterprises and in town politics. A Republican, he left the G.O.P. in 1912 and served as a delegate at the Progressive Party convention in Chicago that nominated Theodore Roosevelt for President.

After significant industry developed in Edwardsville and rails linked it more conveniently with other places, a number of two-story "blocks" for retailers were built downtown: the Tunnell Building on Main, the Henry

J. F. Ammann's Greenhouses, producing fresh flowers, were just east of Woodlawn Cemetery.

Ammann's used this postcard as a sales tool.

Tunnell Brothers Building (below), on North Main facing the St. Louis Street intersection, shown in 1895, is still in service today.

Main Street building in very early photo, taken before 1873.

Trares Block on Main, the Kriege Block on Main, and the Madison Store on Purcell. In 1884, John S. Trares built a two-story multipurpose building on Main Street. On the lower floor were store rooms, while the second story housed an opera house seating 800, with a large stage, a gallery, and dressing rooms. This building still exists on Main Street, at 236-238 N. Main. It was connected by a second-floor walkway to the elegant St. James Hotel, which stood on the parking lot between present-day Edwardsville Frozen Foods and Do Drop Inn.

The Henry Trares Block was typical of thousands of urban commercial buildings built on America's Main Streets: retail, commercial space at street level, apartments or offices above.

Kriege & McKittrick Hardware occupied much of the Kriege building with its handsome detailing.

The Madison Store, on Purcell Street across from the courthouse, used local women as display-window models shortly after opening in 1890. The women were members of St. Andrew's Episcopal Church and earned $1 an hour for their guild. Note plank crosswalk on Purcell, before street paving in 1903. The Madison Store was razed in 1989 to make way for the new county government building.

The St. James Hotel, with its mansard roof and broad, welcoming porch, added a touch of luxury and class to downtown. The location is now a parking lot, but the building at extreme right still stands. It houses an 800-seat, second-floor opera house (still there, but unused for many years), which was connected to the St. James by a second-floor walkway.

The Tuxhorn Brothers, turn-of-the-century hardware merchants, pose for a formal portrait.

Tuxhorn Brothers Store sold many items, including bicycles and fancy baby carriages. In 1959, Mrs. Jessie Springer recognized in this picture the carriage she rode in as a baby; it sold then for $7.50.

Edward Schwarz, second from right, proprietor of Schwarz Brothers Groceries and Provisions, poses with employees and Christmas trees for promotional picture.

Members of the Edwardsville Retail Grocers' Association pose in front of the Tunnell Building downtown in 1895. Sitting on the curb in front, left to right, are unknown, Gus Smith, Wilkie Barnsback, Will Vance, Harry Tartt, Joseph Schneeberger, unknown, Percy Whitbread, John Gessert, George Fiegenbaum, Joseph Schwarz and unknown; second row, seated: Ben Stillwell, Tom Clark, James Flynn, Edward L. Schwarz, Nick Bosen, Charles Hack, William F. Wayne, Ferd Tunnell, Adolph Klingel, Jacob Dornacher and John Sanner; third row, standing: Tom Crossman, Joe Sties, John Bernreuter, Joe Smith, Will Crossman, Tom O'Connor, Ansel Brown, Otto Girnt, Tom Long (behind Charles Hack), Adolph Suppiger, Will Schwarz, James Tunnell, Will Wayne, Ralph Wayne, Alvin Morefield, unknown, unknown, Jacob Hans. In doorway, hat over eyes, Joe Sturm.

J. G. Delicate Grocer, typified the kind of mom-and-pop store that once supplied food and household items for all. With the coming of supermarkets and, later, convenience stores, most of the small groceries disappeared.

At Makler Saloon, on East Vandalia Street at Kansas, the holiday decorations are in place, the polished bar gleams, the spittoons shine and the bartenders' jackets are spotless for a formal portrait in this men-only enclave of yesteryear. The Maklers were Czech and their saloon was torn down to build the Czech National Hall in 1906. There were 29 taverns in Edwardsville in 1907—-the most common small business of that era.

Businesswomen were concentrated in certain trades associated with traditional activities thought suitable for females. Wood's City Directory of 1894 lists 11 females: three "laundresses," three "dressmakers," three "boarding house keepers," a "milliner and dressmaker," and a "domestic". By 1907, the number of women listed had doubled to 25. Sixteen were still "dressmaker", "milliner", or "boarding house keeper". "Laundress" and "domestic" no longer appeared as categories of employment, although women must have done that work. Women employed in the shirt factory remained unlisted. Two women were listed as "nurses," along with one man. Five women gave music lessons, and one woman was a "midwife", Mrs. A. J. Voge at 638 East Vandalia. One woman, Mrs. Margaret Lynch, at 103 Vandalia, listed herself as "photographer."

During the first two decades of the twentieth century, a number of impressive brick structures were added to North Main Street. The three-story Wildey Theater and Lodge Hall went up in 1908; the Palace Store followed in 1909.

The three-story Wildey Theater building was opened in 1909, a project of a group of investors led by the local chapter of the International Order of Odd Fellows and named for Thomas Wildey, an Englishman, who founded I.O.O.F. in Baltimore in 1819. The lodge had a formal meeting room on the third floor; there was a small theater on the second, and on the main floor and in the east end of the building a 1,150-seat theater with balconies and boxes and a stage area equipped for major productions. Big names played here—Al Jolson, W.C. Fields, Douglas Fairbanks Sr., Ginger Rogers. Later came silent movies, then talkies; the last regular film was shown in 1984. Thanks to a heroic private effort, the building was saved, though not reopened as a theater.

The 1909 Palace Store, with its vast retail space, anchored the west side of the 100 block of North Main Street for most of the 20th century. The building bowed out as Fredman Brothers' Furniture and was demolished in 1988; some of the elegant terra cotta ornament was rescued by Southern Illinois University at Edwardsville.

Edwardsville's first true office building, the Bohm, was built by William Bohm, a farmer-businessman, in 1910 and stands today on the northeast corner of Main and Vandalia.

Until the extensive downtown demolitions of the 1980s, the Bank of Edwardsville, a solid, classically ornamented five-story unit in place by 1917, stood on the north-west corner of Purcell and Main, replacing a group of older stores. It was joined in 1922-23 by the five-story Edwardsville National Bank building, with its famous clock, on the corner of St. Louis Street and Main. For 80 years these two buildings were the downtown "skyscrapers." Both are gone now, replaced by more modern structures.

Farmer-businessman William Bohm.

The Bohm Building (1910) is still in service today. Its third floor was added as an afterthought when William Bohm decided he wanted a ballroom. His son, Clarence, studied ballroom dance in California and gave dance lessons in the Bohm Studio for many years.

Three generations of Bohms pose outside the family home off Poag Road near what now is the north entrance road to SIUE. Left to right are William Bohm's son Wilbur, Sophia Blume Bohm and husband Frederick, son William H. Bohm and his wife, Emma, H.C. (Smith) Bohm, holding daughter Bertha, the hired girl, Birdie Martin, and dog Shep.

Fireplace at Bohm homestead was made in 1910 of terra cotta and other material left over from the Bohm Building by workers who came to Thanksgiving dinner that year.

The five-story Bank of Edwardsville building at Main and Purcell streets, completed in 1917, was the city's first "skyscraper." It was impressive, with its dramatic terra cotta ornament, including two four-story Ionic pilasters. The bank moved to new quarters in 1972, and this building was demolished in 1990 to make way for a new county administration building.

This is what the Main-Purcell street corner looked like around 1890, before the 1917 Bank of Edwardsville building. The bank began in 1868 in the light-faced building at left, designed by Edwardsville architect C. H. Spilman.

The Edwardsville National Bank building on St. Louis Street at North Main, is seen in an artist's rendering done for a picture postcard.

The Leland Hotel, with its distinctive corner turret, was a popular downtown gathering place. Most of the hotel was razed to make way for the Edwardsville National Bank building. The portion of the building just to the right of the columned canopy, which housed the Leland Barber Shop on the first floor, lasted for 50 more years, when it was torn down and a small park put there.

REORGANIZATION AND NEW RESPONSIBILITIES FOR CITY GOVERNMENT

Changes in the city's government and the extension of its functions reflected the needs of a population which nearly doubled between 1860 and 1900 and which lived in a world of increasing mechanization and more rapid communication. In September 1872, voters of the town approved the city form of government. A board of trustees, which had governed the town since its official creation by the State Legislature in 1818, yielded to a mayor and council. The vote was 213 in favor of the change, with 89 against it. On October 1, the city was divided into three wards. On November 25, banker and Civil War veteran John A. Prickett was chosen mayor for a short term. By the new city charter, the mayor was to be elected every other year in April. In the first regular April election in 1873, William H. Krome defeated Prickett by nine votes. The mayor's salary, clearly an honorarium, was $100 a year.

The new Edwardsville City Council adopted a city

"Major" John A. Prickett, was Edwardsville's first mayor, 1872-73.

William H. Krome was the city's first full-term mayor, 1873-75.

Edwardsville Architect Charles H. Spilman designed this house, shown in the 1870s, for William H. Krome; its mansard roof imparted a French look. Krome was 31 and fresh out of the University of Michigan Law School when he came here, one of the new, trained, professional lawyers. He became a county judge in 1890 and a justice of the Illinois Supreme Court in 1892. He died in 1917 and his home on Fourth Street was demolished in 1928.

seal and a general code of laws. The police force was to consist of the mayor, aldermen (a total of six, two from each ward), city marshal, superintendent of streets, police magistrate, deputy marshals, and such policemen and watchmen as might have been appointed by the mayor and confirmed by the council. As the city's only full-time employee, the marshal got a salary of $500. Edwardsville only gradually developed a professional police force to assist the city marshal.

The first full-time municipal employee hired when Edwardsville voted to become a city, in 1872, was Argalus G. Stubbs, City Marshall.

Otto Dagenfelder poses proudly with Edwardsville's motorized police patrol car in 1918.

The Madison County Jail building—sheriff's residence in front—is seen in this view published in 1873. The building, located across North Main Street from today's county administration building, was a significant downtown feature from its construction in 1869 to its razing in 1982. When the last prisoners moved out in 1979, the jail was the oldest Illinois jail in continuous use. By this time the county had opened a much larger, modern jail a few blocks away.

Before 1874, Edwardsville had no fire-fighting organization. Volunteer Fire Company Number One was formed in February 1874 with 33 charter members. From 1874 until 1906, the volunteers raced to the firehouse and pulled a hand-operated pump to the site of a fire and then passed buckets and pumped water from either cisterns or available ponds.

In 1875, the City Council authorized the spending of $160 for a fire bell, and during the same year, citizens donated $172 for the department's first uniforms (fire hats cost $4.00 each and shirts $2.50). In 1892, when the city built its first City Hall, located on Main Street at the site of the present city public safety building, it put the fire engine house on the first floor and city offices on the second, with the fire bell on top of the building.

For 32 years, until 1906, when the city council took over the organization of the fire department, the men elected their own fire chief and his two assistants. The department had no paid members until 1906, when the city purchased an almost new combination hose, chemical wagon and ladder truck and a team of beautiful black horses that had been part of the 1904 St. Louis World's

Edwardsville firefighters have restored the first fire "engine" used in the city dating from 1874. In those days, the firemen themselves provided the motor power as they ran to a fire, pulling the wagon behind. The vehicle carried ladders in racks on top, plus leather buckets slung underneath.

Uniformed volunteer firefighters pose in 1896 with their equipment—still hand-drawn. In center foreground, in front of the hose cart, is Dennis Hentz, chief; holding the horse, at right, is Argalus Stubbs, marshal. The scene is Main and Hillsboro; the Clark grocery is part of today's Schwartz Health Mart.

Fair equipment. At this time, the city employed a paid driver. In June 1906, the city bought a third fire horse, "Teddy," and placed an electric fire alarm in the belfry with the bell. The telephone office rang the alarm differently for different districts of the city so that firemen could tell the location of any fire by the number of rings. A new era dawned in 1917, when the first motorized fire truck was purchased to replace the horses pulling the old equipment. The old firewagon was sold to a junk dealer for $16.20. The two horses brought $250. Fire hydrants, connected to city water mains, now replaced cisterns on the major streets.

At the monthly meeting of January, 1907, the department cut its active membership from 35 to 20. At the March meeting, a new set of rules was adopted. Firemen were divided into "Active" and "Honorary" members. Active firemen reported for every fire, while Honorary firemen served as guards at large conflagrations.

By 1940, the city had a paid fire department, but volunteers were still enrolled and were expected for larger fires.

This picture of the 1901-03 city administration, was taken in front of the 1892 city building at 400 North Main Street. Seated, left to right, are Charles Gueltig, city attorney; George Barraclough, police magistrate; Nicholas Bosen, mayor, and Charles Hack, treasurer. Standing are William Harley, streets superintendent; Charles Bartels, alderman; Nick Lanham, city weigher; Jacob Weber, alderman; John Schumacher, alderman; Martin Fischer, night watchman; Dennis Hentz, chief of police; John Daech, Henry Meyer and Thomas Moriarity, policemen; and Joseph Kesl, Fred Bernreuther, Frank Daech and Jacob Dunstedter, aldermen.

Edwardsville City Hall and Fire Station was built in 1892, with engine house below and city offices upstairs. The building was demolished in 1965 to make way for a new city hall. The water tower, behind, served from 1898 to 1964. Posed in front are the famous team of black horses and fire fighters' wagon used in the World's Fair of 1904 and purchased by Edwardsville after the fair was over.

Before the depression of 1893-95 wiped out their treasury, the firemen of Edwardsville in the 1870s and 1880s created their own "safety nets"—- funds to pay members injured on the job and to create a "sick aid fund" for members laid off their regular jobs by illness. Firemen's balls and picnics drew hundreds of people. Firemen's tournaments, in which companies from various towns competed in hose car races, coupling contests, foot races, and ladder climbing matches thrilled spectators and brought dollars into the company treasury in the form of prizes. Edwardsville's department joined the Illinois Firemen's Association in 1889. From August 31 to September 2, 1894, the city blazed with glory as it hosted the Association's state convention, a first for any town south of Springfield. Visiting firemen and city organizations participated in a grand parade and listened to speeches. Chief Dennis Hentz received a gold watch from the businessmen of Edwardsville. More than a thousand townspeople and visitors watched the competitions. In 1904, the company voted to use contest winnings and receipts from balls in its treasury to take out insurance, through the state association, for all of its 39 members, who got benefits for injuries received in going to, at, or coming from a fire and $100 in case of death.

During these years, Edwardsville's fire department produced some outstanding athletes. In 1897, they were county champions in the hose cart race, in which they ran 1000 feet in 40 4/5 seconds. At the state tourna-

Wolf's Lake (Wolf Reservoir) is shown on 1906 map of the south part of Edwardsville.

SIMON KELLERMANN, JR., WHO JOINED THE EDWARDSVILLE FIRE DEPARTMENT IN 1899, REMEMBERS THE STATE CONVENTION OF 1894 IN 1957.

You should have seen the races. You'd have enjoyed them no end. Each event was chock-full of excitement, from start to finish. We had foot races, ladder climbing, a novelty hose race and thrilling hook-and-ladder races. . . . Those boys were outstanding athletes, make no mistake about that.

Yes, it was all so grand. . . . My, that parade—that was really a dandy—horse-drawn carriages and buggies and the gents and their ladies so smartly dressed for the occasion. Our unpaved streets were filled with dancers during the evening hours, and firecrackers exploding everywhere.

Wolf's Lake was at the head of Delaplaine Branch in the near south end of town.

ment of 1900, an Edwardsville team won eight prizes for a total of $110. At the World's Fair in August 1904, Fred Stolze became the World's Champion Ladder Man by running 50 feet and climbing a 24 foot ladder in 6 2/5 seconds. Edwardsville's team at the fair also did well. They placed second in one hook and ladder contest and first in another, took second in the championship foot race, and won first prize for best drilled company. Riding home on their specially chartered railroad car, with their equipment on a flat car behind, Edwardsville's men carried $222.50 for the treasury. Disbanded in 1908, the team was reorganized in 1915 and won the state championship and $375 that year at Blue Island. In 1920, Edwardsville firemen again won the state champi-

onship. They entered seven events and won seven first prizes. At the last state tournament, held in conjunction with the State Fair at Springfield in 1921, Edwardsville's running team won nine of ten events for another state championship. Simon Kellerman III, as captain of the team, won the 100 yard dash for captains. His father, Simon Kellerman, Jr., was president of the Illinois State Firemen during both 1921 and 1922. Beginning in 1922, the old athletic contests between firemen's units were replaced with "fire colleges," where the men met to learn about new techniques and equipment for fighting fires.

> **AN AGE OF ORGANIZATION. LAWYER C. W. TERRY, SPEECH AT FIREMAN'S PARADE, 1894**
>
> *This, my friends, is an age of organization. Interests have become so gigantic that therein is our only safety. The time has come when we exemplify the Bible teaching that no man 'liveth unto himself and no man dieth unto himself.'*

Volunteer firemen were skilled athletes around the turn of the century. These men took part in state competitions. Left to right, on the street, are Pete Rump, Charles Dickerson, James Burns, Ben Bernius, George Hanser, Clarence Tindall, Fred Zeigler, Ben Wood, Julius Schulz (squatting), Charles Somerlad (sitting behind), Edwin Morefield, Nathan Wood and Charles Rau. On the ladder are Simon Kellerman, left, and Henry Faust, right, and Harvey Stone, at top.

Edwardsville's running team at practice for the state games in 1920.

Below is Edwardsville's 1920 State Champion Running Team. Squatting in front, left to right, are Fred Schwager, Oliver McNeilly, Charles Hentz and James Burns; standing, left to right, are Louis Hartung, Simon Kellermann III, Simon Kellermann Jr., Dr. Wilbur Bohm, Tom P. Reilly, E.P. Gilmore, James Brandt and Elmer Bohm. On ladder truck behind, left to right, are Lester Kennedy, George Hartung, Ben Wood, Ferd Rohrkaste, Frank Gusewelle, John Hensley, Eddie Flynn, William Love, Florian Trares and Russell Southard.

ELECTRIC LIGHTS AND CITY WATER

During the 1880s, American life was revolutionized by the development of electric lighting. Many homes did not acquire this luxury until the 1930s, but Edwardsville was among the first cities in Illinois to install electric street lights. In 1887, E. W. Mudge and Associates, a local engineering firm, proposed the building of an electric power plant, and 494 voters petitioned the city government to appropriate funds for the franchise. Mudge installed a generator in the Dunstedter Building on Second Street and operated it on a city con-tract for five years. Fourteen electric street lamps, sus-pended about 35 feet from the ground, burned from twi-light until midnight on nights when the moon provided insufficient illumination and on cloudy, rainy or other-wise stormy nights. Over the next three decades, more streets, business buildings, and many homes were wired. In 1924, the canopy of cables crisscrossing the downtown area was sharply curtailed by putting the electric wires underground. Edwardsville acquired its power from a plant on Second Street until 1927, when current began to arrive from a new plant at Cahokia.

The Edwardsville Electric Light & Power Company, founded in 1892, opened this plant on North Second Street at E Street. The plant, shown in 1895, was destroyed by fire in 1898.

> ### FRED SCHWAGER'S GRANDFATHER GOES ELECTRIC
> *After the Palace Store opened in 1909, Grandfather Schwager had charge of one of the clothing departments. He built a home on Grand Avenue, the first on the street to have electricity. Each night, after work, Grandfather turned on all the lights. Then, he took the dog for a walk up and down the street to admire his house, the only one with electric lights.*
>
> Story told to Dick Norrish, 1996.

An interior view of the Edwardsville electric plant, before the fire.

Once the link of germs to disease was understood after the Civil War, and as the population of the town increased the number of outhouses, pollution of local wells emerged as a public issue. However, engineers called in to do a water plan for the city in 1891 argued that the population, about 3,500, was too small to support a water system. During the 1890s, several efforts by out-of-town companies to develop a pumping station at Cahokia Creek failed. In 1898, a group of local businessmen including W. L. Hadley, Dr. Joseph Pogue, N. O. Nelson, William Kriege and others, incorporated the Edwardsville Water Company and built a pumping station at Poag, 4 1/2 miles west of town, laid pipe along the Wabash tracks, and built a 136-foot-high water tower at the corner of North Main and High streets. Use of city water gradually spread through the community as property owners made the decision to spend the money to connect. In 1912, the Centennial History of Madison County noted that many private wells remained in use. In 1926, the locally owned plant was sold to a national company.

Edwardsville's original water tower, built in 1898 behind city hall by Tuxhorn Brothers Contractors, had a gently tapering, octagonal brick shaft; the catwalk and tank top also were octagonal. The tower was razed in 1964 to make way for a new city hall.

MAIN STREET CLEANED UP

Henry P. Hotz, a banker and lumber yard owner, was Mayor of Edwardsville from 1903 to 1913, a time of crucial changes in the life and appearance of the town. During his first term as mayor, he worked to reconfigure Main Street. Old-fashioned wooden porches in front of many downtown businesses were torn off and replaced by awnings. The dirt road lined with wooden sidewalks yielded, in 1904, to brick paving laid on a concrete foundation. Workmen digging a trench for the city's first sewer line in the middle of Main Street in 1904 found oak boards from the antebellum days of plank roads. Concrete sidewalks with curbs solved the decades-old hazard and inconvenience of mud on major streets.

Mayor Henry P. Hotz spearheaded downtown transformation.

Henry Hotz's home at 516 North Kansas Street, in one of the city's newer neighborhoods.

Goodbye mud! A new North Main Street paved with brick is seen in 1909 view looking south from courthouse square, at right; note new concrete sidewalks.

Here's North Main Street around 1920, the courthouse on the left.

A LEADING MODERNIZER

In December 1895, Charles Boeschenstein, editor and publisher of the *Intelligencer,* proudly published a special supplement, "The Industrial Issue," which described Edwardsville's transformation during the previous 25 years. Boeschenstein, only 31 years old in 1895, had already demonstrated a willingness to experiment with new ideas and technology.

Before his father's death in 1883, young Charles had purchased, at the age of 17, the *Highland Herald,* a floundering English-language newspaper in a community of immigrants where German remained the language of preference. Growing up in Highland, Boeschenstein, the son of Swiss immigrants, had a foot in two worlds. He was proud of his European heritage and yet, he sought to become the epitome of an American businessman. Boeschenstein reorganized the *Highland Herald* and made it go.

Understanding the connection between rapid communication and presentation of the latest news, he successfully promoted the installment of the first long distance telephone line through Madison County to Highland. He bought the first typewriter in Madison County, a Remington. In January 1883 at the age of 19, Boeschenstein purchased Edwardsville's *Intelligencer* and merged it with the *Herald.* He moved to Edwardsville. For ten years, the *Intelligencer* remained a weekly. In 1893, it became a semi-weekly. In 1895, it began publishing three times a week, and by 1907 became a daily, except Sundays. Continuing his application of technology to his business, in 1899 he installed the first Linotype in Madison County. This mechanical typesetting machine, with a keyboard something like a typewriter, was a godsend for the publishing business. As improved machines for newspaper production appeared, Boeschenstein adopted them. Like Main Street, the paper under Boeschenstein changed in appearance. Advertising disappeared from the front page. A want-ad section and more coverage of local and national sports were added. A woman's page appeared every day. On selected days, a men's corner, a children's page and a farmers' page were added. Once a week, the "I" included a page of cartoons and jokes.

Following his father's tradition of civic participation in Highland, Charles ran successfully for mayor of his adopted city, Edwardsville, in 1887. During his two-year term, he talked the city council into illuminating the major streets—- Main, Second and Vandalia—- with electric lights. During the 1890s, Boeschenstein edited his newspaper and successfully entered the banking business, ending as a director and later vice-president of the Bank of Edwardsville. He sparked the organization of the Edwardsville Water Company, which moved the city, during the first decade of the 20th century, from dependence on individual and communal wells to piped water from the present source, aquifers in the American

Industrialist Andrew Carnegie contributed money to build a new Edwardsville Public Library, plus more than 2,800 other libraries in towns across America. Ours was built in City Park and dedicated in 1906. Land for City Park had been set aside in the 1820s by Ninian Edwards and Benjamin Stephenson.

Bottom off Poag Road. It was Boeschenstein who wrote to Andrew Carnegie and asked for assistance in building a public library for the town. Andrew Carnegie's check for $12,000 arrived by return mail. The library soon moved from a room in City Hall to a brand new "Carnegie Library" building.

In other ways too, Boeschenstein's career as civic-minded businessman represents the forces of modernization working on Edwardsville. Many businesses were becoming "professions," journalism among them.

Before he was 20, Charles had been part of organizing the Southern Illinois Press Association and later served as President of the Illinois Daily Newspaper Association. A lifelong Democrat, he participated in the reorganization of the Party after the Republican onslaught of 1896. In a period of rapid change, he wanted to celebrate the present by remembering the sacrifices of past times. Hence, he was a main organizer of the Madison County Centennial of 1912.

Vice-president Thomas R. Marshall, seated left, was a Chautauqua lecturer here in 1914; his host was businessman and civic leader Charles Boeschenstein, right. Standing behind are Elizabeth Barnsback Spilman, Bertha Whitbread Boeschenstein, Charles H. Spilman, Mary West Hadley and Mrs. Marshall.

Boeschenstein's House on North Kansas.

CHARLES H. BARTELS: A GOOD EYE

Between 1899 and 1910, Edwardsville was home to its own documentary photographer, Charles H. Bartels, known to many in town as a barber in his shop at the Leland Hotel. He came to Edwardsville from Hanover, Germany, at the age of 20 in 1884, and lovingly recorded scenes of his adopted town, his neighbors and friends, and local landscape during years of momentous change. He seemed to want to juxtapose enduring values of friendship, family, and community with the hectic pace of modern life.

His own self-portraits reveal a man who took pride in

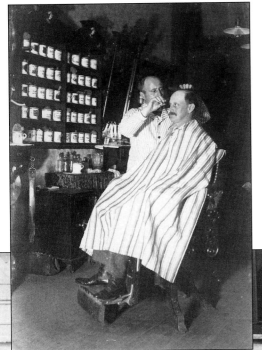

Left: Barber-photographer Charles H. Bartels at work in his shop in the Leland Hotel. Above: An 1899 ad for Bartels' barber shop. Below: Bartels' pictures, like this one of him on his back steps, are rich with details of ordinary life.

his work. We see him in 1899 carefully working on a balding customer, one of many who might have owned one of the private shaving mugs in the rack at the back. Again, he photographed himself with magnificent houseplants on the back steps of his home, now gone, at 416 N. Main. He holds a newspaper, symbolic of his role in the town, where he had been elected Master of the Masonic Lodge in 1901 and member of the City Council during 1903 and 1904. In 1904, Bartels left the barbershop and became a claims agent for the East St. Louis and Suburban Railway and for the Mt. Olive and Staunton Coal Company. Something of a Renaissance man, he collected butterflies, kept a sizable library of books about entomology, and belonged to the American Entomological Association. Most of his photographs, in collections of the Madison County Historical Society, were taken while he was a barber, but one self-portrait, perhaps made in the 1920s, shows us an older man, standing in a field with his butterfly net, his cigar, and his watch on a chain.

Bartels on an outing, with cigar, butterfly net and watch on a chain.

Bartels' residence, seen in 1899, was at 416 N. Main Street, next door to what is now the main fire station. The building housed city offices for a number of years and was torn down in 1993.

Interior of Bartels' home, with baby picture on display easel, right, and framed arrangement of butterflies.

Bartels recorded both landscapes and social moments and conveyed an understanding that they were "historical," passing into memory. On August 9, 1899, he caught the Wabash Continental racing along at 60 miles an hour. A year later, people stood, dignified in their Sunday best, ready to ride the first streetcar from Edwardsville to East St. Louis. Children, his own and others, drew his lens. Little boys perform daring feats. Girls sit among flowers or with their dolls. He shows us scenes of town life: a sleigh in front of a doctor's office in 1900; men playing

This October 1899 scene featured corn shocks.

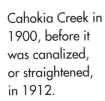

This farmstead, with its split-rail fences, was on Troy Road, where Kmart is now.

Cahokia Creek in 1900, before it was canalized, or straightened, in 1912.

Bartels caught the Wabash Continental running at 60 miles per hour at 9:40 a.m. on August 9, 1899.

Around 1900, Bartels made this portrait of a dignified group, in their Sunday best, ready to ride the first electric streetcar to East St. Louis.

An adventurous group of boys posed for Bartels on a railroad trestle, probably over Cahokia Creek north-west of Edwardsville.

dominoes in the barbershop in 1899; German families posing in front of their homes; the home of Dr. E. W. Fiegenbaum on Main Street, a particularly impressive example of Second Empire mansarded magnificence built in the 1870s and now a funeral home; a club of young fishermen, laughing, trying to be exotic and romantic; the "Floriss Club," neighbors happy on a summer day, who now exist only in family memories and this photograph.

Those back steps again: Bartels' daughter, right, with a friend, and some of the family's collection of houseplants.

Bartels' daughter with doll and Christmas tree.

Walking dollies on a summer day; note the boardwalk around the house, before bricks or concrete were common.

Bartels recorded this game of dominoes in his barbershop in 1899.

The North Main Street home of Dr. E. W. Fiegenbaum, photographed by Bartels, still stands today, though greatly altered, as Weber Funeral Home.

The Floriss Club, shown in 1900, consisted of neighbors who now exist only in family memories and this photograph.

This fun-loving group of young fishermen used Mexican sombreros, corn cob pipes and guitars to add romance to their meetings.

THE GERMAN PRESENCE

From 1860 to 1920, German-born Edwardsvillians were about 25 per cent of the population, and with their children, made up more than half of the town's people. Many of the German immigrants to Madison County between 1845 and 1920 brought with them traditions of skill in working with wood, machines, brick, and in farming.

Two German-language newspapers were published in Edwardsville. The *Madison County Anzeiger* lasted from May 1875 to May 1878. The *Demokrat* appeared for only four months in 1880. Charles Boeschenstein, the editor of the *Intelligencer* who, from 1883 to 1915, participated in many of the most dramatic changes in town life, was the child of German-speaking Swiss immigrants.

Edwardsville's first volunteer fire department, organized in 1874, reflected German interest in this vital institution: two of the three top officers and 14 of the first 20 rank and file volunteers were German-American. As they built institutions and constructed social organizations, Germans left their stamp on the town and the countryside and formed a vital segment of the farmers, businessmen and working classes of the city.

The Germans, however, were not a monolithic group. Many were Catholic; others were Protestants, but of three different denominations: Methodist, Evangelical Protestant (now United Church of Christ), and later, Missouri Synod Lutheran. Until World War I, German was the major language of services in each of these churches. In 1867, German and Irish Catholic families in Edwardsville split into two parishes, St. Mary's, a mix of Irish, Czech and Italian, and St. Boniface, predominantly German.

The German Methodist Church, now Immanuel United Methodist, at 800 N. Main Street, was built in 1890.

The predecessor of today's Eden United Church of Christ, The Free Evangelical Church, was this simple Gothic building at the Eden location, 903 N. Second Street. The old church dates from about the time the original congregation was formed by German settlers in 1868.

This original Trinity Lutheran Church building, at North Fillmore and Chapman, was dedicated in March 1906. In 1984, the congregation moved into a much bigger church a few blocks away. This building has been divided into apartments.

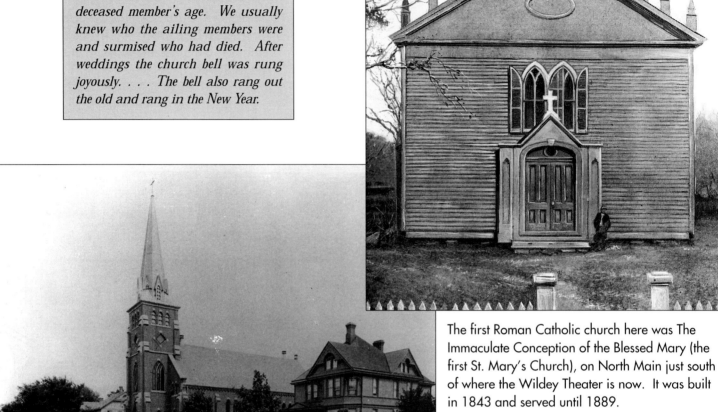

The first Roman Catholic church here was The Immaculate Conception of the Blessed Mary (the first St. Mary's Church), on North Main just south of where the Wildey Theater is now. It was built in 1843 and served until 1889.

St. Mary's II, a Gothic structure with a massive tower, was built on Park Street and dedicated in June 1889. An ample parish house is at right. The congregation built St. Mary's III in the Montclaire subdivision in 1965, and St. Mary's II was demolished in 1982.

St. Mary's confirmation class of 1910 poses in the parish house yard.

From 1855 to 1863, German families supported a German Language School in Edwardsville. Built with community contributions and $90 from two dancing parties, this subscription school cost $400 ($50 for two building lots and $300 for a building). It was part of a house now standing at 314 Clay Street. The teacher, who was paid $25 a year, lived in the building and prepared his meals there. After the new public institution, Dale School, was completed in 1864, the German school was closed and sold for $635, including the furniture. This fund was later given by these German families to the public library.

The Germans of St. Boniface parish established its first school in 1871, with Sisters of the Precious Blood as teachers and administrators until 1896, followed by Sisters of St. Dominic of Racine, 1896-1905, and then Poor Handmaids of Jesus Christ, from 1905. In 1882, a larger building was constructed, and in 1912, the present school, which flourishes today, was built. Enrollment from the beginning was more than 100 students. In 1889, St. Boniface had 103 pupils taught by two teachers.

Edwardsville contains pockets of neat, smaller turn-of-the century homes built by German families who worked in the mines, factories and stores of the town. Street names in Lower Town resound with this heritage: Schiller, Krafft, Ritter, Hanser, along with Eberhardt and Klein Avenues. Because of the numerous ridges and steep hills near Cahokia Creek, German residents called Lower Town *Hexe Buckel,* colloquial German for "witch's back." In other parts of town, Ammann Place, Wolf Street and Schwarz Street bear the names of well-known businessmen of German ethnicity.

Olga Heberer, who was born in Edwardsville, daughter of German parents, remembered that many German

Part of this residence at 314 Clay Street served briefly in the mid-1800s as a German language school.

Fischer home on Union Street was built in 1909 by parents of Kenneth Fischer who, with his wife Marie, still lives there. In the backyard is one of the oldest oak trees in the city.

St. Boniface School and Hall, dedicated in 1913, was modern, designed with future needs in mind. It housed a kitchen, dining room and playrooms in the basement, large classrooms upstairs, and an auditorium seating 600 on the third floor. Note the statue of the parish patron in a niche in the roof-level gable.

families, like the Bartels, grew not only vegetables, but also flowers and fruits. Women made apple butter in the summer. Older residents, remembering notable events for the Madison County Centennial in 1912, recalled that George Frederick Julius Barnsback, who farmed land 3 1/2 miles south of Edwardsville before the Civil War, had returned from a visit to Germany with a pink-scented peony and planted the "first garden in this vicinity devoted exclusively to flowers."

German Edwardsvillians organized much of the musical life of the town. In 1853, a men's singing society, the *Maennerchor,* was formed, with 52 members. Active during the 1850s, the society disbanded during the Civil War and reorganized in 1868 with 14 members. During the 1880s, the Maennerchor presented German-language musicals at meetings of the Druidic Order, a German lodge of about 50 members, organized for the purpose of providing life insurance and sick benefits in a time without Workmen's Compensation and Social Security. For $8 to $10 per year, a member of Franklin Grove No. 26, United American Order of Druids, got $500 worth of life insurance and $5 a week while ill. Another German-language lodge, active between 1890 and World War I, was the United Order Teutonic Brotherhood, which had about 30 members. The Druids and the Maennerchor were most active at about the same time, from 1881 to 1899, when the Druids disbanded. The Maennerchor also dissolved about the same time. An effort was made, between 1905 and 1907, to reorganize the Maennerchor, but in 1907, their music and furniture were given to the Evangelical Church choir.

Adam and Catherina Schwarz came to Edwardsville from Germany in 1844. Their children, especially

This thriving grape arbor was once part of the Neuman Place, off North Main Street in Lowertown.

Olga Heberer, who often sang at local entertainments, strikes a pose on a railroad car.

Helen Watson Herzwurm and Dorothy Watson stir the apple butter kettle on Monroe Street about 1930.

Christoph, born January 19, 1834, and called Chris, sparked much of Edwardsville's musical life for the next eight decades. Chris Schwarz carried one of the family's treasures brought from Germany, a rosewood melodeon (German accordion), to and from St. Boniface in order to play at Masses. He also taught dancing to the music of his own violin in the 1850s and 1860s. Chris's son, William C. Schwarz, organized the Edwardsville Enterprise Band on August 7, 1885. During the 1890s, the band won applause and fame as it took prizes at festivals in Alton, Decatur, and Staunton. The Schwarzes and the Enterprise Band brought to Edwardsville the German custom of serenading newlyweds in their new home. On July 4, 1890, the Enterprise Band serenaded Dr. and Mrs. E. W. Fiegenbaum, who had just returned from their honeymoon, and then marched on to play

The Enterprise Band poses with their leader, William C. Schwarz, in center, in 1895. The four men standing behind are, left to right, Joseph Hotz, James Whitbread, Will Schulze and Ed Overbeck; in middle row are Henry Trares, Elmer Schwarz, C. E. Willis, Henry Fischer, Edgar Gerke, George C. Schwarz, George Brendle, Caspar Vorwald, C. Lorch and Leopold Brendle; front row, Herman Wolf, Albert Stolze, W. D. Kirkpatrick, Charles Schwarz, W. C. Schwarz, George W. Belk, George Roberts, Charles Hoffmann and Will Overbeck.

Here's the Enterprise Band in front of the Madison County Courthouse in 1910, the durable Will Schwarz still in charge, though there have been some changes in personnel.

William C. Schwarz (left) with a cornet presented to him by "the boys" in the band, in 1886.

patriotic music on Courthouse Square. A group of Schwarzes also played together as the Independent Orchestra.

Most famous among Edwardsville's numerous musical groups was the lovely Schwarz Sisters Orchestra, eventually composed of all nine daughters of Enterprise Band leader William C. Schwarz and conducted by William B. Thomas, husband of the eldest daughter, Jessie. They per- formed for enthusiastic crowds at public ceremonies and in many surrounding towns between 1896 and 1910. According to Mary Blixen, a daughter of Estella Schwarz Whiteside who was one of the Schwarz Sisters, the family had to rent two carriages at the livery stable for their trips to neighboring villages. One day, a horse spooked and ran away with the instruments.

Bands continued as a feature of community life.

This Independent Band included violins, guitar, flute and percussion.

The Schwarz Orchestra, in 1901, was a showcase for Schwarz musical talent. Left to right are Herman Wolf, Christoph Schwarz, Henry Trares Sr., Charlie Schwarz, William Schwarz, Henry Trares Jr., Caspar Vorwald, Elmer Schwarz, William Overbeck and George Schwarz. Bow ties were big back then, as well as high-laced shoes.

During 1917, when many regular band members went off to war, William B. Thomas, formerly conductor of the Schwarz Sisters, organized a boys' band.

The Turnverein, a gymnastic society, represented another significant German institution in Edwardsville, a club closely affiliated with the German Evangelical Protestant Church (now Eden United Church of Christ). First organized in 1858, the Turnverein lapsed during the Civil War and then was reorganized with 40 members in 1868. Young men trained to perform gymnastic feats of strength, tumbling and pyramiding. They competed with similar organizations in neighboring communities. By putting on festivals in conjunction with singing by the Maennerchor and by giving annual masquerade balls, the Turners raised money for the church and for rent of a practice hall.

In 1871, the Turner and singing societies of towns in Madison County formed an association, which held yearly competitions. In 1884, the Edwardsville Turnverein qualified in gymnastic trials for admission to the Nord Amerikanischen Turner Bund, the national organization. The same year, they decided to buy the old Presbyterian Church building on Second Street for a permanent Turner Hall, which opened in September, 1884. In 1886, the club had 50 members. Dues for gymnastics classes were 25 cents a month. Other activities at

The Schwarz Sisters Orchestra played many a concert here between 1896-1910, under the direction of William B. Thomas, husband of the eldest daughter, Jessie, the trombonist, at left. The others, left to right, with their married names, present or future, are Etta (Mrs. E. C. Ferguson), Minnie (Mrs. G. W. Bassford), Catherine (Mrs. E. L. Sumner), Ruth (Mrs. W. Rogers), Edith (Mrs. J. F. Keshner), Estella (Mrs. W. C. Whiteside) and Irene (Mrs. Ernest Harpole).

the Hall included German language classes on four nights of the week.

During the 1890s, interest in gymnastics classes declined, perhaps due to the uncertain economy and depression after 1893. Classes started up again briefly after 1896, but Turner Hall continued mainly as a place for social gatherings for Evangelical Germans until World War I, when German language and German organizations were discouraged by wartime propaganda equating such activities with disloyalty.

Clarence Bohm, from a German family who came to Illinois in the 1830s, recalls that German language preaching in the German Methodist Church ended after the U.S. entered World War I in April 1917. In 1928, when German language was readmitted to the public school curriculum after a 10 year absence, there was talk of reviving the Turnverein also, but success was apparently limited. Public school sports now offered an alternative to the Turner form of exercise and competition. As part of the New Deal, the hall was a teenage recreation center in the late 1930s. Later, during World War II, Turner Hall was used as a dress factory and, most recently, again as a church.

Thus, Edwardsville, although not famous as a German community, was in many ways a town whose development reflected the influence of this powerful ethnic group.

THE MEANING OF NARODNI SIN

Czech immigrants, though fewer in number than the Germans, also left their mark on the community. Some farmers arrived before the Civil War in the wake of nationalist uprisings in 1848 in the Austrian Empire, of which the region of Czech- and Slovak-speaking peoples was a part. (Czechoslovakia did not exist on the map until 1919.) After the American Civil War, coal mining and opportunities for skilled craftsmen in construction drew a larger community of Czechs to Edwardsville.

In 1867, 45 Catholic families formed the Bohemian Catholic cemetery, today known as the Buck Road Cemetery in Glen Carbon. In 1875, Rolnik No. 7 Lodge was organized to provide insurance benefits in case of sickness and/or death and also opportunities for socializing in culturally familiar ways. The lodge was formed under the leadership of young Jan Kalal. The familiar Czech names of Sedlacek, Benda, Primas, and Slivka are found on the first membership list. Rolnik means "farmer" in Czech, reflecting the occupation of earlier Czech immigrants and perhaps the hope of later Czech immigrants to own land in their adopted country. According to Frank Novak, historian of Edwardsville's Czechs, early meetings were held in the Wabash Hotel.

As membership in Lodge Rolnik No. 7 grew from 14 in 1875 to more than 50 by the end of the century, an

The "Turner hall" on North Second is currently a church.

This unusual photograph shows a funeral group at the Bohemian Catholic Cemetery (Buck Road Cemetery, on Illinois Route 162, Glen Carbon), in the late 19th century. The picture is from SIUE's collection of photos of Slavic-American life.

Three young members of the Czech *Sokol,* a gymnastics society, stand with their leader, Vaclav Snajdr.

Czech working men used their hall building as a backdrop for this picture. The Snajdr-Schejbal Park Saloon occupied the first floor, or part of it, after 1913.

older two-story building which the Society had bought in 1881 was too small. Through a variety of activities, such as dances and picnics, the Czech community raised money to purchase a lot on Vandalia Street. In 1906, Anton Hlad, of a family that later changed their name to Ladd, built the graceful two-story brick building which still stands at 209 East Vandalia, across from City Park. Ladd Avenue was named for this family of builders. Within the Narodni Sin (National Hall), classes were offered in Czech language. The Sokol, a gymnastic society similar to the Germans' Turnverein, flourished. Until 1958, the language of lodge rituals was Czech, afterwards it was English.

During World War I, Lodge Rolnik supported and helped to finance the Czechoslovak Legion fighting on the side of the Allied Powers in Europe. Membership in the lodge crested at 173 during the 1920s. During the depression of the 1930s, many members had to move out of the area, but the mortgage on Narodni Sin was nevertheless paid off in 1935. Meetings in the building continued until 1971, when directors of Lodge Rolnik No. 7, with heavy hearts, sold the building. Afterwards, monthly meetings continued for some years in the meeting room at Walt Schlemer Realty, 405 East Vandalia.

The 1906 Czech Hall, seen in 1910, decked out for a parade. Narodni Sin means National Hall, and the initials below stand for Cecho Slovensky Podporujici Spolky, or Czechoslovak Protective Society.

In 1933, all Czech organizations were merged into the Czecho Slovak Society of America. Here's the Edwardsville contingent in 1935, on the second floor of Narodni Sin, for the group's 60th anniversary. With the merger, the local Lodge Rolnik No. 7 became Svobodny (Free) Rolnik Lodge No. 26.

MORE FUN

In times before movies, radio, television, and the Internet, many people in Edwardsville participated in amateur theatrical performances or musical groups or other sorts of homemade entertainment. Churchwomen devised unique fundraisers. In July 1889 the Altar Society of St. Mary's Church produced "The Flower Queen," a children's operetta, at the Tuxhorn Opera House. In 1890, women of St. John's Methodist Church presented a "milkmaids' carnival." After weeks of practice drilling in military formation with milking stools instead of guns, Milkmaids Edith Metcalfe, Julia Hadley, Minnie Jones, Mamie and Josie Springer, Carrie Wolf, Mamie and Jennie Keller, Lizzie White, Lizzie Brinkmann, Annie Trares, Veva Mudge, Maud Burroughs, and Dora Judd netted the church $63 in two performances.

Musicians from Edwardsville's African-American community occasionally performed for a larger public. At the St. Andrew's Guild/Enterprise Band joint musical show in 1887, a drill by the African-American lodge of the Knights of Pythias was, according to the *Intelligencer,* "encored with relish." In 1894, when Edwardsville hosted the Illinois State Firemen's Association, an unaccompanied quartet composed of Grant Ward, Mitchell White, Felix Green and Charles Smith was the featured entertainment.

African-American entertainers from out of town also appeared here. Several times after the Opera House opened in the 1880s, community groups brought in Blind John Boon, who, because of his handicap, played entirely by ear. He carried his own beautifully tuned Chickering piano with him. When he performed, he

> **"POUND PARTY"** - *Edwardsville Intelligencer* - 1877
>
> *"A pound package of something was the price of admission and these packages were sold at auction without the contents being known before being purchased. The first package offered by Mr. Metcalfe, who had been chosen to act as auctioneer. . . brought only one bid in spite of the efforts of the auctioneer, and was knocked down for 5 cents. The purchaser got a bargain, as it is recorded that he got for his 5 cents fully as many hickory nuts as could be bought for a dime at any store. [Another man] paid 80 cents for a package that contained one ear of corn. . . . The oyster supper that followed the entertainment was very fine. The affair was under the immediate direction of mesdames John Prickett, A. W. Metcalfe, M. G. Dale, and J. M. Armstrong. The church benefitted to the amount of $62.00."*

Members of the St. John's Methodist Ladies' Aid and guests are ready to dine al fresco in front of the William Erastus Wheeler home about 1904. Mrs. Wheeler is standing, in white, at the right end of the table. The man in the top hat is her brother, a Col. Hatcher. The Wheeler house, at 419 E. Vandalia Street, was built in 1875 and razed in 1928. A smaller home stands there now.

customarily invited members of the audience to come to the stage and play a selection. After hearing it once, he repeated it. According to the *Intelligencer*, on one occasion, Marie Weir played "If I Were a Bird," a piece played entirely on the black keys, which she thought Blind John Boon could not duplicate. "But he did, perfectly," reported the newspaper. Because all-black Fisk University in Nashville, Tennessee, was associated with the Methodist denomination, St. John's Methodist Church brought the Fisk Jubilee Singers to the Opera House on several occasions. In 1891, a capacity crowd heard them sing "Steal Away," "The Lord's Prayer," several pieces by Bach, and "Swing Low, Sweet Chariot."

The Courthouse of 1857, before it was wrecked and replaced by a new building in 1914, continued in use as a community gathering place. On June 7, 1893, the Knights of Tabor, an African-American lodge, and Golden Link Tabernacle, a traveling gospel group, held services in the circuit court room, accompanied by an African-American band from Alton. After the services, people marched to the Knights of Tabor club rooms on Main Street, led by the band. In March 1910, the courthouse provided a stage for a week of YMCA revival meetings, led by A. M. Bruner, the railroad evangelist, of Elgin, Illinois. The Christian message was aimed at male workers in Edwardsville's industries. Afternoon attendance averaged 200, while evening meetings were packed with crowds of 500, not including 200-strong Protestant interdenominational choirs of adults and children. Separation of church and state was apparently not a major issue in turn-of-the-century Edwardsville.

"A Meeting of the Aid Society" was the title of a play these members of the St. John's Methodist Aid Society presented in 1915 at the Gem Theater here. The three women in front are Mrs. Thomas Ramey, Mrs. J. G. Delicate, and Mrs. Joseph Barnett. Behind, left to right, are Mrs. Amos Gusewelle, Miss Emma Hobart, Mrs. Ammie Proctor, Mrs. E.W. Burroughs, Mrs. William D. Harnist, Mrs. Elmer Schwarz, Mrs. J.A. Vance, Mrs. Albert Kriege and Mrs. Ione Sanders. The picture was taken at the Harnist home, 529 St. Louis Street.

Many groups gave "balls"—- even the Grocerymen's Delivery Boys Association, in 1897. The firemen staged such dances every year after the formation of their association in 1874. At first, the Fireman's Ball was a casual dance. For a small fee, anyone could attend. By the turn of the century, it had become a more exclusive event, with admission by printed invitation only. 1884 and 1894 were leap years, occasions on which a group of Edwardsville's wealthier single women invited favored men to a special party. After the Depression of 1893 struck hard in the community, a charity ball was given each year at the Opera House, for the remainder of the decade.

The Tuxhorn Opera House closed in 1906, but with-

This formal ball "programme," with space for one's dance partners, bespeaks Old World refinement in the rough-and-tumble Midwest.

Balls sponsored by the Edwardsville Fire Company were elegant events.

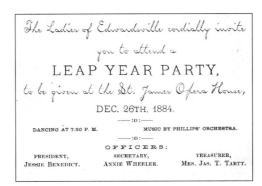

During leap years like 1884, the women felt free to invite the eligible men to gala parties.

CHARITY BALL
EDWARDSVILLE INTELLIGENCER - 1897

The Charity ball is over. . . . Tuxhorn Opera House. . . . was filled as it seldom has been before. The floor was crowded with merry dancers and the gallery was packed with spectators. Between 300 and 400 people were present. Shortly after nine o'clock Brendle's popular orchestra struck up the grand march, which was joined in by nearly all dancers. The march was led by W. D. Harnist and Mrs. C. N. Travous. . . . The program consisted of 24 numbers. . . . It was after four o'clock when "Home, Sweet Home" was played, and the dancers departed. A palatable supper was served at midnight in the dining room of the St. James. . . . The ball netted $95.20. . . . The ball was made possible by Manager A. G. Tuxhorn, who, with characteristic generosity, tendered the use of the Opera House free. . . . The Electric Light Company donated the light, Burroughs & Judd the wax for the floor, and the printing offices the printing matter. The fund will be distributed to the best advantage by City Marshal Stubbs, assisted by Supervisor S. T. Kendall.

Judging from the bit of poetry attached to his dance card, Mr. Terry must indeed have been an eligible bachelor.

in a few years, the Wildey building became a favored spot for dances or "social hops," as they were called at the time. Edwardsville elders, interviewed in 1969, also recalled dancing parties at the larger private homes: "Occasionally at some such house as Slosses', Burnetts', Wheelers' or Pricketts', the furniture would be cleared and there would be a dance with Chris and Charlie Schwarz fiddling lively music to the deep vibrations of Ed Schwarz's bass. Refreshments were served—-pound cake and so much coffee that one who used to make it said she kept it on the stove in a wash boiler."

The pages of the *Intelligencer* reveal the great variety of amusements available here: wrestling matches, carnivals, circuses, visiting opera companies, intercity baseball, picnicking, swimming and wading in Leclaire and Wolf lakes, scouting, interclass games at the high school, and "ragball," for those who couldn't afford to buy a ball and bat. During the 1890s, bicycles appeared in such great numbers that the City Council had to pass special regulations for bicycle traffic. Parades marked many occasions. People enjoyed the pageantry.

The William Russell Prickett Home, 210 N. Kansas, was the scene of elegant parties. The building currently is Mateer Funeral Home.

The Hadley House, 708 St. Louis Street, at West, was another Edwardsville hub of social life. The house was built in 1875 by Edward and Julia West, who lived across the street, and presented it to their daughter Mary and her new husband, William Flavius Leicester Hadley, as a wedding gift. The building was greatly enlarged and remodeled in 1898. Since 1954 it has served as headquarters for the Edwardsville School District.

Gathered for Christmas dinner at Mrs. Kennedy's boarding house in 1886, this octet posed for a portrait. Included are Mr. and Mrs. C.N. Travous, Emily Crane, Dean Gordon, Ansel L. Brown, Bessie Newsham, Grant Dugger and Jessie Prickett.

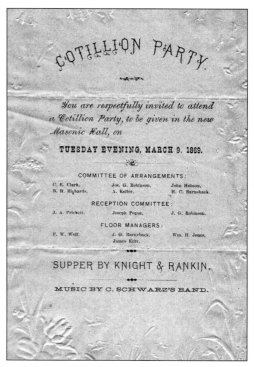

Parties and dances were at the heart of Edwardsville's social life in the late 19th century. At cotillions, formal dancing based on a French model was the featured activity of the evening. Invitations like this were delivered by hand, probably by a boy who would cover the town for a quarter.

ORGANIZATIONS, FRATERNAL AND SOCIAL

Many adults belonged to fraternal lodges with secret rituals and often, a practical purpose of providing insurance benefits for members. The Knights of Pythias, the Illinois United Brothers of Friendship, the Redmen, the Order of Pocahontas, the Grand Army of the Republic, the Catholic Knights of Illinois, the True Redeemer Lodge, the Star Lodge, the International Order of Odd Fellows and the Modern Woodmen no longer exist here, while other groups, such as the Masons and the Knights of Columbus survive. All of these groups flourished in Edwardsville's industrial age.

A number of wealthier young women of the town, both married and single, after 1900 formed The Monday

Proud Knights of Pythias wore buttons with the image of Illinois Grand Chancellor Thomas Williamson, a prominent Edwardsville attorney and civic leader.

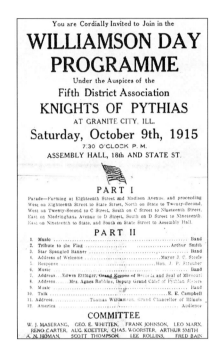

Williamson was the featured speaker on Williamson Day in Granite City.

Membership certificate from 1886 of Edwardsville Independent Order of Odd Fellows Lodge guarantees insurance benefits, including $30 for a funeral.

Here's the original Odd Fellows Hall, located on Second St. and constructed in 1848.

Members of the Edwardsville Knights of Pythias chapter pose for a formal portrait sometime after 1910. Pythias and his friend Damon were characters from Roman mythology. When Pythias was condemned to death for plotting against the Greek tyrant Dionysius, Damon offered himself as hostage while Pythias went away to arrange his affairs. When Pythias returned to be executed, the ruler was touched by the friendship between the two and released them both.

Club, whose name symbolized the fact that, while most women had laundry to do on Monday and thus could not attend meetings, these privileged women belonged to families able to hire laundresses. Members enjoyed concerts, played bridge, entertained themselves with literary readings, and occasionally put on plays. Many also used their leisure to work for civic improvement.

Edwardsville Amateur Gun Club, organized in 1894, met every Saturday "at the driving park" for several years.

This group of riders, shown in front of the public library, took part in a Farmers' Institute parade in 1906 or '07. Left to right are Joseph McKee, Mrs. A.P. Wolf, Lester Geers, Mrs. Thomas Geers, George Mahler, Mrs. J.A. Vance, William Barnsback and Mrs. Barnsback.

Here are some of the senior members of the Edwardsville Monday Club. Left to right are Mrs. William H. Krome, Mrs. B.R. Burroughs, Mrs. Adolph Wolf and Mrs. Greenwood.

Women of the Edwardsville Monday Club donned costumes for a stage presentation in 1914 of Alfred, Lord Tennyson's "A Dream of Fair Women," a poem about a number of famous, tragic women in history. Cast members were Mary Krome, Anne Krome, Katherine Pogue, Mrs. W.H. Morgan, Mrs. Charles Ford, Flavia Hadley, Edna Jeffress, Mrs. F.W. Tunnell, Mrs. A.W. Clark, Mrs. J.F. Keshner, Winifred Hadley, Mrs. George Meyer, Mrs. E.L. Burroughs, Caroline Wolf, Mrs. M.W. Warnock, Mrs. Herbert Crocker and Mrs. Lester Geers.

NEW PUBLIC SCHOOLS

After Dale School was built in 1864 to serve all white children through eighth grade, the population of the town doubled and the facility soon was overcrowded. More and more towns were establishing public high schools. Edwardsville established its first high school classes in 1868, also in Dale School. During the 1870s and later, some classes for white children were held in the Wheeler house on Vandalia, a large mansion now gone. In 1886, a separate four-room grade school building was built on the North Kansas Street site behind Dale School, and the Dale School then became the high school. In 1896, an additional eight rooms were added to the elementary school. In an election of 1909, voters named the new structure, designed by local architect Charles H. Spilman, Columbus School. In 1910, a new high school was completed on the site of the old Dale School.

Teachers in the high school and primary grades around the turn of the century are, left to right, front row, Katharine P. Evans, Nona Barnsback, Rose Cline, Georgia Stillwell, Birdie Barnsback, Josie Springer and Minnie Greenberg; middle row, left to right, Mattie Sherman, Nina Newlan, Mamie Durer, Kate Evans and Edith Metcalfe; back row, left to right, Nina Gardner, Jessie Bickelhaupt, Josephine Hadley and Emma Schwarz.

QUALITIES DESIRED IN EDWARDSVILLE TEACHERS,
1900 -Board of Education

"Professional: equipment, appearance, voice, initiative, use of English. Outside activities. Resourcefulness. Industry. Enthusiasm. Optimism. Loyalty. Definite aims. Sincerity. Self-control. Tact. Sense of justice. Understanding of children. Skill in stimulating thought."

The three-story Dale School, completed in 1864 and named for local Judge M.G. Dale, was the city's first tax-supported school. Originally, it served all grades. It stood until 1910, when it was torn down to make way for a larger building, now known as Columbus School. The original Columbus School (1886) is at left, and stands today, though as part of a larger building.

107

Even after the Constitution of 1870 and a law of 1872 made racial segregation illegal, and after a State Supreme Court decision of 1889 upheld the Illinois State Constitution and said that Alton must abandon separate schools, Edwardsville's white leaders, like their counterparts in many towns in Southern Illinois, defied the law. A segregated public grade school for African-American children was maintained by the all-white school board in the old circuit clerk's office on the town square in Lower Town. Before Lincoln School was built in 1912, the Negro school was called "First Ward." Unlike the public schools, St. Boniface was not segregated. A few black children, even non-Catholics, who could pay the tuition, attended St. Boniface. Most black families, however, were Protestants and preferred the public schools for financial as well as religious reasons.

According to sparsely detailed stories in the *Intelligencer,* which did not "follow up" and develop sto-

Here is Edwardsville's public school (for white children) around the turn of the century. The wing at left is the original 1886 primary school, and the rest of the building, including tower and bay windows, was added in 1896. The whole entire facility, except the top of the tower, is still used and is part of Columbus School today.

The main Columbus School building, fronting on North Kansas Street, was built in 1910 on the site of the Dale School. This building served as Edwardsville High School until a new high school was built on West Street in 1925.

The First Ward School, for "colored children," was opened in 1879 in a 45-year-old building in Lower Town which had housed county offices.

ries about African-Americans in Edwardsville, there were sporadic protests from the black community. During the 1870s, black parents met to plan an end to segregated schools and to petition for political representation in the town. In 1888, David Jenkins ran for the school board. Some black parents in September 1892 tried to register their children in the white school and were refused. These parents protested that the Negro school was near a saloon and on the same grounds as the city jail. They also wanted separate rooms for each class, which was the rule in the white school. In 1892, there were 73 black children of elementary age in Edwardsville. For many

years, Leclaire's kindergarten was the only kindergarten in town. While white children from Edwardsville were welcome to attend, children of color were not admitted. Even though Edwardsville had a high school, until 1912 African-American children who wanted to go beyond eighth grade had to go out of town if they wanted to further their education. The school board arranged for tuition to be paid, but many families did not want to send their children away from home at such an early age.

In 1911, the old clerk's office-school was demolished and Lincoln School, housing all levels of grade school and the first two years of high school, was built on the

Mr. and Mrs. Scott and their children make a serious-looking family group. Because early photographic portraits required long time-exposures, sitters were advised that serious expressions were much easier to maintain over long periods of time without moving than smiles.

GETTING AROUND A "WHITES ONLY" LIBRARY POLICY

"The only [African-American] child that could go in the library was Katie Scott. She was mistaken for white. We waited on the outside while she went in and came out."
Fern Stone, "Growing Up in Edwardsville" - *1996.*

This is the way Mount Joy Baptist Church, an African-American church at 327 Olive St., looked during most of the 20th century, before a new building was built in the 1990s. This building replaced the original 1871 church, which burned. Politicians were not allowed to speak inside the church, but they could post signs, like the one in the picture, on the tree outside.

old town square. Four teachers taught 100 children at Lincoln School in 1912. In 1935, the third year of high school was added to Lincoln, and finally, in 1940 the fourth year was added. Textbooks were often out-of-date discards from the white school. Students who wanted to graduate from high school before 1940 were given a subsidy to go out of town. Some Edwardsvillians went to Lincoln University in Jefferson City, Missouri, while others went to towns such as Decatur which did not have segregated school systems.

Until after World War I, high school classes were small. Eighth grade remained the capstone for most students in Edwardsville and other American towns of the time. Between 1880 and 1911, there was usually a total of about 250 students in Edwardsville grades up to eight, but no class graduating from the high school was larger than 18. And many were smaller. Seven out of 10 high school graduating classes in the 1880s had less than 10 members. In 1890, there were no graduates at all. After 1890, classes got larger. Most had at least 10 students, but the largest class before World War I was the class of 1911, with 30.

Lincoln School, with class-rooms on street level and a basement gymnasium and assembly hall, opened in 1912. It served black students and then integrated classes until it was closed in 1972. Today, the building is a small shopping mall.

School Anniversary Exercises, June 1-2, 1876.

Three Lincoln School belles posed for this photograph at the turn of the century. Left to right: Gertrude Kinchlow Williams, Miss Harper, Roxie Kinchlow Ruffin.

Christopher C. Jones, whose name was synonymous with education of black children for much of the 20th century, accepts an honorary SIUE degree in 1970 from John S. Rendleman, the university president at that time. Jones was Lincoln School principal from 1902-1950.

110

1909: "SCHOOLMARMS PROMISE KISSES FOR SLEIGH RIDE"

Edwardsville citizens are anxious to know whether John Barnsback collected fares. Twenty-three Edwardsville schoolmarms are under grave suspicion of having paid a kiss apiece for a sleighride Wednesday night. . . .John Barnsback, a well-known farmer, who gave the young women the ride, has shown himself worthy of their confidence, if he did collect the fare. When the young women decided that to fail to have at least one sleigh ride while the snow was on the ground would be a burning shame, someone suggested that Barnsback had a fine team and was very gallant. So he was called up over the telephone and readily promised to give the schoolmarms a ride if 'each would pay him with a kiss.' It's said the offer was accepted. At least, Barnsback came in Wednesday evening with a large box sled, and the fascinating twenty-three had a jolly time. When the ride ended no outsiders were present. Hence the mystery.

Edwardsville Intelligencer, January 1909.

Handsome merit cards, given by the teacher, spurred girls and boys to achievement in early classrooms. These two, for grammar and arithmetic, were earned by Louis Klingel.

Eighth graders pose for a graduation picture at ceremonies at the Madison County Courthouse, with Purcell Street in the right background. Until after World War II, eighth grade was as far as most students went in school here, so this ceremony, which included students from rural schools in Edwardsville Township, was important. Lapel ribbons indicate class colors.

This 1911 state teachers certificate for Florine Henson, whose specialty is music, has the OK of county school superintendent John U. Uzzell. Persons with two years of high school, who passed state exams, were certified to teach elementary pupils.

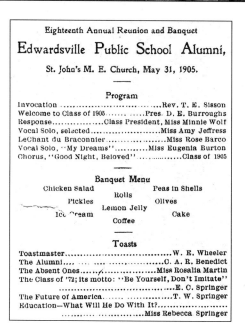

Edwardsville High School kids from around 1900 show the photographer they're having a good time.

In this happy group are Theodore Cullens, Louise Mudge Overton, Maud Barnsback, Courtland Bradshaw, George Crossman, David Fiegenbaum and John Sutter.

Eighteenth Annual Reunion and Banquet

Edwardsville Public School Alumni,

St. John's M. E. Church, May 31, 1905.

Program

Invocation ....Rev. T. E. Sisson
Welcome to Class of 1905.............Pres. D. E. Burroughs
Response.................Class President, Miss Minnie Wolf
Vocal Solo, selected........................Miss Amy Jeffress
LeChant du Braconnier....................Miss Rose Barco
Vocal Solo, "My Dreams"...........Miss Eugenia Burton
Chorus, "Good Night, Beloved" ....Class of 1905

Banquet Menu

Chicken Salad   Peas in Shells
       Rolls
    Pickles   Olives
      Lemon Jelly
   Ice Cream   Cake
      Coffee

Toasts

Toastmaster.......................................W. E. Wheeler
The Alumni.... ....C. A. R. Benedict
The Absent Ones.....√................Miss Rosalia Martin
The Class of '72; its motto: "Be Yourself, Don't Imitate"
....E. C. Springer
The Future of America...... ....T. W. Springer
Education—What Will He Do With It?........................
....Miss Rebecca Springer

Program of 18th Annual Public School Alumni Reunion.

Minnie Wolf (Kriege), EHS Class of 1905, is the picture of elegance in this formal portrait.

In 1898, sports were added as an extra-curricular activity in the high school. Football and basketball games began that fall. Track started in spring. The new gymnasium in the high school building of 1910 was much appreciated. In 1914, Edwardsville High School published the first edition of The Tiger. Jetty Deitz, who graduated from Edwardsville High School in 1920, remembers playing on the women's basketball team. They played only within the school in two teams, the Marathons and the Olympians, and wore "broadcloth bloomers that were pleated and came almost to your ankles [and] middie blouses with those big ties. You didn't," she noted, "move around very fast."

Members of the EHS 1903 football team were, left to right, back row: Paul Luekel, James Stubbs, Manager Will Estabrook, Coach Stroud, Sam Overbeck and Ferd Tunnell; middle row: Florentine Fischer, Arthur Stubbs, Edward Stolze and John Burroughs; front row: Henry Overbeck, Douglas Hadley and Harry Tartt. Because of a lack of protective gear and because rules permitted a rougher game, football in the early days was more dangerous than it is today. Reforms came as the result of a White House conference on football, held by President Theodore Roosevelt.

Girls basketball became very popular at EHS around 1900; this is the 1903 team. Left to right, in front, are Hazel Crossman, Bonidell Sisson, Clara McCune, Minnie Hack, Cecil Barnsback and Hortense Corbett; behind are Florence Dippold, Ann Krome and Hazel Kirkpatrick.

MR. KENNETH SHAW, BORN NEAR LECLAIRE, 1901, REMEMBERS "RAG BALL"

"In 1909, we didn't have money to go to the movie shop. In summer, we played ball most of the time on the Leclaire Campus. The big boys played on the baseball diamond. We smaller boys played on the south end. A ball cost one dollar and a quarter. We made our own balls. A lady who lived near us was a "string saver." I used to do work for her. She let me use one of the big balls of string. We used rag for a center and wound the string tightly around it. Made a ball the right size. Then we got a darning needle and sewed squares around the whole thing. We didn't have bats. Tree limbs didn't work. Sometimes we'd get a spade handle about the right size. It was surprising how long a ball would last that way."

EHS boys basketball team of 1904. Left to right, in front, are George Shaffer, Douglas Hadley and Ferd Tunnell; behind are Florentine Fischer, Sam Overbeck and Will Estabrook.

EHS track team of 1904. Left to right, seated, are John Burroughs, Paul Sebastian and George Shaffer; standing are Homer G. Baird, Sam Overbeck, Ferd Tunnell and Charles Eaton. At this date, high school girls did not participate in track and field.

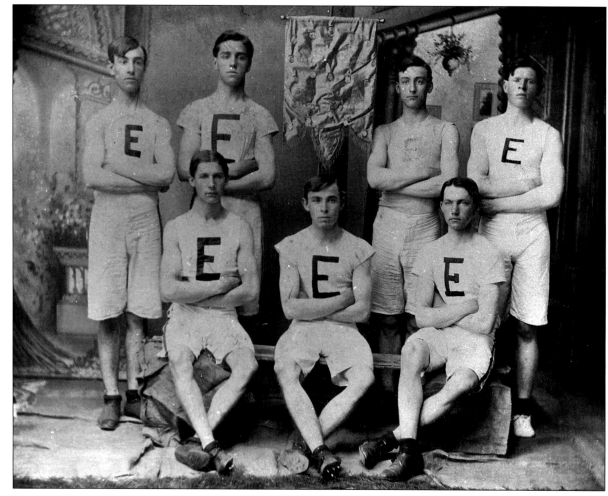

WOMEN MORE VISIBLE IN COMMUNITY LIFE

As Edwardsville became a modest urban center with offices, and as businesspeople, families, and individuals in the town adopted new technologies, such as the telephone, more job opportunities appeared for women. A manual published by the Edwardsville Public Schools lists the occupations of all the high school graduates from 1880 to 1913. Before 1900, most female graduates became homemakers very quickly, although a few taught school. Sara Coventry, for many years the town librarian,

graduated in 1880. Librarianship and teaching school were thought to be compatible with a middle class woman's ideal status as pious homemaker and upholder of community virtue. Although they could become teachers, women were not usually chosen as school administrators. According to Judy Isselhardt, an historian of women in Edwardsville, Edwardsville's first woman principal, H. Lilvinda Moore, who was asked to head the high school after a Mr. Ford left at mid-term in 1906, made a mistake when she asked the school board for more money after serving for three years at the salary of a regular teacher. Mr. Ford was hired back at much more than Ms. Moore had asked for. After 1900, "stenographer" and "bookkeeper" appear as occupations, along with "teacher" for many female high school graduates. Beginning with Maud J. Tetherington in 1902, it became customary to have at least one woman clerk in the courthouse. Some Catholic women became nuns and opted for a life of community service, often in socially approved managerial roles.

In 1912, Maria Tabor built her family's home, with the assistance of her husband. The unusual circumstance of a woman carpenter furnished a short story for inclusion in the Centennial Edition of the *Intelligencer* in 1912.

After 1898, when Edwardsville acquired a telephone exchange and several hundred subscribers, the telephone operators and their immediate supervisor were

Two Edwardsville nuns from the early years were Sister Mary Magdalene (Isabelle Crane), left, and Mother M. Therese (Eleanor Kellerman).

Maria Tabor gave new meaning to the concept of women's work around the house as she and her husband built their own home here in 1912.

women. Women who finished eighth grade could become telephone operators. Stenography, bookkeeping and working the telephone exchange were thought to be particularly suited to women because women, familiar as many of them were with needlework, were thought to possess greater inherent ability to work with intricate machinery. Before World War I, however, the title "secretary" was reserved for men only.

Ms. Lyda Lax, who managed the Bell Telephone Company's Edwardsville office, recruited new phone users, worked at the switchboard, and collected the bills from 1898 until her retirement in 1924, was for many years the only woman manager with Bell. Mr. Lax, her husband, served as mechanic for the system, made repairs, and extended wires over town and country.

Progressive women, many of them teachers, and some men, spearheaded organizations, such as the Civic League, which in 1909 began to promote a twice-yearly cleanup of the town's trash, cutting of dead trees, and planting of new trees and grass in public places. Seventy-six persons paid $1 to join the League. During the week of April 12, 1909, 300 loads of trash were hauled to the dump by members of this organization. Perhaps this began the town's tradition of a twice-yearly large-item pick-up of broken furniture, old appliances, and other bulky discards.

Charles Boeschenstein of the *Intelligencer* applauded the women teachers' organizing of this effort and also hinted at his expectations for the public schools. "We want," he wrote, "women who will insist upon cleanly conditions, who will seek to educate the children of the town to realization of their citizenship, who instill into them a love of nature and more idealism together with a practical interest in domestic science and manual training."

In these years, single-sex associations and clubs were more common than organizations which included both men and women. Women's role in history was recognized by the Old Settlers' Association, which included both genders.

Lyda Lax, behind the bars at left, managed the Bell Telephone exchange in Edwardsville for 26 years starting in 1898. Operators at the switchboard, shown in 1902, left to right, are Christine Klingel, Lydia Dornacher, Mabel Ash and the night operator, Hallie Williams.

Officers of the Madison County Old Settlers Association in 1910 were, left to right, W.W. Barnsback, president; Mrs. William H. Jones, secretary, and W.K. Blackburn, vice president.

To join the Madison County Old Settlers Association, or Union, formed in 1887, you had to be a 50-year resident of the county, or simply be at least 50 years old. Members, who were interested in county history, met annually into the 1920s; some of them organized the Madison County Historical Society, which functions to this day. Here is the group in June 1913. Seated, left to right, are Edwin Woods, Margaret Springer, W.B. Johnson, Mary Willoughby, Margaret Fruit, Dr. S.P. Wiedmann, Mrs. M.A. Skinner and Mrs. Burton. Standing, left to right, are Mrs. S.H. Lanham, C.D. Kneedler, Mrs. T.V. Whiteside, Anton Wienke, Mrs. White, Joseph Bosomworth, Mrs. C.D. Kneedler, Eliza McKittrick, Mrs. Robert Friday, Mrs. R.A. Phillips, T.V. Whiteside (rear), Mrs. R.C. Gillham, Jesse Renfro, Mrs. Schaefer, and C.C. Buckley.

THE PUBLIC LIBRARY

Women also secured for the community a public library. In 1819, some men of early Edwardsville had established one of the earliest lending libraries in the new state of Illinois. But, by 1825, this institution had vanished and a new Edwardsville Library Association was not created until a group of interested women revived it in May of 1879. Susan Lucco, librarian and historian of the Edwardsville library, wrote that "the Library was open one day a week, Saturday afternoon and evening. An early home in the Episcopal Church found the books neatly arranged on the front pews, as there were no shelves." Eventually, in 1894, the Library was granted a room in the new City Hall.

Townswomen raised money for books from 1879 to 1903 by raffling quilts, giving card parties, putting on operettas, such as Gilbert and Sullivan's *Mikado,* and holding ice cream and strawberry socials. This library was open only to those who paid a $2 annual fee, until it became a free public library in 1903. In that year, Andrew Carnegie, millionaire founder of U. S. Steel Company, America's largest corporation at that time, donated $12,500 for a new building, and, as part of the bargain, the city agreed to budget $1,250 per year for library expenses.

The new library was dedicated on June 28, 1906. The women of the Library Association donated all the books they had collected and all the Association's bookcases to the new public library. Charles Boeschenstein, who had persuaded Carnegie to pay for the building, was appointed by Mayor N. E. Bosen to head a new Public Library Board, all male, which he did for the next 34 years. However, Sara Coventry, librarian from 1891 to 1937, remembered the role of women in the founding: "Too much honor and credit cannot be given to these ladies, who planned and labored so faithfully so many years to give Edwardsville a real standard library. . . ."

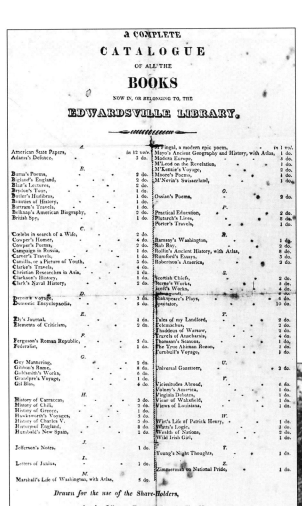

This catalog of books available in the Edwardsville Library as of Nov. 13, 1819, is one of the city's oldest documents. It was printed in the shop of Hooper Warren, pioneer publisher here.

Sara Coventry was Edwardsville librarian from 1891-1937, longer than any other so far.

Postcard view shows the library and the surrounding block-square City Park shortly after the library was dedicated in 1906. Note the worker cutting the grass using a push-powered, reel-type lawnmower.

EDWARDSVILLE WOMEN AND
NATIONAL REFORM MOVEMENTS

Edwardsville women also participated in several national reform movements of the period 1870 to 1920. From after the Civil War until the prohibition amendment was ratified in 1919, Edwardsville's local temperance organization, the Royal Purple Society, was active. In March 1879, when local option for prohibition was on the ballot, the *Intelligencer* ran an advertisement asking women to pray for men to vote right on temperance. Prayers failed. In June 1881, Edwardsville hosted the Madison County Temperance Convention at which Frances Willard, the founder of the Women's Christian Temperance Union (WCTU), spoke. Ms. Willard's reform agenda also included women's suffrage. Mrs. E. W. West represented the 17th Congressional District at a national temperance convention in 1881. For a brief time in 1883, members of Edwardsville's WCTU opened a coffee house on Purcell Street in an effort to offer males an alternative to the town's many saloons.

In 1904, Carry Nation (1846-1911), of whom the WCTU disapproved, visited Edwardsville for one day. Alighting from the Wabash train at 8:30 in the morning, she checked her trunk at the depot and asked the dispatcher to show her "the nearest hotel that hasn't a saloon attached." For five years, beginning in 1899, convinced of divine guidance, alone or sometimes with a few other women, she had been targeting famous larger Midwestern saloons, entering them at peak hours, singing a hymn or two and then smashing bottles and pictures which she regarded as "pornographic." Almost six feet tall, with a strong, grandmotherly face, she always wore black. A hatchet swung from her belt. Many times jailed and the mother of an ailing daughter, she had been forced on to the lecture circuit to pay her fines and debts.

She came to Edwardsville seeking to speak at a local revival meeting, but the pastor in charge refused to let her appear. Local Baptists agreed to let her talk at their afternoon meeting. Before noon, she was arrested by Argalus Stubbs, the town's policeman, who took her to see Mayor Henry P. Hotz, who warned her against using violent language. She responded by calling him anti-Christ for using tobacco. Released, she took to the streets to sell some small enameled hatchets, which bore the motto, "Carry Nation, Joint Smasher." Later that day, the Baptist Church was packed. A spectator remembered her as "motherly, with grey hair, gold rimmed spectacles, and a small black bonnet perched so far back on her head that it could scarcely be seen from the front." She hawked her recently written autobiography, claimed 25 jail sentences, and asked for donations for a home for drunkards' wives and mothers in Kansas City. Taunted by a jeering crowd of young men as she boarded the night train, she turned to them and shouted, "Don't forget that the devil is wider awake than his enemies."

Some Edwardsville women worked hard to secure women's suffrage in national elections. Mrs. J. W. Terry belonged to suffrage reformer Susan B. Anthony's Equal Rights Association, which supported Belva Lockwood for President of the United States in 1884. Ms. Lockwood got 1,008 votes in Illinois that year, all from men, since women did not vote. Young Charles Boeschenstein reported this information in a one paragraph item on an interior page of the *Intelligencer.* In March 1885, Ms. Lockwood visited Edwardsville and was welcomed by a banner across Main Street. In 1895, the *Intelligencer* reported that Mrs. F.A. Geers and Miss Minna Crocker were also active in the Equal Rights Association.

Edward Gardner Lewis (1868-1850), like N. O. Nelson, was a businessman-reformer whose efforts affect-

American Women's League Chapter House at 515 West High St. dates from 1909; it stands today, as a private residence.

Here's the Edwardsville AWL Chapter House on dedication day in 1909. This house was the first of 38 built in the United States in a women's movement founded by a St. Louis businessman and reformer.

ed Edwardsville history between 1903 and 1912. While developing University City, the new area of St. Louis west of the World's Fair grounds, he published women's magazines and, in 1908, created an organization, the American Women's League (AWL), both to sell his publications and to promote womanly citizenship in anticipation of women's suffrage. Lewis believed that women's most important role was to educate, guide and protect children, but he also encouraged women to enter business and to pursue careers in arts and crafts. Charter Members of the AWL had to sell $52 worth of Lewis publications in one year. By dividing profits from magazine sales between his company and local chapters, Lewis planned to build permanent American Women's League chapter houses in a number of cities all over the United States. Eventually 38 chapter houses were built, 10 of them in Illinois.

Edwardsville's AWL, named the Terry Chapter for Mrs. J. W. Terry, venerable suffrage supporter, received the first AWL house built in the United States. It was dedicated on July 20, 1909. Now a private residence, it still stands on West High Street. Designed by the St. Louis firm of Helfensteller, Hirsch and Watson, the house reflects the influence of the Prairie School of Chicago architects led by Frank Lloyd Wright. Though Lewis furnished the house with Mission Style oak furniture, rugs, and a $250 Columbia Concert Grand phonograph concealed in a Mission Style table, none of these items survives.

Who belonged to the AWL in Edwardsville and what did they do? According to Pauline Meyer, historian of this group, "Many AWL members were associated with the N. O. Nelson Company and lived in Leclaire." She notes that women studied law through a "People's University" sponsored by the Lewis Publishing Company.

At weekly meetings, they discussed principles of active citizenship. In a room of the chapter house, they sold their handiwork, sewing and such, and Lewis' publications. The chapter house was also rented out on a regular basis to other groups, such as the Monday Club. Mrs. Agnes McKee, of Edwardsville, presided over the League's national convention in 1910.

In 1912, Lewis, who in the meantime had declared bankruptcy but continued as a reformer, reorganized the League into the American Woman's Republic. Women, he thought, could better understand the government of the United States if they had to govern their own republic. In June 1912, at a meeting in University City, Mrs. H. J. Springer and Miss Minnie Crocker of the Terry Chapter signed a Declaration of Equal Rights and voted with hundreds of others to adopt a Constitution of the American Woman's Republic written by a committee under the direction of Belva Lockwood, who was attorney general of the American Woman's Republic. Mrs. Lewis (Mabel Gertrude Wellington) was elected president. Lewis borrowed money to buy land in Atascadero, California, and in 1913, proclaimed the American Woman's Republic to exist there. The flag of the Republic had stars representing the 10 states which had adopted full woman suffrage by 1913. After 1920, when the national suffrage amendment was adopted, the League faded from history. The chapter house in Edwardsville was sold as a private home in 1920.

Here is the chapter house as a private home, in a June 1977 photo.

A number of Edwardsville women attended the 1910 AWL convention in St. Louis. The event was presided over by Agnes McKee, of Edwardsville.

MADISON COUNTY CENTENNIAL, 1912

For eight days in 1912—- September 14-21—- Edwardsville greeted visitors with 200,000 square yards of bunting and flags coordinated by a fleet of committees headed by Charles Boeschenstein, president of the Centennial Association. Planning had begun in May 1911 when the State Legislature appropriated $5,000 for a Madison County Centennial Monument—- which still stands in City Park east of the library. A plaster of Paris triumphal arch, designed by local architect M. B. Kane to suggest a similar structure in Paris and to recall the St. Louis World's Fair, greeted visitors entering the front door of the courthouse. Every day, wondrous aeroplanes recently designed by the famous Wright brothers took

North Main Street sported lots of bunting for the Madison County Centennial, September 1912.

Some of the downtown stores added special decorations for the centennial.

This plaster of Paris triumphal arch was erected at the main entrance to the courthouse for the centennial. The arch, designed by Edwardsville architect M.B. Kane, recalled the Arc de Triomphe in Paris and similar structures at the St. Louis World's Fair, which had been held just eight years before.

off and landed in an open field. Alton, Collinsville and Granite City were honored with special "days." A combination Farmers' Day and Good Roads Day closed the celebration. Publication of a new encyclopedic *History of Madison County* by Norton was timed to coincide with these public activities.

At 10 o'clock on the morning of Homecoming Day, Saturday, September 14, Eleanor Boeschenstein, Charles Boeschenstein's teen-aged daughter, surrounded by a bevy of her friends, opened the festival by firing the first of 100 rounds from a five-pound cannon set up near Leclaire Lake. Factory whistles blew and bells rang in all county towns. Edwardsville crowds then welcomed Mrs. Mary Lusk Sloss of Memphis, Tennessee, 82-year old daughter of pioneer John T. Lusk and the oldest living native of Edwardsville, and hundreds of other natives who had come home for the party.

On Sunday, September 15, all Protestant ministers of the county were instructed to make some mention of "progress" in their sermons. At special ceremonies coordinated by lawyer and civic leader Thomas Williamson, members of early families, Paddocks, Flaggs and Atwoods, raised flags at Fort Russell (see photo on page 15) and at the building of Thomas Kirkpatrick in Lower Town, where W. R. Prickett was master of ceremonies.

For a week-long historical exhibit at the public school buildings on North Kansas street, members of old Edwardsville families contributed mementoes: a pair of spectacles worn in 1808 by early settler Jacob Gonterman, a dried bouquet 60 years old, R. C. Gillham's military commission of 1814 signed by Ninian Edwards, a bill from the Wabash Hotel dated 1827, old books and family Bibles, a copy of *The Federalist* dated 1788, a brush used by Edward Menk's grandfather to care for the King of Germany's clothes, two crocheted baby caps worn by generations of Mudges, Dr. Joseph Pogue's father's naturalization paper, a framed issue of the Edwardsville *Spectator.*

A graceful and permanent feature of the Madison County Centennial was this 16-foot-high Centennial Monument, sculpted of Georgia marble by Charles J. Mulligan, of Chicago, and shown here in 1927. It stands today in the middle of City Park, its four sides representing Plenty (at left in this picture), Virtue (the veiled maiden, to the right), plus Justice and Wisdom. Shields behind the heads support a globe. This view looks north-west, with East Vandalia Street in the background. Mulligan studied at the Ecole des Beaux Arts in Paris, and had done a figure of Henry Clay, in Lexington, Kentucky, and decoration for the Illinois Supreme Court building. One inscription reads: In Grateful Memory of the Early Settlers, Who by Courage, Industry and Endurance Transformed a Wilderness into a Land of Order, Peace and Plenty.

This view looks southwest on St. Louis Street from North Main during one of the Centennial parades. The Leland Hotel is at left; the Courthouse Square, at right.

Just nine years after the Wright Brothers' first successful flights, airplanes were making the rounds of celebrations like the county centennial. Mary Lusk looked determined as she became the first county woman to ride in one of the new contraptions, on September 14, 1912. The pilot is Eugene Heth. Several others took flights the same day: Viola Gueltig Gamble, Charles E. Gueltig, Katherine Lanham, E. L. Lax, Joseph A. Barnett, E. L. Witherell, Georgia Lusk and Mary Lusk's husband, Percy P. Lusk. After Percy died in 1927, Mary became the county's first woman insurance agent.

The Centennial was the time for family gatherings, like this one at the home of Mr. and Mrs. W. R. Crossman, 220 W. Park Street. The group surrounds the family matriarch, Margaret Bickelhaupt, seated in center. On the porch are Edmond Bickelhaupt, in hat, and Sam V. Crossman. The others, left to right, are Hazel M. Crossman Williams and Dr. Byron P. Williams; Hazel's mother Julia B. Crossman; Julia's sister Emma Bickelpaupt Versen, and William Robert Crossman, holding four-month-old Ella Margaret Williams.

Eleanor Boeschenstein gets ready to open the centennial festivities by firing the first of a hundred shots from a cannon set up in Leclaire Park. The hour was 10 a.m. on the opening day of the Centennial, Saturday, September 14, 1912.

On Monday, September 16, Governor Charles Deneen, a native of Edwardsville, plus judges of the Illinois Supreme Court and 15 other officials arrived in a special car via William Brown McKinley's Illinois Traction System ("The Interurban") from Springfield. At 11 o'clock, the governor and his entourage climbed onto a reviewing stand in front of the courthouse and watched a parade of 50 automobiles decorated with flowers. In the afternoon, Governor Deneen spoke to a crowd of several thousand in City Park and unveiled the Centennial Monument. Governors Day concluded with the dedication by the Daughters of the American Revolution of a monument in the courthouse to Madison County men who had fought in the American Revolution.

Governor Charles Deneen and his birthplace.

This is the home in which Charles Deneen, later U.S. Senator and Governor of Illinois, was born. The house originally stood on the southwest corner of Center and Benton streets, a location obliterated in recent years by the new Madison County Jail. It was relocated to 412 Randle St., where it stands today, somewhat altered.

Governors Day at the Centennial concluded with the dedication of this memorial plaque for Revolutionary War soldiers, by the Daughters of the American Revolution.

Fifty decorated automobiles were entered in a Centennial Governors Day auto parade, the first such parade in Edwardsville and one of the earliest in Illinois. Virtually every auto in the city was entered, along with some from other cities. This is the car of L. D. Lawnin and family, decorated to suggest a Japanese tea garden. Lawnin is at the wheel—which is on the right side, as with most of the cars shown here. Mrs. Josephine Lawnin Robinson, of San Antonio, Texas, is next to him. Standing is Eleanor Rock, of Kansas City, Missouri, and with her on the rear seat are Mrs. Charlotte Lawnin Crawford and Mrs. Julia Lawnin Gordon, both of St. Louis.

Decorated with pink and white bunting, white roses and white butterflies was this car owned by Ralph C. Wayne, but driven by Paul Schwarz. The others, left to right, are Caroline Wolf, and Mr. and Mrs. Charles O. Nash. Wayne was at the head of the parade, in one of the pilot cars.

"My Most Emotional Impressions [Madison Co. Centennial]"
by Rachel L. Travous, participant

About 10 A.M., Saturday, Sept.14, a shrieking of whistles announced the birth of a new century in the county's history. Church bells followed, and for five minutes the two were heard alternately and in unison. At 10 minutes after 10 came the first roar of canon. . . . The canon continued at intervals until a 100-gun salute had been given. At night the streets blazed with lights strung for the occasion.

The Sunday celebration at Fort Russell was most solemnly impressive, particularly the flag raising by a small Owens girl-child.

The festivities seemed actually to start with the flower parade Monday morning.

Rain interfered with Children's Day on Tuesday.

What appealed to me when Collinsville paraded on Thursday was the carrying of a small bell by every person marching.

Friday Granite City, parading, tossed small granite pans to the watchers.

. . . . Truly Edwardsville was outdoing herself. I liked too the miners' parading in blue and white with a good drum major leading the band.

But the closing Saturday brot disappointment. Rain fell, and when the farmers arrived, many of them having driven thro heavy mud for miles, the exhibits had been removed.

With a deer head mounted up front, Mr. and Mrs. Thomas Williamson and family entered the Boy Scout group of floats.

Dr. E.H. Schwarz, one of the first owners of autos in Edwardsville, pilots his 1907 Ford runabout "Butterfly Car" in the Governors Day parade. With him is his daughter Dorothy.

Henry Trares Jr., left, is at the wheel of his car in the parade. With him are his brother-in-law, J.T. Mooney, and, in the back seat, Mrs. Trares, left, and Mrs. Mooney, with their nephew Edward Pauly Jr., of Granite City, between them.

Mayor Henry P. Hotz and his family decorated their car with white bunting and artificial snowballs. With him are his wife, and daughters Coleta, Gladys and Eloise.

124

NEW FEDERAL BUILDING: POST OFFICE, 1915

The story of Edwardsville's postal services represents the growing role of the federal government in everyday life of the 20th century. The first post office opened in Edwardsville in 1822. Until the federal government provided a building in 1915, the location of the post office changed with every postmaster. In 1889, the total staff was Thomas M. Crossman and his daughter, who took care of four mails a day. People still came to the post office to pick up their mail. The total budget for the post office in 1889, including rent for the building, was $2,100, $1,700 of which was the postmaster's salary.

During the 1890s, rural services began as two star route carriers took mail to designated dropoffs in the country. In December 1902, rural free delivery to each country home began, and Edwardsville acquired six rural carriers. Town mail was now delivered to each address. In July 1904, because of the amount of business, Edwardsville's post office designation changed from third class to second class. Although only 40 persons used it initially because of the strength of local private banks, after August 21, 1911, federal postal savings was available as a public alternative to private banks. In 1912, with 14 mails a day and a staff of 15 persons, the postmaster commanded a budget of $17,580. The new post office, completed in 1915, provided a striking reminder of services provided by the federal government.

EDWARDSVILLE POST OFFICE STAFF AND SALARIES, 1912

Postmaster	$2,400
Deputy Postmaster	$1,200
Chief clerk	$1,100
Deputy clerks (2)	$1,000 each
City carriers (2)	$1,100 each
City carrier	$1,000
City carrier	$ 900
Rural carriers (3)	$1,000 each
Rural carriers (3)	$ 960 each
Vacation salaries	$ 900

Rural mail carriers have their horses and buggies ready to go outside the post office in the Prickett Building, 109 Purcell Street, prior to 1905. The men are H. C. Miller, J. H. Wohlbrink and P. W. Sommerlad.

Ground was broken on a snowy day in December 1913 for a new U.S. Post Office at Hillsboro and Commercial, a block from the courthouse. Wielding the shovel is young W.M. Crossman Jr., a grandson of the postmaster, T.M. Crossman, at right. The others, left to right, are William Probst, excavation contractor; Eugene Sheets, construction superintendent; W.M. Crossman Sr., assistant postmaster, and V.E. Taylor, building contractor.

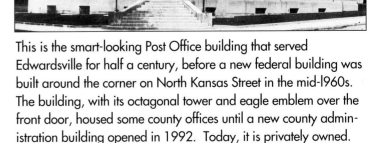

This is the smart-looking Post Office building that served Edwardsville for half a century, before a new federal building was built around the corner on North Kansas Street in the mid-1960s. The building, with its octagonal tower and eagle emblem over the front door, housed some county offices until a new county administration building opened in 1992. Today, it is privately owned.

THE FOURTH COURTHOUSE:
A NEW BUILDING FOR THE NEW ERA

A movement to build a larger and more modern courthouse commenced in 1904, soon after Edwardsville's major streets were paved and sidewalks installed. In November 1907, however, county residents voted down a new courthouse in a county-wide ballot. In 1913, voters approved the expense, and construction of the building, designed by St. Louis architect Robert G. Kirsch, began in February 1914.

As in earlier times, other towns plotted to steal the county seat from Edwardsville. Altonians, with their 1910 population of 17,528, were hopeful, but Granite Citians took action. Granite City had boomed from a town not listed in the census of 1890 to an incorporated area with a population of 9,903 in 1910, compared to Edwardsville's 5,014. According to Attorney Leland Buckley in 1964, Republicans met in convention at Granite City in April 1913, in anticipation of the referendum on the new courthouse in November 1913. The county was "strongly Republican" then. "But the Lord saved Edwardsville that day," Buckley wrote. "A strong April wind came up and sand blew in everybody's eyes and the tent almost blew away and no vote was taken." Edwardsville secured the new building, which finally cost $301,960.12, not extravagant by later standards but a fortune in those days.

On October 11, 1915, county officers began moving from their temporary headquarters, a hastily constructed building at Vandalia and Johnson streets, to their new quarters. Monday, October 18, was declared a county-wide holiday. A committee composed of D. H. Mudge, H. T. McCrea, T. A. Desmond, Louis Borman, T. P. F. Reilly, J. M. Bandy, Frank Troeckler, Simon Kellerman, George E. Little, and C. H. Spilman coordinated the dedication. "Uncle Joe" Cannon of Danville, a nationally famous Republican politician and former Speaker of the U.S. House of Representatives, agreed to give the major address. So Edwardsville ended an era of growth and social change with another new courthouse.

Here's a "birds-eye" view of downtown looking southwest, probably from the water tower behind city hall at 400 N. Main Street, taken around 1900-1910. In the foreground is the mansard roof of the 1865 John Trares Home (now Weber Funeral Home), and beyond that is the St. James Hotel—both the squarish part and the wing with the chimneys and dormers just beyond. The 1857 courthouse, slated for demolition in 1914, is the big building at upper right, with the gables and chimneys; St. John's Methodist Episcopal Church and its tall bell tower are right of it.

This group of citizens reorganized the Edwardsville Commercial Club in 1914 to raise money for a temporary home for county government during construction of the new courthouse. The temporary building, at West Vandalia and Johnson streets, kept at bay those demanding to move the county seat to Alton or Granite City. Seated, left to right, are B. H. Richards, George Shaffer, Dent E. Burroughs, Edward W. Burroughs, Thomas Williamson (named president), Judge Dick H. Mudge, Fred Pfeiffer and August Selzer. Standing, left to right, are William L. Estabrook, M. D. Powell, Charles V. Truxhorn, Frank Campbell, Peter Dresch, Sam V. Crossman, J.F. Ammann, (unknown), F.A. Eisele, Judge George W. Crossman, (unknown), Thomas J. Long, Mr. Moser (campaign director), John Dierkes, (unknown) and M.L. Burroughs.

CONSTRUCTING THE COURTHOUSE

Wreckers are busy tearing down the 1857 courthouse and its 1890 annex in this view looking southwest in March 1914.

Footings for the new courthouse are seen in this view looking northeast in June 1914. The flag and the crowd are for cornerstone ceremonies.

Lee Little, daughter of Mr. and Mrs. George E. Little, helps set the first courthouse stone on top of the cornerstone. On the preceding day, the cornerstone itself was set, containing a copper box filled with photographs and other documents. George Little was a sheriff and county treasurer.

127

Construction of the new courthouse, clad with white marble, is up to the second floor in this northeast view from St. Louis and Second streets.

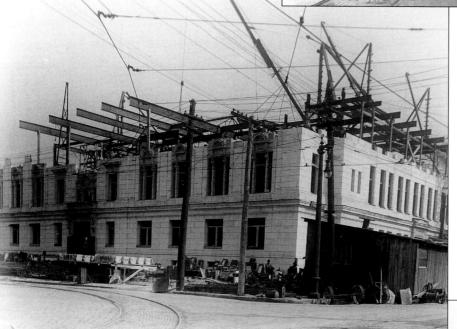

Up and up. Structural steel for the third floor is bolted together as the second floor is finished. This is the Purcell Street (left) and Second Street corner of the building.

The courthouse is nearing completion in this view looking northeast at the St. Louis Street (right) and Second Street corner. The architecture, which is more elaborate on the Main Street side, is described as Classical Revival, with a French influence. The architect was Robert G. Kirsch, of St. Louis.

Fred Tegtmeier Sr., of Edwardsville and Pin Oak Township, was the only person to work on the 1857 courthouse (as a boy) and see it torn down at age 74. A German immigrant, Tegtmeier worked at a local brickyard as a teen-ager and hauled many a load of brick to the construction site. At times, the bricklayers would allow him to lay a few bricks. He is seen in 1928, at age 88.

Thousands jam Purcell Street on the north side of the new courthouse for dedication ceremonies on October 18, 1915. Republican Congressman Joseph G. "Uncle Joe" Cannon, of Danville, who had been U. S. House Speaker from 1903-1911, was featured at the ceremonies. Cannon can be seen down front, in center, hand on rail, turned toward the courthouse with right arm extended, declaiming on the latest addition to the downtown cityscape.

CHAPTER 5: FROM WWI TO WWII: CHANGE AND STABILITY

EDWARDSVILLE IN THE GREAT WAR FOR DEMOCRACY, 1917-1918

On March 31, 1917, a week before the official Declaration of War was approved by Congress, N.O. Nelson wrote to his officers and managers in Edwardsville suggesting that a contingent, led by himself, volunteer for military service. "While my age. . . precludes my enlistment I think my unimpaired physical condition will allow me to enlist. I want to raise," he wrote, "one or more companies of men who have been associated with me in business. As I am tired of bossing, I shall insist upon being a private and take the fare and work of all the rest." Shortly after war was declared, 37 of Edwardsville's well-known Civil War veterans, both black and white, all older than 70, wrote to President Wilson offering their services for war duty.

On September 20, 1917, 172 young men, the first large group of draftees from this district, boarded the eastbound train at the Clover Leaf Station, bound for Camp Taylor at Louisville, Kentucky. Congress had declared war on April 6, but mobilization took time. J. F. Amman, respected businessman, headed the Draft Board in Edwardsville. Waving and cheering for the new sol-

diers, 3,000 relatives, friends and townspeople sang "Hang the Kaiser from a Sour Apple Tree" as the train pulled out.

During the previous evening, the soon-to-be dough-boys had been honored with a banquet at the Leland Hotel, complete with cigars courtesy of Fred Yeager. After dinner, every seat at the Wildey was taken. Over

Group of draftees aboard train.

Edwardsville Intelligencer
MADISON COUNTY'S HOME DAILY

Congress Votes for the War
President Signs Measure

The *Intelligencer* marked America's entry into World War I with this banner headline, on April 6, 1917.

Crowds jam the curbsides as Edwardsville's military heroes parade down North Main Street, in the 100 block, with the courthouse in the background, and in the 200 block.

1,000 were turned away. As the audience rose to sing the "Star-Spangled Banner," the curtain lifted, revealing the honorees seated on the stage backed by a giant American flag. The Reverend J. R. Sager of the Presbyterian Church delivered the invocation. A quartette of local women sang "The Flag Goes By" and "Forward, March." Mayor Henry Hotz awarded each man a key to the City, followed by more speeches and a benediction. The next morning, at 7 o'clock, the corner of Main and St. Louis Streets hummed, as paraders assembled for the march to the station. Accompanied by a band and three flagbearers, the draftees lined up in fours, followed by the Boy Scouts' Bugle and Drum Corps, members of a newly organized Children's Loyalty League of America, various automobiles, honking, and a crowd of residents. Two hundred employees of U.S. Radiator Corporation marched, each carrying a tool or finished product of the plant. After leaving the station, the train stopped at Richards Brick so that Jack Campbell, in charge of the draftees, could take roll.

Then, with a blast of steam and a lurch, the boys eased away from Edwardsville.

As the war progressed and more men volunteered or were drafted, townspeople attempted to make each send-off a memorable occasion. This was true for both black and white soldiers, although the banquets for each were held in separate halls. At 5:22 on the chilly morning of April 29, 1918, according to the *Intelligencer,* nearly every African-American person in Edwardsville came to the Wabash Station to bid farewell to seven recruits, who marched to the station from Lincoln School, where they had been honored by their families and friends with dinner, an all-night party and early breakfast. More than four hours later, 2,000 people gathered at the Wabash Station to say goodbye to 94 white recruits.

The Edwardsville Concert Band played for both groups of soldiers.

C. H. Spilman, who had taken over the *Intelligencer* from Charles Boeschenstein in 1915, appears to have done some thinking, during the war, about democracy at

MT. JOY BAPTIST "Our Members in the Service"

Sgt. Daniel Wolford	Sgt. Raymond Curtis
Corp Wilbur Brandom	Priv. William Scott
Priv. Albert Richardson	Priv. Harry Penelton
Priv. Bertrum Searcy	Priv. Benjamin F. Leurs
Priv. Frank Jason	Priv. David Fair
Priv. Harry Samuels	Priv. Wilbur Martin
Priv. Henry Rice	Priv. William L. Brooks
Priv. Paul Tandy	Priv. Lilland McMurry
Priv. Archibald Rollins	Priv. Priv. Albert Spiller
Priv. William Brown	Priv. Thomas Bradley
Priv. Benjamin Jason	Priv. John Wolford
Priv. William Robinson	Priv. Dewey Rice
Priv. Joseph Mitchel	Priv. William LaPorte
Priv. Oscar Ward	Priv. Arthur Martin
Priv. George Brewington	Priv. Dennis Gambol
Priv. Charles Green	Priv. Samuel Green
Priv. William Mitchel	Priv. Robert Shaw
Priv. Fred Coleman	Priv. Eli Stringer
Priv. Daniel Curtis	

GRAND ARMY VETS WHO OFFERED SERVICE TO U.S. IN 1917

Dr. Joseph Pogue, age 82	Dr. H. T. Wharff, 73
C. C. Buckley, 84	Winfield Hall, 75
W. R. Prickett, 80	W. H. Shaffer, 75
S. O. Bonnet, 79	Louis Bode, 72
A. P. Wolf, 76	Henry Barnsback, 78
C. H. Nash, 79	Simon Bradley, 76
A. M. Sparks, 78	Henry Langwisch, 78
F. W. Overbeck, 72	George Washington, 76
B. M. Tabor, 72	William Reid, 76
Ed Dickerson, 75	F. G. Bernius, 73
Thos. Morton, 71	Levi Scott, 76
Frank Daech, 76	James Dees, 79
C. H. Lynch, 79	John N. Daniels, 74
Dan A. Lynch, 75	Jasper Smith, 72
Samuel Reid, 74	George W. Putnam, 73
C. C. Peterson, 75	David Voyles, 76
Edward Naehr, 75	Geo. D. Shaffer, 73
Thos. Barnett, 74	Oliver Secrest, 75

Edwardsville gave its departing servicemen a big sendoff, first with a downtown parade, seen from the courthouse square, and then at the Clover Leaf railroad station on Wolf Street (with N.O. Nelson Mfg. Co. buildings and water tower in the background.)

home in the United States. Sometimes his editorials suggested connections between a war for freedom and the end of prejudice and discrimination in Edwardsville.

War spending had some impact on the local economy. During 1918, some Edwardsville companies signed contracts with the U.S. Government to produce war supplies. Employees of U.S. Radiator made six-inch artillery shell casings. Bran from Edwardsville's Blake Milling Company fed army horses and mules in Europe. (The company proudly displayed a letter from the feed manager of the 33rd Division, A.E.F.) Michael Desmond's machine shop on St. Louis Street near the Wabash tracks repaired railroad wheels and supplied roller bearings for wartime trains. E. A. Fresen, of Edwardsville, chaired District 82 of the U.S. Fuel Administration and prepared regular reports on the tonnage of coal available from this area.

Other local firms faced hardship. National Roofing Materials company had just begun to make asphalt shingles, a much safer option than wooden shingles for homeowners using coal furnaces or wood-burning stoves, in February 1917, at a factory located along the Clover Leaf Tracks south of Madison Coal's Number Three Mine. By July 1918, the plant had shut down because the war had diverted needed materials to other uses. In 1919, John Stolze bought the property from the Bank of Edwardsville and laid it out in building lots.

People throughout the community raised money for Liberty Loans and tried to be thrifty with food and other strategic supplies. Employees at the N. O. Nelson Brass shop subscribed to $1700 in bonds. Edwardsville hotel owners, in November 1917, adopted a plan to serve no meat on Tuesday and no wheat bread on Wednesday to conserve food and win the war. Rationing of food and

"NO DISTINCTION" - EDITORIAL FROM *EDWARDSVILLE INTELLIGENCER*, APRIL 30, 1918

"When Second Number Four pulled out of the lower Wabash station at 9:40 this morning, Edwardsville had sped on its way the second contingent of soldiers for the day. Number Six, four hours earlier, had carried the first contingent, composed of colored boys.

At both departures there were huge crowds of people. The Lincoln Council, which managed the colored boys' departure, had not asked for the band. . . . But the band boys decided that a soldier is a soldier and they would honor them all alike. So they got up at 3:30 this morning, assembled at the court house at 4:15 and marched to the Lincoln school, and were enthusiastically received and provided with hot coffee and lunch. Then they headed the procession to the lower station. . . .

It was a splendid demonstration of the right spirit. When the boys go over the top there will be no distinctions and there should not be when they leave on the Great Adventure. In the trenches of Europe, there are people from eighteen different nations fighting side by side. . . . They are allied in a common cause, and while they have different complexions and speak different languages and worship different gods, their hearts and their minds are concentrated in the one great cause of democracy, liberty and humanity for the whole world."

RIDING THE YELLOWHAMMER TO EAST ALTON, 1918

During World War I, the little car ran "specials" morning and evening to and from Western Cartridge Company in East Alton (now Olin-Mathieson). These "specials" (two or three cars long) were loaded with people, mostly women, on their way to work helping make powder and bullets for our much admired young soldiers, many of whom had gone right from high school to the army. The women were for the most part a jolly laughing crew, waving and calling from the open windows as they passed, happy to be helping with the war effort.

Evelyn L. Stine, born in 1905, remembering in 1985

This World War I Renault tank was brought here in the summer of 1918 to stir up patriotic feeling and raise money for the war effort. The machine was later described by historians as "clumsy" and unbearably hot inside. But it seemed to have been a crowd pleaser as it clanked down St. Louis Street at the courthouse.

fuel in World War I was voluntary. Streetlights in the town were shut off each night at midnight to conserve fuel. As a wartime measure, the Illinois Traction System abolished round trip and excursion tickets. Members of the Monday Club donated $1273 to the Library War Fund in Washington, D.C., which provided magazines and books for "the caps," slang for soldiers. During the summer of 1918, a tank of the sort used by the American forces rolled through downtown, stirring enthusiasm for more purchases of war bonds.

The local chapter of the Red Cross, headquartered in the Bohm Building, sponsored a wild west show on July 4 staged by cowboys from the National City Stockyards. An audience estimated at between five and six thousand enjoyed the rodeo. Charles Boeschenstein served as County Chair of the Red Cross, and Mrs. Roy S. Barnsback was Chair of the local branch. Canteen

Committees organized by the Red Cross met troop trains going through Edwardsville with coffee and cheer.

Familiar community leaders organized the wartime sacrifices. William Stullken and L. D. Lawnin served on the State of Illinois Council of Defense, which attempted to coordinate local efforts to conserve food, sell bonds, and promote patriotism. Mrs. W. D. Harnist chaired the Edwardsville Branch of the Women's State Council of Defense, with headquarters on Second Street. Thomas L. Tandy chaired the Lincoln Branch of the State Council of Defense, which met at Lincoln School Mrs. Thomas Williamson headed the very successful Edwardsville National Woman's Liberty Loan from an office in the Meyer-Trares building on Purcell Street. Edwardsville's quota for the Third Loan was $278,000, but 3,000 subscribers bought $455,000 worth of bonds! Attorney C. W. Terry served as local food administrator, coordinating vol-

A Wild West Show was staged on July 4, 1918, by the Madison County Chapter of the Red Cross as a fund-raiser. The show, which was held on the William H. Schwartz farm, just south of Center Grove Park, drew big crowds to see steer roping and bandits holding up a stagecoach. The participants came from the National City stockyards.

The Liberty Bond Committee maintained this headquarters at Main and Hillsboro.

untary efforts to conserve meat and wheat in the town. In June 1918, he asked all grocery stores to make only one delivery a day to each customer. Terry was also in charge of Four-Minute Men, who gave patriotic talks about the war to any group requesting their services.

L. D. Lawnin, vice-president of N. O. Nelson Manufacturing Company, implemented Thrift Gardens on 15 acres of unsold house lots in Leclaire during 1917. Ground was plowed and seeds furnished at the expense of the company. Children between 10 and 14 grew easily preserved vegetables--- potatoes, cabbage, tomatoes, carrots, and parsnips. Hoeing and weeding for one to three hours a day, they received a wage of ten cents an hour paid by the company and a share of proceeds from sale of the crops. Thrift Gardens spread from Leclaire to many of the city's empty lots, where they were tended by unpaid volunteers.

With small change, school children could accumulate stamps in a Liberty Book to be redeemed, with interest, after the War. The *Intelligencer* reported on May 9, 1918, that pupils in all Edwardsville schools, public and private, had bought $4,090.35 worth of "Thrift Stamps" and that pupils and teachers held Liberty Bonds amounting to $23,450. Edwardsville school children also donated large quantities of clothing to be sent to homeless Belgian children. The Young Ladies' Club of St. Mary's Church organized musical evenings, proceeds of which were directed to Belgian relief. During 1918, school children saved nut shells and peach seeds for use in the manufacture of soldiers' gas masks. Children at the Lutheran School, sixty in 1918, made rifle wipers for the soldiers.

Due to the many German families in Edwardsville, there must have been some tension as the Federal Government's anti-German propaganda machine heated up. According to Clarence Bohm, German-language services at Immanuel Methodist Church on Main Street stopped soon after war was declared, but both German and English services continued to be offered at Eden Evangelical Church. In 1918, Eden's congregation pur-

FOUR MINUTE MEN GET SOUVENIR FROM GERMAN U-BOAT
Edwardsville Intelligencer, July 3, 1918

"*C. W. Terry. . . . yesterday presented nine men with emblems for their services. Each is entitled to wear a small button with the letters and figures '4 M. M. 4' engraved upon it. . . . The buttons were cast from the metal of a German submarine captured some time ago. . . . Those who secured the insignia are C. W. Terry, C. H. Burton, Thos. Williamson, D. G. Williamson, Geo. D. Burroughs, M. L. Burroughs, D. H. Mudge, Jesse L. Simpson, Geo. A. Lytle and M. D. Powell.*"

Here are views of a popular summertime activity—a fish fry. This is the Firemen's Fish Fry, held in 1918 at the Turner Hall.

134

G.A.R. vets, both black and white, were photographed on memorial Day 1916. Though elderly, many of them offered to join the U.S. military in World War I.

THRIFT JINGLE

Mary had a little card
(Of savings stamps, you know)
And everywhere that Mary went
That card was sure to go.
And every time she earned some change
For doing well at school,
She'd save it for another stamp,
And soon her book was full.

The American Legion put up this sign at the southeast corner of the courthouse honoring those who served in World War I. Six men were killed in action and 10 died of other causes, such as illness. Edwardsville's black soldiers were not listed on this sign.

chased and displayed on a new pole what must have been one of the largest American flags ever to fly in the city, eight by twelve feet. On April 5, 1918, the school board announced that study of German language at Edwardsville schools would stop. As reasons for its decision, according to the *Intelligencer,* the Board noted little interest among students and the fact that "schools of practically every city around here--Alton, East St. Louis,

BATHS

RICHARDS BRICK CO

THE PALACE

SCHOOL SUPPLIES!

Quincy and dozens of other places have done away with the study of German in the public schools." It was not resumed until fall term, 1928. At Trinity Lutheran School, which had opened in September 1915, the board decided that, starting in September 1918, all instruction would be in English instead of German.

Committees of citizens "visited" people who were suspected of disloyalty, and, because a group of local Protestant patriots suspected him of pro-German sympathies, a priest was forced, first to leave town and then to resign from St. Boniface parish. But the physical violence, the lynching and tarring and feathering of so-called "slackers" that marked many other communities, did not occur in Edwardsville.

As the war drew to a close in October and November 1918, many people became ill with influenza, part of a world-wide epidemic that year. A reported 25 to 30 cases in early October grew to 600, with 19 deaths by early November. On October 10, 1918, by proclamation of Mayor Hotz, all schools were closed in an effort to check the spread of "Spanish flu." No church services were held during October. To no avail. Schools reopened a month later, on November 18, only to close again on December 2, this time to reopen only after Christmas. Because of the number of sick employees, businesses, from October 22 to the end of 1918, closed at 4:00 p.m. Lodge meetings and public entertainments were also cancelled for more than two months.

As lavishly as it had sent them off to war, the town welcomed the troops on their return after Armistice Day, Six men had been killed in combat, while another 10 had died from other causes while in the service. On July 22, 1921, the body of Henry "Hank" Ostendorf of Edwardsville, who had been fatally injured in France on August 2, 1918. Guarded by George Berleman and Edwin Wood, the coffin rested for a day in the rotunda of the Court House so that the town could pay its respects.

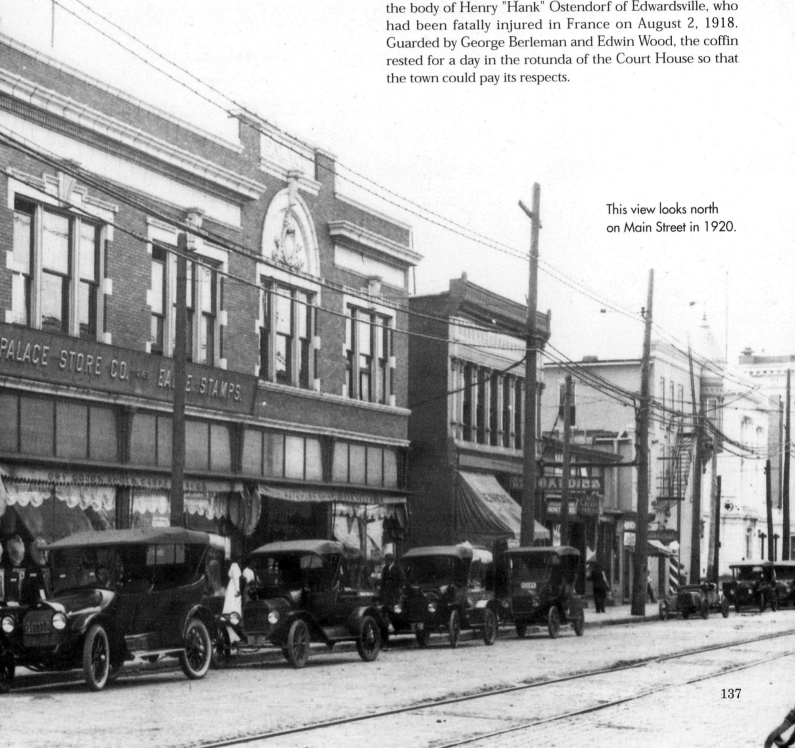

This view looks north on Main Street in 1920.

An early Trinity Lutheran School building, dedicated in 1915.

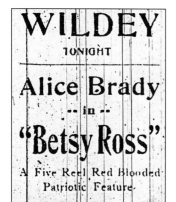
Ad for Betsy Ross Film at the Wildey.

ARMISTICE DAY, A POEM

How well I remember the day and the date
Out there on the Western front
It seemed we were doomed as sure as fate
With our outfit bearing the brunt
****
Then all at once the glad signal came
To cease firing---it's all over at last.
You see fighting a war is a sacrifice game
But we were holding on to the task.
****
Our nation stands 100 per cent freedom from fear
Freedom of speech, the right to live with pride
We fought for the country we loved so dear
That wide wide democracy might always abide.

By William O. Scott, African-American
"Soldier Poet" of Edwardsville

William O. Scott, member of Company A, 365th Infantry, 92nd Division, A.E.F. in World War I, came to be known as Edwardsville's "Soldier Poet." This photo was taken in the 1920s.

It was a time for posing proudly for pictures in front of the Leland Hotel and of marching, marching, marching (in the 200 block of North Main.)

Edwardsville Intelligencer

MADISON COUNTY'S HOME DAILY

Thursday, Nov. 7, 1918

PEACE!

Armistice Signed at 11 Today

GERMAN SURRENDER

Unconditional Giving up of the Last Autocracy

The *Intelligencer* appropriately trumpets the end of hostilities in Europe on November 7, 1918; the official armistice was signed four days later, on November 11. The date was called Armistice Day for many years; several wars later it became Veterans Day.

The body of war casualty Henry "Hank" Ostendorf lies in state in the atrium of the Madison County courthouse in July 1921, with George Berlemann and Edwin Wood as honor guards. Ostendorf was injured on August 2, 1918; he died five days later and was temporarily buried in France.

Here's Mr. Catalano's Fruit Store on wheels, in 1927.

This—or Bobbed?

Be honest now—which do you think is the more beautiful? You may not be able to grow a head of hair like this, but what you have or can grow we can surely make lovely on you. Our expert treatments insure that.

Nancy Jane Beauty Shoppe

5TH FLOOR
EDWARDSVILLE NATIONAL BANK BUILDING
EDWARDSVILLE,   ILLINOIS

The Nancy Jane salon urged women to adopt the shorter, more comfortable hair styles.

VELIE SILENT SIX

The difference that is paid for a QUALITY CAR
is refunded again and again through the cash value
of the satisfaction it gives   ::   ::   ::

WM. C. KRIEGE CO.

EDWARDSVILLE   ILLINOIS

From The Tiger for 1921, an ad for a "quality car."

A store operated by James Fagg, across from the Wildey Theater, sold radios and phonographs, which brought a new world of sound right into the home. The picture is dated June 1927.

A NEW ERA

Many national trends associated with the postwar era also appeared in Edwardsville. Flappers bobbed their hair and allowed their legs to show in photographs. "I had bobbed hair and smoked," Jetty Deitz, age 93, remembered with a smile in 1996. Radios and phonographs were sold on Main Street. Housewives were urged to abandon the ice-box for an electric refrigerator. Delivery trucks and automobiles gradually replaced the horse- and mule-drawn vehicles of an earlier time. Although automobiles zoomed through dreams and reshaped business and the landscape, many families in Edwardsville did not own an automobile until after World War II.

This 1934 *Intelligencer* ad promoted electric refrigeration, which must have been a god-send for busy housewives.

Chain stores appeared for the first time in the New Era. In April 1923, a new Kroger store opened; in July 1925, Tri-City opened a grocery store in a new building on the northeast corner of South Buchanan and Schwarz, now the home of Edwardsville Cyclery. In the Delicate Building at Main and Hillsboro, the A&P welcomed customers in 1928.

The Travous house is considered the first modern house in Edwardsville, built about 1940 on Center Street.

LOUISE TRAVOUS, E. H. S. CLASS OF 1911, WRITES TO FLAPPERS IN *THE KICKAPOO,* JANUARY 20, 1928

"In order to get a thorough understanding of each other right at the start, I am going to tell you straight out from the shoulder what I think about you. All things considered, it's my opinion you're a pretty fine lot, in spite of all the adult anxiety we are wasting on you. You know more than we did in our generations (but so does the rest of the world for that matter). And as a whole you're better, and more comfortable, looking. We has-been flappers, who on cold days bore resemblance to a piece of overstuffed, lament the scarcity of your clothing. But I believe at that you have the grippe and tonsilitis less often than some of us who wore red flannel."

MARMON

HARWOOD GARAGE
MOTOR EXPERTS
EDWARDSVILLE, ILL.   Phone 345

This Marmon touring car was advertised in the 1922 Tiger.

Streamlined locomotives came into use in the 1930s as speed became more and more important in travel. This is the Illinois Central's Green Diamond on one of its St. Louis-Chicago trips. IC passenger service between the two cities was inaugurated on May 18, 1936.

Electricity continued to transform the landscape. The City Council in 1924 decided to create a White Way Lighted District downtown. In August 1924, removal of Main Street's bricks began for laying the cables underground. More and more Edwardsvillians enjoyed telephones. According to the *Intelligencer* of October 12, 1927, the phone directory listed 2056 customers. In 1927, the Palace Store installed the first downtown sprinkler system. Traffic lights, Edwardsville's first, were installed at Vandalia and Main on July 1, 1928.

A number of new businesses were established after the war. Returning from military service, William A Rohrkaste, Sr., bought a farm on the site of what is now Southern Illinois University at Edwardsville and a 40-head herd of milk cows. From a site at 1003 N. Main, he at first delivered milk to customers with a horse and wagon. Women brought pails to the wagon to be filled with a dipper. Later, Rohrkaste delivered the milk in bottles. Rohrkaste Dairy, in the 1970s, became the Senior Citizens Center. From 1921 to 1928, American Canneries Company operated a plant on St. Louis Road at the foot of West Street. Between 1922 and 1925, C. F. Scholl of Troy Road manufactured and marketed a liquid cleaner for furniture and stoves called Kleen-Rite. Young Ernest E. Tosovsky decided in 1922 to establish Home Nursery, its name signaling that it was to serve local customers. Helped by J. J. Ammann, Edwardsville's leading florist, Tosovsky gradually built up the business that continues today. In 1925, a plant which treated railroad ties with creosote was established south of the city on Center Grove Road. In 1927, city realtors organized the Edwardsville Real Estate Board.

The Edwardsville Chamber of Commerce, an advocacy group for local business, was founded in 1923, with Gilbert S. Giese, publisher of the *Intelligencer,* as its first president. In 1928, the Edwardsville Chamber affiliated with the Chambers of Commerce of the United States, the national organization.

In 1927, grain elevator operators Louis C. Abenbrink, John A. Fruit, John A. Buhrle, Martin Jensen, and John G. Klueter founded the Edwardsville Creamery Company (ECCO) at Park and Johnson Streets. The new plant processed 30,000 pounds of milk on its first day in operation. In 1929, doing a million-dollar-a-year business in condensed milk, the company doubled the size of the plant. In 1930, bottled milk was added and also ice cream, evaporated milk, butter, and skim milk powder. The company sold milk directly to stores and to drivers who made home deliveries.

After World War I, women were more visible in the city's public forums and workplaces. The Nineteenth (Suffrage) Ammendment allowed women to vote in national elections for the first time in 1920. In 1891, the Illinois State Legislature had permitted women to vote in school elections. Mrs. E. W. West, who ran for the Board of Education in 1892, got 15 votes. But in 1924, Mrs. George Handlon became the first woman elected to Edwardsville's Board. During the War, some married women and many single women had taken full- or part-time employment. In February 1929, a group of the city's working women organized a chapter of the Business and Professional Women's Club with 71 charter members. Members discussed working conditions for women, studied leadership and national affairs, and funded some college scholarships for women.

African-American women also contributed to community betterment through the Women's Federated Club, organized in 1927. Led by Mrs. Malweda Jason Thomas and Mrs. Susie Jones Scott, club members cleared land at Springer's Woods for a children's playground.

Starting in 1927, and for about half a century, Edwardsville produced ECCO milk, the end product of Madison County dairy herds, according to this 1930 newspaper ad.

Here's the Edwardsville Creamery Company (ECCO) plant on Park Street (right) at Johnson Street.

142

ODE TO EDWARDSVILLE, PROBABLY COMPOSED IN THE 1920S

O Edwardsville, old Edwardsville, on seven hills like Rome.
Thy Wand'ring sons, in exile drear, turn longing eyes toward home.

Thy avenues on tree-crowned hills are bordered all in green.
In verdure clad, bedecked with flowers, thy vallies lie between.

There all along her winding streams, the red man once held sway.
There built his wigwam, lit his fire and lived in primal way.

Here courts and order first prevailed---the church, the school, the law.
An empire in the wilderness the early Fathers saw.

Through all the coming centuries, this prophecy we speak.
No true born son will cause a blush to burn upon thy cheek.

Found in home of Alfred Raut in wooded area off Franklin behind Leclaire School in 1974. Possibly written by Raut, county agent here, 1920-1929.

SAM OVERBECK REMEMBERS SATURDAY NIGHTS DOWNTOWN

In those days [1920s], on Saturday night, the stores were open until 9 o'clock. It was shopping day for the farmers. Dad would get the sedan and park it on Main Street, which had angled parking. In the evening, our family would shop and then sit in the car and watch people. It was a Dodge car. It was like going to the mall today. I was 12 in 1928. There were lots of people downtown.

WHAT HAPPENED WHEN WOMEN GOT THE VOTE?

Mrs. M.R. (Dot) Grainey recalled what Mr. and Mrs. Harnist of Edwardsville did. One of them was a staunch Republican; one a strong Democrat. On election eve, they sat down to discuss the upcoming election. It was decided that since their ballots would cancel one another, the Harnists wouldn't vote. The next day, they met at the polling booth!

Judy Isselhardt,
"Illinois Women and the Vote," 1987

The Governor Edward Coles monument, erected in 1927 by the State, is in a corner of Valley View Cemetery, facing Route 157 and Lewis Road.

Valley View Cemetery opened in 1925 on the St. Louis Road (now Illinois Route 157); this is the cemetery building.

A POSTWAR BUILDING BOOM

During the 1920s, Edwardsville acquired a number of notable edifices, nearly all of sturdy Richards brick, which permanently altered the look of the town. Today these monumental structures dot the landscape, reminding viewers that people in the 1920s intended to leave their mark upon the distant future.

On February 10, 1924, Presbyterians dedicated their new church on the corner of Kansas and College. Membership had grown from 164 in 1912, with 204 in Sunday School, to 355 members and 320 in Sunday School during 1919. A smaller country church, the Columbia Presbyterian Church, located in Hamel Township near the Fruit store and elevator, had decided to merge with Edwardsville. Rural families were acquiring automobiles, and a "hard" road linked Hamel and Edwardsville. The old Presbyterian church at Kansas and College, built in 1885, could not accomodate the extra 15 families. Presbyterian membership by 1924 was 390. According to Professor Jack Ades, historian of the First Presbyterian Church, The Young Ladies Club of the church secured $3500 for a new organ by borrowing $2400, taking pledges, and cashing in "one or more Liberty Bonds."

A second large church, erected on St. Louis Street in 1924, a downtown landmark which echoes the rectangular feeling of the Courthouse, is St. John's United Methodist. The present building is the fourth Methodist church on a site donated in 1828 by James and Sarah Mason, early residents of the town. Leland H. Buckley, a well-known local

The original First Presbyterian Church building, on North Kansas Street at College, was built in 1885.

The present First Presbyterian building dates from 1924—still on North Kansas. Like many local churches, it has built additions to the original structure and has bought up adjacent property for more parking.

Modern windows made of vibrantly colored glass set in a heavy black matrix were installed in the First Presbyterian sanctuary in 1983, as part of an ongoing remodeling of the building. The windows are the work of the renowned St. Louis firm of Emil Frei & Associates. The church has an ambitious music program and is known throughout the area for choral and instrumental concerts.

144

lawyer, coordinated the raising of $70,000 for the new church and donated generously himself.

Its ample size permitted St. John's to be used for meetings by other community groups. In 1925, more than 40 businessmen formed a chapter of Rotary Club International, which began meeting at the new St. John's.

Reflecting the spirit of their mottoes, "Service Above Self" and "He Profits Most Who Serves Best," the club established a college scholarship given each year to a boy from Edwardsville. Perry Hiles served as the first president, while Clarence Gerke was secretary for many years.

This is St. John's Methodist Episcopal Church in about 1910, at the same location as the present church, Second and St. Louis streets. This building, built in 1884 combining Gothic and Romanesque elements, was torn down to make way for the present building, erected in 1924. This building faced Second Street and the courthouse square.

An old grocery store just north of the 1924 St. John's Methodist building, part of which is at left, became a church annex in the late 1950s. It was razed to make way for a Memorial Chapel of modern design, the work of local architect Edward A. Kane Sr., which was consecrated in 1960.

Here is the present St. John's, now called St. John's United Methodist, which faces St. Louis Street. The design is Classical, echoing the Classical look of the new courthouse built 10 years earlier across Second Street.

Eden United Church of Christ, one of Edwardsville's largest churches, was built in 1926 at a cost of $112,000. More than 900 persons can be seated in the worship area. This American Gothic building replaced an earlier, plainer brick church of the 1870s. Congregation members cleaned the bricks from the earlier structure to reuse them in the new.

A smaller Gothic church, St. Andrew's Episcopal, completed in 1916 on the site at Hillsboro and North Buchanan, also replaced an earlier brick structure, dating from 1872. The congregation of St. Andrew's thus anticipated a post-war trend of church construction in the city. Reporting on the first Easter services held in the new building, the *Intelligencer* noted prophetically that "the opening of the church" was "an important event for Edwardsville. It will, no doubt, prove an incentive to other congregations and lead to a rebuilding of other churches."

Downtown, a new home for the *Intelligencer,* on Second Street after 1921, where it remains today, joined the Edwardsville National Bank and the Bank of Edwardsville among the newer structures. Their square, modernist second-story windows contrasted with the gently rounded windows of earlier eras. At the northwest corner of Commercial and Hillsboro, the handsome Masonic Temple, completed in 1927 at a cost of $52,000,

The present Eden United Church of Christ, successor of the original German Freie Evangelische Kirche, is at 903 North Second Street and has one of the biggest congregations in town. Church members helped build this building in 1926-27; they salvaged brick from the old church and cleaned it for re-use.

The present St. Andrew's Episcopal Church (1916), simplified Gothic like the first, is on the same site, at 406 Hillsboro. The building, shown in 1941, looks pretty much the same today, but without the rampant ivy.

welcomed members of many city organizations, who also used it as a gathering place.

Masonic Lodge 99, which counted more than 300 members in the 1920s, held a charter acquired in 1851 and documents which record an earlier Lodge, Libanus No. 29, meeting in Edwardsville as early as 1819. Lodge 99 included among its founders many of the celebrated names in Edwardsville history, including John H. Weir, Matthew and David Gillespie, John A. Prickett, William Glass, and Thomas O. Springer. During the early 20th century, men from Edwardsville occupied state and national offices in the Masonic Order. C. H. Spilman succeeded former Governor Frank O. Lowden as Grand Orator of Illinois in the autumn of 1922 and, in 1927, gave up the editorship of the *Intelligencer* and moved to Boston to be Grand Secretary General of the Scottish Rite Masons of the Northern Jurisdiction. In 1928, Spilman presented Lodge 99 with a gavel and block made from wood of the historic U. S. naval frigate *Constitution,* constructed in 1794 and rebuilt in 1928. Although the new temple received its first use in December, 1926, it was not dedicated until September, 1929.

This is the Hillsboro Avenue side of the new Masonic Temple, completed in 1927. The dark brick is accented with terra cotta; the Masonic emblem tops the design.

Members of Masonic Lodge 99 break ground on Hillsboro at Commercial for a new temple.

The Edwardsville *Intelligencer* building at 117-119 North Second Street, as it looked in the 1970s. The facade is topped with battlements, a popular architectural feature of the early decades of the 20th century. Accents are in light-colored terra cotta, a much-used material which, like brick, was durable and could be mass-produced.

A featured architectural style in Edwardsville housing constructed during the postwar era was the "California bungalow."

Early in the 1920s, the Schwager brothers took a trip to California and returned with the new style, which caught on immediately. Dozens of these homes were constructed in Edwardsville neighborhoods by the Schwager Company. Because these homes were comfortable, sturdy and well-designed for families, many of them remain today.

Before 1920, Victorian homes with occasional softly curved windows and lacy woodwork so popular in the 1880s and 1890s yielded to less ornamented and sparer styles. A notable prewar example of a "Prairie Style" house in the manner of Frank Lloyd Wright was constructed at 705 St. Louis Street in 1910 by Ralph D. and Julia Hadley Griffin. Mr. Griffin's brother, William Burley Griffin, one of Wright's apprentices, designed the structure. It is known as Edwardsville's only example of modernist architecture.

In 1922, when N.O. Nelson died in California, employees of the Edwardsville plant each contributed one day's wages toward a memorial fountain. Designed by Victor S. Holm of Washington University, St. Louis, and placed in 1924, the cherub riding on a turkey originally stood north of the Leclaire Kindergarten building.

During the 1920s, as enrollments in Edwardsville's public high school soared, voters in March 1922 approved purchase of land behind the Hadley house as the site for a projected new building. In March 1923,

Another bungalow is this one, completed in 1923, at 215 commercial Street, the home of Dr. Eugene Wahl, who was company physician for the Illinois Terminal Railroad, Nickel Plate, Wabash, Litchfield & Madison, plus Wagner Electric and U.S. Radiator. For more than four decades after 1922 his office was on the top floor of the Edwardsville National Bank building.

The Griffin House, 705 St. Louis Street, was the first of "modern" design in town. It was built in 1909-10, designed by Griffin's brother, Walter Burley Griffin, an associate of Frank Lloyd Wright, in Wright's distinctive horizontal Prairie Style.

Joseph, John and Wilbur Schwager built this "California bungalow" in 1928 for their mother. The builders saw the new style of residential architecture on a trip to California and brought it back here. The house, at 1013 Grand Avenue, was modern, with central heating; it replaced an older house heated with stoves. The cost of the house, including lot, was $2,500.

they voted to build a new facility, and in August 1923, in a special election, by a margin of five to one, they approved new school taxes. The school census of September 1924 showed 139 boys and 130 girls enrolled in Edwardsville High School.

Designed by local architect Ed Kane, the new high school received its first students in September 1925. Its three stories of south windows commanded the heights above the St. Louis Road, now Highway 157. With double entrances facing east, the structure seemed to welcome hundreds of new students to the richness of education beyond eighth grade.

Since many more families could now afford to send sons and daughters on to high school, high school athletic and musical events began to attract community crowds as they do today. In June 1921, the Board of Education approved a regular course of athletics for the public schools' curriculum. In April 1927, town voters approved a bond issue to add a gymnasium and auditorium to the recently opened high school.

In fall 1930, Edwardsville joined surrounding towns in adding lights to the football field. The original football field can still be seen west of the 1925 high school. A community organization, the Edwardsville High School Athletic Association, paid for the lights by selling season tickets to all football games for $2.50. In 1930, one hundred tickets were sold. Ten years later, Edwardsville High School's football team tied with East St. Louis as Co-Champion of the Southwestern Conference.

The Boy on a Turkey memorial to N.O. Nelson was a fountain with a pool in front of it, erected in 1924. The design was appropriate because it is said Nelson loved children; the turkey in those days was considered a symbol of strength. The fountain was moved in 1970, minus its water connections, to the traffic circle in front of a new N.O. Nelson School, built across town three years earlier.

This is the original Edwardsville High School, opened in 1925.

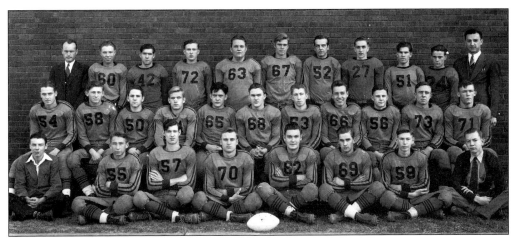

The first undefeated EHS football team was the Tigers of 1940, who shared the Southwestern Illinois High School Conference championship with East St. Louis. In first row, left to right, are John Morgan, manager, Tom Kolesa, Ed Agles, co-captain Leonard Menoni, Bill Rohrkaste, Robert Brumitt and Robert Bartless, manager; second row, left to right, are Don Zajicek, Blaine Stermon, George Demos, Bennett Hensley, Jack Parker, Harold Lankford, Paul Stafford, Wilbur Volz, Bill Martin, Melvin Kuethe and Maurice Gregor; third row, left to right, are Coach Glenn C. Smith, Robert Eads, Norman Merkel, Ed Utechtt, Clifford Schmidt, Dwaine Moore, Charles Hogue, Tom Shrier, J.C. Ritchie, Bill Holt and Assistant Coach William Dragalin. Missing was George Lautner.

American Legion Park, an Edwardsville landmark, also appeared during the 1920s. The Legion as a national organization with branches in most towns of any size developed as a voice for veterans in the years after World War I. Its founding convention met in St. Louis during May 1919. Here in Edwardsville, according to local historian Ray Rathert, "about 40 ex-servicemen" led by Charles E. Gueltig, met to organize in September 1919 in the Probate Court Room of the courthouse. The new post first met in the W. A. Edwards building on St. Louis Street and organized dances, which were held in the courthouse and at the Wildey, and a basketball team. By March 1920, Post 199 had more than 100 members. By 1922, a women's auxilliary had been formed. The search for a permanent organizational home ended in 1924, when members voted to buy a 42-acre tract of land on St. Louis Road near the site of the new high school for $7,950. The first picnic was held in the new park on July 4, 1924. In April 1925, citizens of Edwardsville voted to bring the park within the city limits. During the years 1930 and 1931, a golf course was added and a new clubhouse was built.

The Veterans of Foreign Wars (V.F.W.) organized the Fischer-Weeks Post in Edwardsville in May 1932, meeting

RAY C. RATHERT RECALLS THE CONSTRUCTION OF LEGION PARK

"They [the members] practically built the golf course, built the greens (sand), hauled the sand in by truck, sowed the fairways, oiled the sand for the greens, even went to St. Louis to get the oil. Members even helped mow the fairways. They built the clubhouse and beer stands, laid water pipe and sewer lines, installed septic tanks, laid sod, planted trees and shrubs. You name it, they did it---and most of the work was done on Saturdays and Sundays. It was no wonder Mrs. Fink asked Leroy if he married her or the American Legion."

For God and Country *(1979), p. 11.*

The old American Legion Post 199 clubhouse dates from the 1930s.

Leclaire's kindergarten class of 1922 or 23 proudly holds their diplomas. Standing, left to right are teachers Mildred Shaw and Pearl Wilson. Back row: Virginia Hunt, Rodney McNeily, Ethel Davis, Frances Morton, William Crossman, Nigle Klausing, Edith Long,_____ Schwager, _____. Sitting: Bobby Ferguson, Dorothy Schaefer, Clifford Karnes, June McCune, Harold Highlander, Ona Lingner and Alistar Stewart.

first at the American Legion clubhouse. On February 16, 1934, the anniversary of the sinking of the battleship *Maine* in the harbor at Santiago, Cuba, in 1898, wives and sisters of V.F.W. men organized the V.F.W. Auxilliary.

In May 1926, the Madison County Tuberculosis Sanatorium, located on 50 acres of land adjoining Troy Road south of town, was opened. Designed for 90 to 100 patients, the three-story structure, which had been built on land undermined by the Donk Coal Mine, began to sink a few weeks after it was opened. Along the northern end of the building, subsidence reached a maximum of twelve inches. The structure, which still stands today, was saved by exceptional engineering, which included placing several hundred screwjacks around and under the foundation and heavy beams against the north end of the building to check the slippage. After nearly two years, when all evidence of sinking had passed, the jacks were removed and the spaces filled with brick. Inner and outer walls were then covered with a new coating of plaster, and treatment of patients proceeded. By 1945, 45 people were employed at the sanitarium.

The opening of Valley View Gardens Cemetery in 1925 on the St. Louis Road (Highway 157) and the dedication of a monument to Governor Edward Coles in that

The Madison County Tuberculosis Sanatorium was opened in 1926, but immediately began to suffer the sinking effects of coal mine subsidence. The building is seen resting on jacks, with beams shoring up the north end.

Massive screw jacks under the sanatorium could be adjusted until the subsiding stopped after a couple of years.

The sanatorium is seen from the southeast corner toward the end of the 1920s repairs. Two sunroom wings are on the south side of the building. The building became the Madison County Nursing Home in the 1960s after the construction of a TB outpatient treatment center on the grounds, as tuberculosis declined and aging became more of a problem.

cemetery in 1927 added two more now-familiar places to the town's historic heritage.

Along with these many new structures, the town in the years after World War I also valued some of the old. Herbert C. Crocker, a young reporter for the *Intelligencer*, who, like Charles Bartels earlier, seemed determined to document features of Edwardsville, photographed some of the more venerable buildings still in use. In 1930, the Edwardsville High School *Tiger* was dedicated to history and featured photos of historic buildings in the town and county.

This picture of the historic Samuel Judy House, built in 1808 at what is now Glen Carbon, is from the 1930 EHS Tiger, whose theme that year was local history. Col. Judy and his family were the first permanent European settlers in Madison County and his residence was the first brick house in Illinois north of St. Clair County. The building stood for 125 years; it was demolished in 1933 because it would have been too costly to renovate.

The nicely proportioned Madison County Jail Residence, where sheriffs lived for many years, was built in 1869, Charles Spilman, architect. The cellblocks were behind the house. This picture, taken in 1928, appeared in the 1930 EHS Tiger. When a new jail was built a few blocks away in the late 1970s, the county had no further use for this building and it was demolished in 1982, despite efforts by preservationists to save it. Only the iron fence at the front sidewalk remains.

The Madison County Home, of bold, Italianate design, is seen in 1923, with James Stallman, superintendent for many years, and Mrs. Stallman on the porch. The place has been variously named over the years: the County Hospital, the County Poor Farm, the Madison County Nursing Home and, most recently, the county Sheltered-Care Home, for persons who don't need the supervision of a nursing home. It was described in the 1873 Brink, McCormick County Atlas, thus: "This farm is one of the best located improvements of the kind in the State, and its buildings, for the accommodation of the county's unfortunates, are large, substantial and convenient."

HARDY PEOPLE FACE HARD TIMES: THE GREAT DEPRESSION AND THE NEW DEAL IN EDWARDSVILLE

People who remember the Great Depression as it affected Edwardsville are survivors. They were able to stay in the town. They are alive now and tell stories, but their memories of hard times are generally muted. Seen in the glow of the "good war" that followed, hard times have become a momentary inconvenience, best forgotten.

The depression came gradually to the town, not suddenly. It was, Studs Terkel has said, like the air leaking slowly out of a punctured tire. Numerous wage workers had experienced hard times during the 1920s. After World War I, three of the four coal mines were often shut down. In September 1932, only the East Side and Henrietta mines were operating, the former employing only 12 to 14 men. Elder Manufacturing Company, which employed 100 to 110 people making shirts and, after 1925, coveralls, closed in 1932 and reopened in 1933 with a force of only 60. The U. S. Radiator plant cut its work force gradually after the war and, by the mid-30s, the only employee was Mrs. Mary Paproth's father, Elsie "Doc" Bryant. As foreman of the company, he was kept on as a watchman. The Bryants had a house on Springer Avenue then. Only a fence separated the house from the radiator plant. Mr. Bryant built steps along the fence, so that he could climb the steps, make his rounds at the plant and then rest on his back porch between watches. Other companies also reduced their workforces, as the economy plunged after 1929.

N.O. Nelson Company experienced decline and reorganization before the onset of the Great Depression. The marble shops were closed and the building torn down in 1925. The smokestack at the brass shops collapsed the same year. In 1928, the company sold the waterworks in Leclaire to the Edwardsville Water Company.

One result of the pressure of the Great Depression on profits of the N. O. Nelson Company was the annexation of Leclaire to Edwardsville in 1934. According to Robert Blain, an historian of Leclaire, maintaining of the village's streets and sewers had become an intolerable burden for the company. In 1933, the company took bids for the wrecking of the social center. In June 1933 Nelson Lawnin, President of N.O. Nelson, suggested to Edwardsville city officials a plan for Leclaire annexation. After a community referendum approved, the annexation was completed on January 31, 1934. Between 1920 and 1930, Edwardsville's population had grown from 5,336 to 6,235, an increment of 899. Leclaire added another 1,773 to make the 1940 population 8,008.

Joe Rotter, who was 21 in 1932, remembers that summer as a time when "no one had a job." He had just returned from college and passed time with other unemployed young men playing fast pitch softball. Rotter pitched 63 games, including 11 no hitters, and lost only six games that summer. In 1933, with his college education, he got a job jerking sodas at Ballweg's. By September 20, 1933, 650 families in Edwardsville were on relief rolls. (Nationally, 25 per cent of the workforce was unemployed by 1933.) Local farmers also suffered. Prices fell and drought meant less grain to market. In 1930, only 18 inches of rain, less than half the normal amount, had fallen by the beginning of September. Jetty Deitz, who lived with her family on Union Street, remembered a second dry summer in 1933. Between June and October, "it didn't rain one drop of rain the whole time. When you walked across the grass it just crackled." According to the *Intelligencer* of October 14, 1933, the average farm in Madison County lost $291 in 1930, $359 in 1931, and $424 in 1932.

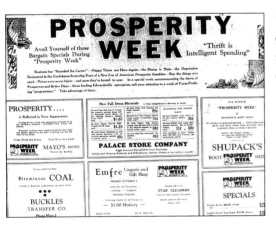

"Prosperity Week" was declared in October 1930 and used as an advertising gimmick in the *Intelligencer* as a way of fighting Depression blues.

Joe Rotter did find employment, at the *Intelligencer,* where he sold advertising for 43 years. Meanwhile, he ran for city treasurer in 1941, and won; he was treasurer for 10 consecutive four-year terms, which was an Illinois record when he retired in 1981.

JOSEPH F. ROTTER
— CANDIDATE FOR —
CITY TREASURER
EDWARDSVILLE, ILLINOIS
— ON THE —
CO-OPERATIVE TICKET

Election: Tuesday, April 15, 1941

Your Vote and Support Appreciated

(1)

A majority of Edwardsville voters, beginning in 1930, shifted their allegiance, which had been Republican during the 1920s, to the Democratic Party. Warm enthusiasm greeted efforts by the Roosevelt Administration to fight the depression.

After 1933, the New Deal created significant local temporary employment through a number of construction projects. In January 1934, for example, men employed by the Civil Works Administration (CWA) raised bleachers for the athletic field at Edwardsville High School. In August 1934, the city secured a federal loan of $199,000 to build a sewage plant. Also during 1934, 25 painters employed for 6 hours four days a week refurbished the Tuberculosis Sanatorium. In September 1935, Camp Wheeler, a Civilian Conservation Corps Camp housing 223 men, opened northeast of town. The young men dug culverts and planted 20,000 trees all over the county. In March 1936, Works Project Administration workers began to drain, dredge and beautify Leclaire Lake, which was filling with mud. Using $83,799 of federal funds, they gave the lake a sand bed and built the rock walls around it. In September 1936, a federally funded recreation center for young people opened in the old Turner Hall on Second Street. Malweda Jason worked at the center and organized a club for teenage girls. Workmen cleaned up the ruins of the old Koehler Mill, which had burned 50 years ago, to prepare a place for horseshoe pitching in connection with the recreation center. In the summer of 1937, $30,000 of federal funds and $300 of city monies were spent cleaning up the site of the closed Henrietta Coal Mine and creating Voge Park. Shafts were filled with rubble, structures torn

Edwardsville's NRA Celebration An Outstanding Success

Edwardsville Intelligencer, Madison County's Home Daily. 71st YEAR—NO. 249. EDWARDSVILLE, ILLINOIS, SATURDAY, OCTOBER 21, 1933. TEN PAGES. WEATHER: Unsettled and possibly showers, much cooler tonight. Tomorrow fair and colder. Temp. today at 2 P. M., 78.

Edwardsville jumped onto the National Recovery Act (NRA) bandwagon with a parade on October 20, 1933, attended by an estimated 7,000 to 8,000 spectators. The parade ended at City Park, with speeches. The National Recovery Administration, which administered the Act, came up with an immensely popular Blue Eagle symbol, like that at the left end of the Intelligencer nameplate. This logo, which appeared everywhere, was intended to show support for New Deal efforts to pull America out of the depression.

Led by a color guard, marchers carry the NRA banner past the courthouse as somber crowds line North Main Street on a rainy October 20, 1933.

Camp Wheeler, a Civilian Conservation Corps camp was constructed northeast of town, near what is now Vadalabene Park. The camp is in the center of the picture, which looks northwest, across the diagonal of U.S. Route 66 (now Illinois Route 157) and the parallel tracks of the old Litchfield & Madison Railway Company (now the Chicago & Northwestern/Union Pacific).

154

Ed Ballweg Jr., at his drugstore in the mid-1930s, with East Vandalia Street in the background.

Ballweg's Drugs, located in the Bohm Building corner from 1932-38, sports the NRA Blue Eagle in one of its entranceway windows.

In the 1950s and 1960s Ballweg's Drugs served its customers at this location.

William C. Straube, Edwardsville's "New Deal Mayor."

Proud WPA workers put their name on many Edwardsville sidewalks.

down, and the site graded to make a ball field, which remains today, although the park has been renamed to honor Sam Vadalabene. The Works Progress Administration also replaced many of the city's brick sidewalks with concrete walks. Federal money supported major road-building efforts in the county, including the rebuilding of U.S. Route 66 through the city in 1938-39, the construction of the Edwardsville-Wood River Road, and the resurfacing of the center of the city's streets after three electric railroad lines abandoned their routes through Edwardsville. In April 1940, another of the New Deal's public works projects, the Rural Electrification Agency, brought the first electric lights and power to a number of Madison County farms. Administration of local public works and relief projects was headquartered in the Bohm building on North Main.

The Madison Construction Company designed their own pavement pulverizer for repaving U.S. 66 through Edwardsville in 1938-39. A very big jackhammer mounted on the side of the truck did the job of smashing the old brick paving and its concrete foundation. The hammer could strike 60 to 70 blows per minute. It is seen just west of the East Vandalia Street railroad tracks.

As the highway system flourished, the electric rail lines lost riders, and three trolley companies pulled out of the city. But they left their tracks behind in many places, and this caused problems for the city as street resurfacing continued. During 1938, a federal WPA (Works Progress Administration) project paid for removing the tracks and patching the streets. This view looks north on Second Street from St. Louis Street.

East Vandalia Street is all torn up in front of the Hi-Way Tavern during the repaving of Route 66. The building dates from about 1918.

The Hi-Way Tavern was doubled in size some two decades after this picture was taken. A restaurant was added to the left, in front of the house that can partly be seen, and another house acquired for parking. Today the business is Neumann's Tavern, (no restaurant), 461-63 East Vandalia, owned by Paul and Rose Neumann.

The New Deal also subsidized some intellectual projects in Edwardsville. Researchers paid by the Federal Writers' Project compiled an annotated index to the *Intelligencer* covering the years 1862 to 1937. They also inventoried items owned by the Madison County Historical Society and investigated historic structures in the town.

As part of the New Deal's support for works of public art, Miriam McKinney, an artist in many media whose works are now found in museums around the country, created murals for the Edwardsville Public Library. McKinney, who lived in Edwardsville for 30 years, until 1959, was married to Donnell Hofmeier, a local lawyer. During the 1930s, the town and its environs were among her favorite subjects. With their bleak beauty and strong lines, her landscapes suggest an age of anxiety, while her

Earth movers rearrange the landscape to make way for a new road to Wood River (now Route 143), replacing a narrow, twisty Old Alton Road dating from horse and buggy days—and probably before. Old Alton Road is still there, serving rural residents, primarily.

An outfit capable of laying down 800 to 1,000 feet of highway slab daily is seen at work on the new Wood River road in 1939.

Rural electrification, another New Deal project, came to Madison County on April 13, 1940, when a switch was thrown in a substation on Route 66 northeast of Edwardsville. Left to right are Victor Kallal, superintendent for the cooperative; Mrs. Henry Talleur, a director of the Southwestern Electric Co-op, Inc.; W.E. Callaway, superintendent for Cater Construction Co., of Kansas City, Mo., builders; George Hawes, district manager for the Illinois-Iowa Power Co.; G.G. Pape, vice-president of the Southwestern Co-op, and county Farm Adviser Truman W. May.

The brick portion of this structure was found by WPA researchers to be the oldest brick building in Edwardsville, built before 1819 as a store for the Pogue brothers, Robert and George, who came here from Philadelphia to trade with the Indians. The building stood on North Main Street across from the old town square (later Lincoln School), and is believed to have housed the first post office and the land office. Later, it was the home of Isaac Prickett, another early merchant, and his wife, Nancy Lamkin. Since the 1940s, Rusty's restaurant and bar has been here, with some of the original 1819 brickwork carefully preserved through a number of add-ons and remodelings and exposed on interior walls.

WHAT REALLY DID HAPPEN, ANYWAY?

The details of human events are so ephemeral. People who witness the same happening ususaly come away with different impressions, different versions of what actually took place. Writing about events years later can be a trying exercise in weighing evidence, deciding which sources are the most reliable and weeding out fanciful stories. Take the story that Amelia Earhart flew her plane into Edwardsville and landed on the American Legion golf course. She was here, all right, but she didn't arrive like that.

Miss Earhart was the famous young woman who courageously attempted to fly around the world in 1937 and, tragically, disappeared without a trace with her co-pilot in the southwest Pacific. What happened to her and her plane has been a major 20th century mystery. There have been many attempts to get to the bottom of the mystery, with no result.

What Amelia Earhart did in Edwardsville the year before her ill-fated flight was easier to determine. We asked two people who were there. Dorothy Fink, a deputy Madison County clerk for many years, was a brand new member of the Business and Professional Women's Club here when the BPW invited Miss Earhart to speak here on October 21, 1936. Infact, she went to Lambert Field in St. Louis with other BPW members to pick up the young flyer and bring her to Edwardsville. Mayor William Straube had arranged for a limousine for the purpose, and Miss Fink was chosen to ride in the limousine. She was a last-minute replacement for someone else who backed out, and Miss Fink said she was surprised she was chosen because she was so new.

But BPW President Eulalia Hotz, Madison County Clerk and Miss Fink's boss, said she wanted a young member of the club with her and Miss Earhart in the limo. The driver, Miss Fink remembered, was John Soehlke. And there were state police escorts for the car—both Missouri and Illinois. It was all very impressive.

The plan was for everyone to go to the Madison County Country Club (now Sunset Hills) and have dinner, and then go to the high school where Miss Earhart would give a public speech. Miss Fink still has her placecard from the dinner, autographed by Miss Earhart. It's one of her most prized possessions.

Helen Delicate was busy as a young housewife and not a BPW member, but she did go to the high school for the speech. She said, "There was a big crowd to hear her speak, and it was so interesting. I thoroughly enjoyed it. She was a woman ahead of her time, all right." Miss Fink recalled how unassuming the flyer was: "She was just like one of us."

You had to buy a ticket to hear the speech, so the Earhart visit here was undoubtedly part of a fund-raising tour in anticipation of her world-circling flight.

How could the Legion golf course rumor have started? The Legion is across St. Louis Road (Route 157) from EHS, so it makes a certain amount of sense to put together the country club, with its gold course, a daring young pilot, and come up with landing a plane at the Legion.

Except it didn't happen that way.
— ***Richard Norrish, 1996***

scenes of daily life offer reassurance and hope. "Because I thought it would be fun," she told an interviewer in 1980, "I did several things with local color. . . ." Her most famous Edwardsville painting shows regular customers at the soda fountain of Mottar's Drug Store, which occupied 206 N. Main for 42 years. McKinney's studio was across the street from Mottar's.

William D. Mottar Sr., and son John A. Mottar Sr.,in the 1930s.

This view looks south on Main Street past Mottar's to the Hillsboro Avenue intersection, where the people are bunched up. The building with the big awning, on the corner, is the Gerber Building, which housed a Woolworth's for many years. All of these buildings are gone now.

McKinney included herself, sketching at left, in a lunch-hour scene at Mottar's Drug Store. Other customers are Louis Smith, next to her, a Mottar's "fixture" said to have died of a heart attack in that seat; Irene Harrell, who has a book with her name on it, and Frank Stanley, manager of the Wildey Theater. In the background are John Mottar, his father William D. Mottar Sr., partly hidden, and Nancy Weeks, a young girl.

The St. James Hotel, a Main Street showplace, was irreparably damaged by fire in 1932. Artist McKinney found poignant beauty in the ruins and the result was this oil painting, done in 1934.

In 1958, Mckinney created three Mother Goose murals which today add color to the children's room of the library. Two are shown.

REMEMBERING THE THIRTIES

"Nobody had anything," said Fred Gillham, who was born in 1931 and lived with his family on Springer Avenue. He remembered that most of the families on his street raised chickens. Food was often shared with those less fortunate. People did not throw away clothes. Churches got involved in rummage sales. Families made vegetable gardens in the depression and canned supplies for the winter. "Then," he added, "when World War II came along, they had victory gardens, but everyone knew how to garden anyway."

"Growing up in the 1920s and 1930s was an experience difficult for many to understand," noted Fern Jason. "However," she added, "it was a joyous time." The Jason family lived on unpaved Schwartz Road in the 1920s and 1930s in a house like those of most other black families, without inside plumbing, telephone or electricity. Since television did not exist, children made their own entertainment. "We played games, went for walks in the woods and gathered flowers, found a spring and cupped our hands and drank from it, read. . . ." From wheels, axles, and boards supplied by Theodore Randles, a general hauler, the children made their own wagons and scooters. On Memorial Day, Mr. and Mrs. Jason and their children packed a picnic and headed for Silver Creek. "We usually chose not to go to the movie," Fern Jason remembered, "because we had to sit in peanut heaven. . . . The band concerts on Thursday nights in the City Park were enjoyable. That was the only time you were allowed to get on the grass." The children walked two miles to Lincoln School and "attendance was very good." On the first of May, she recalled, George Cathcart on East Vandalia treated every child on the way home from school with an ice cream cone. Like many other Edwardsvillians who were children in these years, Fern Jason recollected the delights of George Coukoulis' Candy Kitchen. A child could enter Coukoulis' shop "any time with two or three cents and point out four or five different kinds of candy we wanted." "Candy Kitchen George," always threw in extra

Edwardsville children of an earlier day loved to stop by George Coukoulis' candy shop downtown. This ad is from the 1924 EHS Tiger.

The Gillham House, sometimes known as the William Tyler Brown House, at 104 Springer Avenue, is one of the city's most elegant homes, dating from 1850.

Basketball was something new for the students at Lincoln School in the late 1930s. here's the team from 1936-37 or 1937-38. Kneeling are Ed Jones, Junior Shaw, Robert Hughes and Roland Brown; standing are Wes McMurray, Bobby Penelton, Carroll Williams and Thomas Hornberger.

pieces. Customers "could also get a double dip ice cream cone with strawberry syrup, marshmallow cream and crushed peanuts on top for five cents."

Sam Overbeck, who graduated from college in 1938, remembers the wonders of dating in the thirties, when a movie, hamburgers and cokes for two cost less than $1.00. At Rusty's, 10 cents bought "a whopping big ham-

burger, a big slice of onion, a pickle and a radish." Cokes were five cents. Cathcart's Cafe was "the main place for high schoolers in the 1930s." They had a long counter and three or four nickel slot machines. Customers' cars were parked all the way up to St. Boniface.

Cathcart's Cafe, on East Vandalia Street at Brown Street, was a hangout for high school kids as well as a popular restaurant for travelers along U.S. 66, which followed Vandalia through town. This ad is from the 1938 EHS Tiger.

Need wheels? Butler Chevrolet, 120 W. Vandalia Street, can provide, according to the 1936 EHS Tiger.

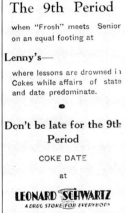

The lunch counter at Schwartz Drugs was promoted as an after-school hangout for students in this ad from the 1936 Tiger. The lunch counter at Schwartz Health Mart today is popular with everybody, in the heart of downtown across from the courthouse.

The long counter at Cathcart's Cafe.

Hurst Pontiac Co., on North Main Street across from City Hall, introduced the steering-column gearshift in 1938. This ad is from the EHS Tiger.

In 1937, the Edwardsville Bottling Works advertised its Orange Kist "refreshing drink."

St. Boniface students posed for this group shot in 1939.

Here are two active young people of the 1930s: Jlm Weeks, on the golf course, and Dorothy Somerlad Weeks by the family car.

The St. Boniface Bowling Alleys, in the basement of St. Boniface School, were the idea of Fr. Ernest J. Eckhard, pastor of St Boniface for 35 years, from 1919 until his death in 1954. He believed that young people should enjoy more opportunities for recreation. The alleys, installed in 1928, were later paved over and the area now is part of the school cafeteria.

Many enjoyed dirt track racing in the 30s. Jack Zika is the driver; Clarence Hoppe leans on door, and Jim Vanzo watches at the far right.

163

Mary Barnsback Byron was born in 1933 at 122 1/2 N. Main, where her father, Dr. Roy S. Barnsback, maintained both office and home on the second floor of a building he had built in 1904. Every morning, her father got up, swept the long flight of stairs, and unlocked the door. Office hours were from 8 to 10 a.m., 1 to 3 p.m., and 7 to 8 p.m. For 58 years, he never charged more than $2.00 for an office visit, including medicine. In the back of the building, Mary, her brother and sister played in a shady, fenced playyard with a sandbox and a double swing. From the wooden seat of the radiator in their bedroom, the Barnsback children could watch cars and trucks deliver coal to all the "little holes" in the sidewalks below.

According to the City Directory for 1932, Main Street in these years housed a dozen different grocery stores. Mary Byron remembers twice weekly shopping trips with her mother. The stores still offered their wares, such as dry beans, in barrels, vegetables in bushel baskets, and fruit in wooden boxes. At the back of these grocery stores was usually a "meat case." In 1942, when Mary was nine, the family moved to the Travous house on St. Louis Street.

During the 1930s, downtown Edwardsville experi-

There were many small grocery stores in Edwardsville in the early decades of the 20th century. This is 231-233 North Main Street, in the 1930s. The City Directory for 1932 shows Joseph Schwarz as the owner of the 231 business. Note the wares displayed outdoors on the sidewalk.

Waldo Vuagniaux at Tom Boy Meat Department, 132 N. Main, in 1938.

A sampling of cars on North Main Street downtown in the 1930s.

A birdseye view looking north on Second Street in the 1930s.

This snowy view looks northwest along the curving right of way of the Wabash Railroad spur past a grain elevator at West Vandalia and Johnson streets, left, operated in recent decades by the Farm Bureau adjunct, FS, with the Dippold Brothers elevator on St. Louis Street in the distance. Both are gone now, as the grain elevator business moved out of town.

Ray, Frances and Mary Jones in front of their Jones Shoe Shop on North Main Street in the 1930s.

BLACK-OWNED BUSINESSES IN THE 1930S

T. L. Tandy's. . . . [blacksmith] shop was still on Main Street in 1933. Other Black-owned/operated businesses were: Harry Daugherty's dairy farm in Pin oak Township, Ray Jones' Shoe Repair Shop on Main Street, Dr. Walter Williams — a really good doctor who would attend to you at any hour of the day or night, Dr. Cochran— foot doctor, and Mr. Bias Jackson (Miss Alma Aitch's husband) was a contractor. Bill Johnson had a night club. Miss Rae and Brister Donald had a restaurant. . . . Dora and Buster Scott had a barbecue business. . . . For a while my mother, Isola Turner, ran the boarding house at the Tie Plant. During the depression, we were among the rich. My father was a tie carrier.

Rose Turner in *Lincoln School Memories*, 1986

Far left: Ernest E. Tosovsky, Sr., founder of Home Nursery, photographed in the early 1970s.

Left: Frank Fink, leader in community music circles during the 1920s and 1930s, receives a life membership in the Edwardsville Musician's Union, 1946. He was president of the union for 25 years, manager of Edwardsville bands for 27 years and pianist in the Star Orchestra for many years.

enced two disastrous fires. The first, in July 1934, said by the *Intelligencer* to be "the most expensive fire in city history," started in the Star Hotel at Main and Vandalia and swept through Schwartz Furniture, the Palace Store, the Cloak and Suit Company, the Beauty Mart, and Kallinger's Buffet in the 100 block of North Main. Firemen from Collinsville, Granite City, and Wood River assisted. A second major fire in November 1937, hit Silverbloom's Department Store, which had been established at 118 North Main since 1928.

Fortunately, the Edwardsville Fire Department had been modernizing during the 1930s. After the annexation of Leclaire, the E.V.F.D. gained five men. In June 1934, the Department purchased a small automobile to

Fire broke out in Silverbloom's department store in the 100 block of North main in November 1937.

Firemen got the blaze under control, but the fire already had done considerable damage.

The firemen take a break for coffee at Wolf's Cafe, 108 North Main, after bringing the fire under control.

transport an inhalator, first aid equipment, and a hand extinguisher for small fires. In 1936, a new pumper truck was added that could spew out 750 gallons a minute. Pensions for both paid and volunteer members of the force were established in 1937. In November 1937, city workers removed the old firebell from the firehouse on Main Street. From now on, the telephone and sirens would summon volunteer firemen to assist the paid force at big blazes.

Music remained an important part of community life during the 1930s. Municipal Band Concerts graced the summer. Among Edwardsville's popular orchestras for hire were the Star Orchestra, led by Joseph Dippold, Lindbeck's orchestra, conducted by Carl Lindbeck, and Joseph Ladd's Orchestra, founded in September 1931. The first band in Edwardsville schools was organized in 1930 by Willis C. Varner. All of the members came from the Junior High School. Starting in September 1931, band instruction entered the High School curriculum. By 1933, with 90 members, the band entered its first state contest at Urbana and won a first in its class. In 1934, the band again received a first-class rating. The St. Boniface School Band got started in 1936. During the late 1930s, Trinity Lutheran School's children's choir developed a fine reputation. Edwardsville's tradition of musical quality enriched the lives of community members in the 1930s, as it does today.

These five officers of the Edwardsville Volunteer Fire Department set a record in 1945 for longevity of service as officers of any Illinois volunteer department, and perhaps for any other Illinois organization as well. The picture was taken in the City Hall council chambers on December 11, 1945, after the annual meeting of the EVFD. Left to right, with years served, are Simon Kellermann Jr., secretary, 45 years; Charles E. Judd, treasurer, 16 years; Ben Wood, president, 31 years; Raymond Rohrkaste, vice-president, 10 years, and Edward Weeks, sergeant-at-arms, 10 years.

Joseph Ladd and his Orchestra was a popular ensemble in the 1930s. Members in addition to Ladd were Irwin Dollinger, Udell Mason, Arthur Dippel, and Gerald Stroud.

The Edwardsville Fire Department shows off its equipment in August 1937, including its magnificent new (1936 model) Seagrave "Sentinel" Service Ladder Truck, which was to serve the city for more than 30 years.

On June 20 to 22, 1940, Edwardsville celebrated the coming of summer with a festival of floats, two nights of parading and prizes. According to Herbert Crocker of the *Intelligencer,* "thousands of persons" were attracted to the city. Perhaps people understood that the depression was lifting and that Edwardsville and the nation would soon enter another historic world struggle.

The Edwardsville High School Band, organized in 1930 by Willis C. Varner, had 90 members when this picture was taken for the 1937 Tiger at a band competition.

The EHS Band looks sharp as it practices marching on the football field in 1938.

Music began growing in popularity in church worship in the mid-20th century. One lively group, which made many public appearances, was the Trinity Lutheran Children's Choir, shown about 1940.

Edwardsville's first summer festival was held on June 20 to 22,
?40, and included back-to-
k evening parades. The
l Order of Moose float, with
ng Statue of Liberty, won
ze in the opening parade.

Second place, on the second
parade night, went to this float
entered by the Madison
County Automobile Insurance
Company—now known as
Madison Mutual Insurance.

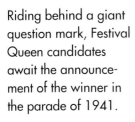

Riding behind a giant
question mark, Festival
Queen candidates
await the announce-
ment of the winner in
the parade of 1941.

THE SECOND WORLD WAR

The Roll of Honor set up on the grass at City Park in January 1946 listed the names of 975 men and women. All residents of Edwardsville, they had served in various branches of the armed forces during World War II.

Edwardsville's economy gained new vigor during the War. Several firms had war contracts. Others were stimu- lated by full employment and fatter paychecks. Evaporated milk from the Edwardsville Creamery Company smoothed the coffee of soldiers as far away as England, Africa and China, while bottled milk from ECCO was used at Scott Field in Belleville. The American Radiator Company received federal contracts to build radiators for military training camps. From the South,

This honor roll sign went up in City Park early in World War II, paid for by public donations , to list local residents serving in the armed forces. The names, in alpha- betical order, were on individual plates so they could be rearranged as more were added. When this picutre was taken in January 1946 there were 975 names of men and women listed, all from Edwardsville.

John Gemoules, 18, the son of a Greek immigrant, left high school before graduation in 1943 to join the U.S. Army. He was killed six months later during the invasion of Italy. Eight sons of the Gemoules fami- ly served in the armed forces during World War II.

In 1995, the *Intelligencer* saluted World War II veterans on the 50th anniversary of V-J Day (Victory over Japan), August 14, 1945, with these displays of faces from the era.

about 200 black workers came here, recruited by Elisie "Doc" Bryant, to work in "the Radiator." During the war, the Madison County Housing Authority, with offices in Madison, rented 50 units of trailer housing on Schwartz Road to radiator factory employees. As millions of tons of wartime supplies crossed the country on rails, the tie plant on Center Grove Road boomed. Farmers in Edwardsville's market area did their part too, growing food for all of the world where the Grand Alliance was fighting. The war witnessed the passing of some old-fashioned technology used to produce wheat, such as threshers propelled by steam engines. After the war, farmers used "combines," machines which employed gasoline engines to power a combination of mower and thresher.

Lieutenant Joyce M. Bardelmeier, U.S. Navy pilot, strikes a gallant pose.

Bardelmeier receives the Distinguished Flying Cross for making a direct hit on a Japanese destroyer and sinking it, during the Battle of Saipan in July 1944.

Three former Intelligencer employees stopped by the newspaper in May 1944 while on furlough, and were photographed in the press room. Left to right are navy Ensign Kirk Stafford; his brother, Army Tech-5 Paul Stafford, and Ensign Harold F. Metzger. Metzger was killed in action in February 1945. During his first mission over the Philippines he bagged a Japanese "Zeke" fighter. Kirk Stafford was a Navy flyer in the Pacific, and brother Paul was with the Army Engineers in Europe.

Joe Carnella, commander of Veterans of Foreign Wars Post 1299 of Edwardsville, is flanked by the four Bode brothers, veterans of World War II, on the night they all joined the VFW post, June 6, 1947. Left to right are Seaman Ralph Bode, who served in the Pacific; Staff Sergeant Eugene Bode, southwest Pacific and Japan; Carnella; Tech. Sergeant Robert Bode, with the Air Corps in England and Germany, and Tech-4 Charles Bode, who spent his time in England and France.

Here are some of the veterans of World War II who were awarded Edwardsville High School diplomas on June 5, 1946. They were given credits for their service, and passed U.S. Armed Forces Institute tests. Seated, left to right, are Ramond A. Maass, Wilbur A. Schmidt, Homer E. Rhodes, Alvin J. Arth, Almont Edwards, Gerald B. Orman, John T. Davenport, Harold Shaffer and Gerald Kershaw. Standing, left to right, are Harley W. Schneider, Donald F. Zajicek, Lauren Weishaupt, Rudolph H. Wild, Bruce L. Barth, Clifford F. Goff, Norman W. Merkel, Thomas R. Lamb, Gilbert H. Highlander, Louis H. Highlander, Owen L. Moore and Vernon H. Meyer.

With the war almost over, the Army foresaw the need for more railroad workers to move material and returning troops. A promotional steam engine on tires made the rounds of the St. Louis area to drum up interest. It is shown here on North Main Street at the courthouse, with a number of servicemen returned because of wounds, plus two women in the service. Second from right is Louis G. Rupp, president of the Chamber of Commerce and manager of the U.S. Employment Service; at right is Edward Fick, Rupp's employer relations representative.

Here is the first self-propelled, one-driver harvester-thresher used in the Edwardsville area, during the summer of 1945. The McCormick-Deering machine was purchased by Wesley Schmidt, a custom thresher, through the Edwardsville Motor Co. Schmidt, who lived near Peters Station, could harvest 35 to 40 acres of wheat daily, at $4 to $4.50 per acre.

The Edwardsville Sewer Reduction Plant was inundated in the spring of 1944 as Cahokia Creek flooded. A long stretch of the Wabash Railroad tracks nearby also was under water. The plant was out of service for a month.

Just a few days after the December 7 attack on Pearl Harbor, Edwardsville's civilians again began to mobilize for victory. The Red Cross on December 16, 1941, began a drive to raise $6,500 by asking for "a day's pay from those who work for those who fight." Before Christmas, the Board of Supervisors removed decorations made in Japan from the Courthouse. Scrap drives to gather scarce metal for recycling began almost immediately. In November 1942, veterans took a World War I English cannon weighing more than six tons from the American Legion park, where it had stood as a war memorial. The men hauled it through the streets of Edwardsville to the Mack Junk Yard and added it to the scrap pile. The Kiwanis Club raised money to underwrite sending cartons of Chesterfield cigarettes to service personnel overseas. Rationing of items such as gasoline, tires, sugar, butter, and meat got fully under way by 1943, and many residents remember this aspect of the war. Andrew Foehrkalb headed the county Rationing Board. Joe Rotter, Advertising Manager at the *Intelligencer,* was responsible for distributing information on rationing coming from Washington, D.C., to all county newspapers. Rotter also headed the Rationing Appeals Board for Madison County. In August 1943, as part of a war bond drive, Edwardsville was visited by a "captured Japanese two-man suicide submarine."

The election of Eulalia Hotz as County Clerk in November 1942, symbolized the entry of women into the workforce in greater numbers than ever before in American history. "Uke" Hotz, who served the County for 31 years, retiring in 1973, became a legend in her job and in the local Democratic Party. In 1969, she was the first woman to be elected president of the Illinois Association of County Officials. During the 1950s, she campaigned for office in a 1925 Model T Ford, painted a hot pink, her campaign color, and emblazoned with her slogan: "Good old-fashioned courtesy and service combined with modern efficiency." Among other innovations during her years in office, she encouraged "branch" voter registration centers in grocery stores and other public places, a practice later adopted throughout Illinois. She once said, "I'm not a politician, but I am a public servant. I think there is a distinction. I don't try to elect committeemen. I stay strictly to my own office, take as good a care of it as I can, and I don't interfere with other offices." Hotz's ethic of service foreshadowed a theme of postwar Edwardsville history.

County Clerk Eulalia Hotz. She was the first female Madison County official, elected in November 1942. Her brother, Norbert Hotz, held the office before her, and her father, Joseph Hotz, was clerk before that.

A captured, two-man Japanese suicide submarine was shown on North Main Street on August 19, 1943, to promote the sale of War Bonds. The 81-foot sub, mounted on a special truck, had been brought to the United States for study by naval engineers, and then sent out on fund-raising tours. The boat was powered by storage batteries and carried two torpedoes, plus enough explosive to blow it up after the torpedoes had been fired.

This six-ton English cannon from World War I stood at the American Legion as a memorial for many years, but in 1942, it was scrapped to help the World War II cause. Here, it is shown at the Mack Junk Yard on South Buchanan Street ready to be scrapped.

BECOMING SUBURBAN

From the 1940s until the early 1960s, Edwardsville was a stopping place on U.S. Route 66, the transcontinental highway of its time. Climbing Mooney Hill on the northeast, now Route 157 from Hamel, entering town on Hillsboro to East Vandalia, then through downtown, riders turned left at Hadley House, passed the High School, ascended Tanyard Hill, passing Legate's Motel on the right, and zoomed out of town. Route 66 was made obsolete in the 1970s by the new Interstate Highways. Traffic patterns through downtown Edwardsville, however, remained heavy. Jack Minner, whose Phillips 66 Station at 141 West Vandalia abutted first Route 66 and then Highway 157, reports that traffic remains heavy. "The difference is that today's traffic is daytime. In the days of Route 66, we stayed open to midnight. When Route 66 moved 25 years ago, we switched to closing at 9 o'clock."

Suburban development in Edwardsville began before World War II, as some homes were built on Florida Street near what had been the Banner Brick Works. In 1946, two daughters of Henry Steinmeyer gave their venerable home at 1020 St. Louis Street and several acres of land to Lester Brockmeier. As homes were built in this area, it was called the Steinmeyer addition.

Dunlap Lake, named for energetic Orie T. Dunlap,

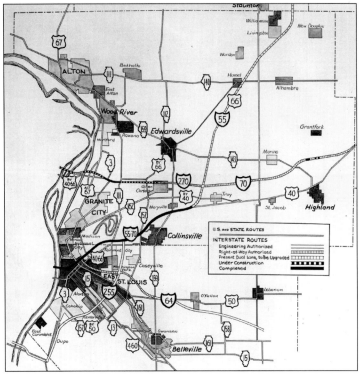

Site station on old Route 66 at 139 St. Andrews Street, now Mark's Muffler, 1948. Charles Hogue stands at left. At right is his father, Robert "Blackie" Hogue, who was well-known as a man who would loan money ($10 to $20) and take various things in repayment. Once he received a goat.

In 1963, Dick Norrish made this map of local, state and interstate roads under construction. These new highways made Edwardsville an accessible site for development of suburban housing.

Home of Henry Steinmeyer, acquired from Judge M. G. Dale in about 1890, located at 1020 St. Louis Street.

Here's the original A & W, opened in 1954 by Mel Kaufmann, at 604 St. Louis. It has since been renovated, but car-hops still bring food and drinks to customers in their cars.

From 1964 to 1968, Dog 'n Suds was a favorite spot for high school students. Located south of Montclaire Shopping Center Road. The popular hangout was owned by Jim Ginalick. On the weekends "kids would ride from Rohrkaste's Dairy down Main Street and Troy Road. Then they would turn around in Dog 'n Suds and go back. Everyone would drive the main drag. You had to keep your hands on the horn." Peggy Wehling

contractor, was created beginning in 1939, when a dam was constructed. It took three or four years for the 138 acre lake to fill, and then, the war intervened. In 1947, 527 lots were approved for sale. The first houses had wells and septic systems.

Among early residents at Dunlap Lake was Max Autenrieb (1891-1987). A painter of many subjects, Autenrieb was best known for his religious frescoes and murals. More than 1,200 of them grace 400 churches of all denominations in the Illinois, St. Louis and elsewhere. Born to a family of woodworkers in Reutlingen, Germany, young Max attended the Royal Academy of Fine Arts in Munich. During World War I, he had painted posters for the German government. In 1923, Father Ernst Eckhard, parish priest at Edwardsville's St. Boniface from 1919 to 1954, came to Schwabenland in Germany looking for an organist and recruited Wolfram Schaefer, who later moved on to New York City. Schaefer

Beside the large Hotz home on East Vandalia, now the Honeybee, were guest cottages for travelers on Route 66.

The Stolte House on Hillsboro was a Guest Home for tourists on Route 66. Rooms were $1 a night and at times 30 to 35 people slept there, some on the floor.

This aerial view of Steinmeyer Addition, taken in the early 1970s by Dick Norrish, shows the shale pit in the foreground, Woodlawn Gardens Greenhouses next to the edge of Woodlawn Cemetery at upper left, and the new neighborhood just above and to the right of the pit. Below the Steinmeyer houses, traces of the old Banner brickworks can still be seen.

176

took Father Eckhardt to the studio of his friend, Max Autenrieb, whom Father Eckhard then invited to come to Edwardsville to make frescoes as part of a redecoration of St. Boniface.

After spending two weeks here, Autenrieb knew that he would be staying in Edwardsville. Asked about homesickness, he replied, "For my family, yes. But America is the land of opportunity." And here, Max Autenrieb found plenty to do. His technique of painting directly on the plaster was rarely practiced in the United States. A year after Max came to Edwardsville, his wife, Lydia, joined him. A diminutive man with a cherubic smile, Autenrieb made friends easily and enjoyed playing the violin, flute, bass fiddle and lute. When he died in 1987, he was the oldest active member of St. Boniface.

During the 1950s, Edwardsville acquired two more notable suburban enclaves, Montclaire, east of Troy Road and south of Hadley Avenue, and Grandview,

Max Autenrieb is shown reproducing a 1923 painting of The Treaty of Edwardsville in the National Bank, 1965. The painting is now hanging in the Madison County Administration Building.

"Glory Be," located in St. Boniface Church and dedicated to Lydia Autenrieb, who died in May 1984, was Max Autenrieb's last mural and, he said, the most meaningful to him of his many paintings.

Max enjoyed working with pupils at the Senior Citizens Center in the 1980s.

between the County Home and Legion Park, south of E. Schwarz Road. In April 1952, Earl C. Wilson, head of Homesite Development, Inc., purchased a 42 and a half acre tract, then known as the old Bollman farm. The 150 homesites laid out on this land became Montclaire, the largest single development associated with Edwardsville since the village of Leclaire, built in the 1890s. Just off Troy road, in a six acre tract, Wilson laid out a shopping district in 1958 with parking for 800 cars, Edwardsville's first shopping center.

In January 1953, the City Council adopted ordinances annexing Montclaire and also Grandview, a subdivision on 65 acres, developed by Oscar W. Schmidt and Otto Homann. Grandview was subdivided into 165 building lots. These early subdivisions heralded the appearance of numerous others over subsequent decades, for example: Esic, which stands for Edwardsville Southern Illinois Commonnage Inc., a development of 900 acres which accompanied the building of the University in the 1960s; Ginger Creek, which began in the 1970s and is

Earl C. Wilson, developer of Montclaire subdivision and Shopping Center.

In the 1960s, Dick Norrish took this aerial view of Montclaire development. The large building on the left is the Montclaire Bowl. Above it is the shopping center. The new St. Mary's church and school can be seen, and at the bottom of the picture are fields which, by 1996, were covered by more housing and businesses.

still growing; Goshen Woods of the late 1970s; various sites around the Country Club in the 1970s and 1980s; extensions of Esic, such as Prairie View, Meadowlark Meadows, Cobblestone, Applegate, Pinebrook and Stonebridge, in the late 1980s; and Gerber Road in the 1990s. By 1987, the city was issuing more than 100 building permits per year. Jeff Lantz, a developer of Esic, said in 1987, "It's astounding. Nothing like this has ever happened in Edwardsville. We have seen the development of the Grandview and the Montclaire subdivisions, but

those took quite a period to fill up. It's a lot different than what the city is used to." To meet demand for classrooms, the community taxed themselves to build a Junior High School in 1959, N.O. Nelson School in 1967 a new Leclaire School in 1969, and a new high school on Center Grove Road.

Segregation of the public schools officially ended in 1951. African-Americans requested that the district comply with the laws of the State of Illinois beginning in fall 1950, but they agreed to wait one year. Unfortunately,

Enjoying the employment created by postwar prosperity, left to right, are Ben Hensley, Bill Werner, and Nick Ladd, working on a Montclaire house at 1403 Madison Avenue in the 1950s.

The *Intelligencer* published this ad for Montclaire homes in 1954.

In 1996, the original four Montclaire homes line tree shaded Madison Avenue.

integration was not complete. Even though their educations equaled those of many white teachers in the Edwardsville system, none of the African American teachers at Lincoln School were hired when the dual school systems merged in 1951. The first African-American teachers were not hired until the decade of the 1960s, beginning with Winston Brown at the Junior High School. Much to Edwardsville's credit, the school system was the first in the area to integrate. Edwardsville's first elected black public official, Professor Rudy Wilson of SIUE, won a race for the School Board in 1972 with the support of many white voters. George Johnson Jr., became the first black man on the City Council. He had been appointed by Mayor Hartung to fill a vacancy, and was later elected by the people.

In 1973, a schoolbus pulls up to pick up a child at the entrance to Esic subdivision at the foot of Tanyard Hill.

Here's the intersection of Center Grove Road and Highway 157, taken in the late 1960s before suburban development. Center Grove School, which closed in 1950, appears to the left of Highway 157, surrounded by junked cars.

A popular and effective administrator, E. L. Alexander was Superintendent of Schools from 1937 to 1957.

Education Professor Rudolph Wilson of Southern Illinois University at Edwardsville, was the town's first elected African-American official to the school board.

N.O. Nelson School was dedicated March 19, 1967. A symbol of suburban growth, this building would have been unrecognizable to folks in the 19th century used to one-room schools. On a 15-acre site, with 23 classrooms, it had a student capacity of 700. Pearce and Pearce, Inc. designed it.

Edwardsville High School Class of 1908 gathers again in 1958. Left to right are Wilma Gusewelle, Eleanor Keller, Milton Harnist, Cooper Groves, Don Proctor, Bertha Barnsback, Josephine Hadley, Abe Tuxhorn, Clifton Corbett.

Suburban neo-European country-style homes constructed in the late 20th century in Pinebrook Estates.

181

Suburbanization has brought thousands of new people to the city and a new character to the town. In 1989, Maureen Kinsella, an artist who enjoyed photographing townspeople and businesses, observed that Edwardsville "is really a very interesting town. It really has a special spirit to it, but I don't know if you're going to see it stay this way because of all of the planning, the new housing and the malls."

Edwardsville Frozen Foods, an old-fashioned, hometown meat market and locker plant, still offers customers personal service and advice of experienced local butchers. It's in the 200 block of North Main Street.

"You'll have to sell me along with this rocking chair," says Mrs. John Kesl of Edwardsville to brother-in-law Martin Smola. This picture was taken in September 1965, at Smola's farm, off U.S. By-pass 66, now Highway 157, just southwest of Edwardsville, near the site of Madison Mutual Insurance Company. It illustrates the selling of farmland for other purposes, such as suburban development.

EDWARDSVILLE'S POPULATION, 1950-1990
1950 - 8,776
1960 - 9,996
1970 - 11,070
1980 - 12,480
1990 - 14,600
1995 - 18,350

The last of the hardware stores in Edwardsville to carry a local family name is Kreige Hardware on East Vandalia. They have been in this building since the mid-1940s. The store has an oiled wooden floor and an extensive stock of materials.

EDWARDSVILLE'S MAYORS

Edwardsville has had 26 mayors since they first began electing mayors in 1872. Terms in the early days were two years—only one year for the first mayor, John A. Prickett. Later, they were lengthened to four years, as they are today.

Three of the mayors served multiple terms, that is, terms separated from each other by the terms of other mayors—Henry P. Hotz, William C. Straube and Raymond O. Rogers. Two mayors were cousins—John A. Prickett and William R. Prickett. And two were father and son—William C. Straube and William G. Straube. All of the mayors, so far, have been men.

Here are the mayors, their dates taken from a wall of the City Council chambers at City Hall.

1872-73	John A. Prickett
1873-75	William H. Krome
1875-77	C. E. Clark
1877-87	Alonzo Keller
1887-89	Charles Boeschenstein
1889-91	E. B. Glass
1891-93	William E. Wheeler
1893-95	William H. Hall
1895-97	William R. Prickett
1897-99	John Stolze
1899-1901	John T. Crocker
1901-03	N. E. Bosen
1903-13	Henry P. Hotz
1913-17	Dick H. Mudge Sr.
1917-21	Henry P. Hotz
1921-29	Frank L. Nash
1929-33	Charles E. Gueltig
1933-41	William C. Straube
1941-49	Oscar Schmidt
1949-53	William C. Straube
1953-57	George L. Moorman Jr.
1957-61	William C. Straube
1961-69	Raymond O. Rogers
1969-73	William G. Straube
1973-77	Clyde L. Hartung
1977-81	Steve Ellsworth
1981-85	Kenneth L. Evers
1985-89	Raymond O. Rogers
1989-93	Dennis DeToye
1993-	Gary D. Niebur

"Young Bill" Straube, Mayor of Edwardsville, 1969-73, throws first pitch at "Edwardsville Night" Cardinals game at Busch Stadium.

INGLIS FLETCHER, AUTHOR

In 1959, Inglis Fletcher published her autobiography, Pay, Pack, and Follow in which she wrote of life in Edwardsville from the 1880s to the 1890s. Although born in Alton, Fletcher grew up here and graduated from Edwardsville High School in the 1890s. Her father managed the Leland Hotel here. Then, her name was Minna Clark. She left Edwardsville after graduation, married a mining engineer, Jack Fletcher, and lived in many places in the world, finally settling on Bandon plantation near Edenton, North Carolina in 1944. By 1959, Fletcher had published 11 successful novels, many of which were dramatizations of historical events and people of colonial North Carolina. She was honored by the class of 1948 in the dedication of their "Gay 90s Tiger Yearbook." In her greetings to the class, Fletcher wrote: "The thing that I regret most of all is that I was not a better and more conscientious student of the important and vital history of the region in which I lived."

The home where Inglis Fletcher lived during her youth in Edwardsville. Built in the 1850s, it is now the offices of Henderson Associate Architects at 234 Leverette Lane.

"MOTHER, WHAT CAN WE DO FOR OUR COMMUNITY TODAY?" THE POSTWAR ETHIC OF SERVICE

Men and women who had been away from Edwardsville during World War II, as well as people who had participated locally in the war effort, were eager during the 1950s and 1960s to enjoy peaceful civilian life in a generally prosperous economy. Their willingness to volunteer and to raise money resulted in many benefits for the town. They joined service organizations which helped the needy and funded a new YMCA building. They generated a range of summer activities for youngsters. They built parks. Full of energy and community spirit, this generation of Edwardsvillians built lasting monuments.

Little League represented postwar idealism in the community. To all accounts, the beginning of Edwardsville's Little League in 1955, came from John Schramek,

Postwar paraders in the late 1940s honor World War II Veterans.

who had seen Bunker Hill's baseball program. He came into Vanzo's and presented the Little League idea to buddies there. The fee for a charter was $10. Lou Gilmore went out on the street and ran into Earl Herrin, who gave Lou the $10. Little League was launched and within 10 years youngsters were playing in a lighted field on the site of the old Leclaire athletic fields.

In a campaign coordinated by Clarence Hoppe in 1960, each of Edwardsville's locally owned banks loaned $5,000 to light the field. "To pay for the lights," Clarence Hoppe remembered, "We had fish fries every Friday night for years. The payment was $3333.33 every year. We paid it off." Volunteers who felt they were creating a worthy community institution nurtured the organization as it grew from eight teams in 1956 to over 100 teams in 1996. Starting in 1956, the annual Little

Signers of the note that brought lights to the Little League field at Leclaire gather here in 1964, with Joe Lucco, master of ceremonies at the burning of the note. Left to right, they are Clarence Hoppe, Ray Lynn, Ed Winkle, Olin Schwalb, Les Gebhart, Jerry Kershaw, Kirk Stafford, "Beets" Paproth, Frank Vanzo, Norman Rosenthal, and Joe Lucco.

184

League Parade became a feature of community life.

In 1965 and 1966, wanting more ball fields for Little League, Clarence Hoppe also led in developing the old city dump into what became Hoppe Park. He was able to gain the support of the U.S. Army Reserves. "We had to move and shift 87,000 yards of debris around," he noted. The smaller diamond in Hoppe Park is, according to Mr. Hoppe, "built in size for small boys so that, should they accidently pop the ball over the fence, they can get a home run." The bigger diamond in Hoppe Park is 350 feet deep, "as big as Busch Stadium," adds Mr. Hoppe.

The first four commissionsers of Little League pose here with Miss Little League of 1964, Nancy Fry. Left to right, they are John Schramek, Edward W. Tibbles, Olin Schwalb, and Clarence Hoppe.

Clarence Hoppe, right, and Leo Dustmann, President of the Bank of Edwardsville, watch the debt for Little League's lights go up in smoke.

Little League parades became a town tradition after 1956 to usher in the summer baseball season for kids. Here, our elected state legislators wave from a convertible in 1970: State Representative (later Senator) Sam M. Vadalabene, in center, and State Senator Merrill Ottwein (sunglasses).

REPRESENTATIVE VADALABENE

Mark Hofeditz chauffeurs the EHS cheerleaders, right to left, Kathryn Stullken, Debbie Hoppe, Darla Bridwell, Christy Mainer, and Aretha Rice in the Little League parade of 1970. Terry Hartley (with bubble gum) and Richard Hutton march behind.

St. Boniface School Band marches in a Little League parade around 1960.

Here's an early Little League team, the Cards, photographed at Leclaire diamond in 1958.

Members of the Lions Club delivered Easter eggs to children, victims of a tornado in Bunker Hill, 1948. The Lions Club had been organized in Edwardsville in 1944. Left to right are R. W. Runft, a Red Cross director, Major James F. Miller of Scott Field, Miss Clara Simon, a Red Cross recreation director, R. W. Heidelberg, president of Edwardsville Lions and Attorney R. W. Tunnell, district governor of the Lions.

FRANCES HOPPE REMEMBERS in 1996

We've been married fifty-three or fifty-four years. Clarence used to get up at 3:30 to 4:00 in the morning, jump out of bed and say, "Well, Mother, it's time for us to see what we can do for the good of our community. Then he went down to drag the ball diamonds before he went to work."

Showing post-war commitment to service, the Moose donated an iron lung to the City in 1946, before Jonas Salk's vaccine for polio had been developed. The Moose had been part of Edwardsville's social life since 1914. Left to right, are Fire Chief Dennis Hentz, Eugene H. Schmidt, governor of the Moose, City Treasurer Joseph Rotter, an Intelligencer employee who was "patient" for the demonstration, Mayor Oscar W. Schmidt and Clem Nischwitz, secretary of the lodge. The equipment cost $1,100.

Hoppe Park, named for Clarence Hoppe, who wanted to provide more athletic fields and playgrounds for Edwardsville youngsters, is shown here. This early picture of the "little diamond" at Hoppe Park was taken in 1966.

After World War II, many organizations became well-known for their community service. Junior Service Club, which is still active in social and fund-raising projects, started in 1938. Past club activities included selling hand-blown decorated Easter eggs, producing fashion shows, and follies. Today, along with many other activities, this club provides house tours, supports blood drives, and raises money by an auction. This group has always supplemented the budget of the head school nurse in the Edwardsville school district. Nursing home bingo games provide recreation for elders in the community. When the YMCA needed a coffee urn, when children needed shoes, when a family could not afford an operation, when mass immunization against polio was a community goal, when residents of the County Home wanted a sewing machine—in these small and large ways, Junior Service members contributed to community welfare. Today, many of the members are women who work outside the home. They continue to find time for projects devoted to community welfare.

African-American women, organized in the Women's Federated Club, which had been started in 1929, continued their prewar tradition of community service by collecting for the annual cancer drive, assisting with SIU surveys, and securing window space from downtown businessmen for the annual Halloween window painting project sponsored by an umbrella group of town organizations. The club also took home-made baked goods to patients at the Alton State Hospital and delivered Christmas baskets to shut-ins in the community. An important goal of this group was promotion of interracial understanding.

Edwardsville Jaycees, young businessmen, ages 21 to 35, eager for community service and leadership development, received their charter on March 5, 1960. Charles W. McConkey was president of the 21-member group. In the early years of what is still a thriving group, the men sponsored seat belt installation clinics and the local preliminary contest for the Miss America Pageant, planted trees on Main Street, picked up Christmas trees and disposed of them after the holiday, and taught a safety program for young children in the city's grade schools. Today, among many activities the Jaycees sponsor a summer event, the Fun Days. Jaycees membership now includes young businesswomen also.

The League of Women Voters organized in Edwardsville during the 1950s and reflected women's interest in public affairs on local, regional and national levels. Mrs. James Reed and

Miss Louise Travous organized 54 women into Edwardsville's first LWV chapter in 1954. Over more than 40 years, the League's campaigns of study and community action have led to recycling within the city, to investigation of equal housing opportunities, to recommendations for health services, and to the appointment by the City Council of an Historic Preservation Commission, among many other achievements. With 85 members in the 1990s, the League continues as a respected source and developer of non-partisan information on local, state, and national issues of interest to all citizens.

Development of a thriving Young Men's Christian Association (YMCA), with a range of activities for individuals and families from throughout Edwardsville, represented a major achievement of coordinated community action in the postwar era. In early 1948, a group of Edwardsvillians, including H. U. Landon, E. L. Alexander, Leland Buckley, Judge Gillham, Laurence Scott, Don Lewis, Ray Foster, Clyde Fruit, Frederic Springer, Sol Mack, and J.C. Wetzel, met with a member of the Illinois area YMCA staff, Leo Kahnmaster, who was very pessimistic about starting a full-facility YMCA in a town as small as Edwardsville. Nevertheless, the community showed will and offered means. A majority (21 of 39) of those responding to a survey of community leaders showed interest in establishing a "Y", and in 1948, more than $6000 was raised.

Chartered as a non-profit corporation in 1949, the YMCA of Edwardsville then rented two rooms above the Madison Store on the corner of Purcell and Second Street for use as an office. The first program was a swimming program. Boys and girls were bused to Alton pools for lessons. During the first year, 530 youth participated in clubs, softball, basketball and bowling activities. Ten years later, in 1962, numbers of persons of all ages participating in YMCA-sponsored events approached 2,000. In December 1949, Miss Ella Tunnell, on behalf of the Madison County Historical Society (MCHS), offered the YMCA the use of the former C.W. Terry residence, which Terry had willed to the MCHS, for use as a headquarters.

In fall 1957, the newly organized League of Women Voters campaigned successfully for a tax increase to finance the new Junior High School. The women in this picture are unidentified.

By April 1951, the YMCA had moved to the Terry House. For six years during the 1950s, along with 25 other different program activities, the "Y" was headquarters for Tiger Town, a teenagers' recreation center fondly recalled by those who were high schoolers in that decade. Staffed by parent volunteers and led by elected teen officers, offering pool tables on the first floor and dancing in the large, open third floor space, Tiger Town was "the place to be" after games and on Saturday nights. Eventually, it was relocated to the Moose Hall on North Main.

As Edwardsville's suburban population grew, the Terry House became inadequate. In 1969, after a two-year campaign that raised more than $350,000, a new YMCA facility with a swimming pool, a multipurpose room, lockers and an office was dedicated at 1200 Esic Drive. During the 1980s, under the leadership of Gary Niebur, the "Y" was repaired and refurbished. In November 1989, using another million dollars raised in the Edwardsville-Glen Carbon area through a campaign coordinated by Edwardsville attorney Gordon Broom, a new addition doubled the size of the "Y". The new wing included two racquetball courts, a new gymnasium, a new physical fitness center, a gymnastics center, and a renovation of the upper floor for expanded pre-school programs. In the summer of 1991, thanks to an anonymous donor's gift of $50,000, a second 42 by 75 foot pool was opened in January 1992.

In many ways, the YMCA, bustling with individuals and families of many ethnic backgrounds from all over the greater Edwardsville area, symbolizes the new town of the 21st century. Built by donations, large and small, offering a meeting place for old and new residents of the town as they bring children for swimming lessons or use the other facilities, the YMCA continues as a creator of community, overcoming the anonymous and privatized life of suburban America. In 1996, the membership exceeded 7,800 individuals and families.

C.W. Terry House on Fourth Street, home of the YMCA, 1951-1969. Built in 1868, it was originally a farm house. From 1848 to 1949, it was owned by Charles Willys Terry, who left it to the Madison County Historical Society for use as a civic center.

Edwardsville 1975 YMCA swim team with long-time coach, Virginia Brown.

YMCA facility, including 1969 building and new addition of 1989, photographed in 1996.

TIGERTOWN TEENS OF THE 50S

We wore big hoops; the can cans were starched. We always dressed up. There were benches [at the YMCA's Tiger Town]. Underneath we kept our records...a lot of Silhouettes, Kansas City, Rock Around the Clock, Primrose Lane. There were always chaperons (parents). They kind of observed. We loved our parents being there. We played spin the bottle with parents there! . . . Basketball was THE thing. The sun rose and set with the basketball team. . . . When we were going steady, we wore the boy's class ring. [To make it fit], we wrapped it with thread and then painted it with frosted nail polish. . . . We belonged to a group called "The Prissies"—eight girls. If all of us didn't have a date, none of us did. We had our picture taken with black sweaters and pearls. The [George] Mussos took people everywhere in their stationwagon. We had slumber parties in the jail [residence]. He locked us in once.

—*Donna Brockmier Hart, Nancy Giacomelli Suhre*

CELEBRATING MADISON COUNTY'S SESQUICENTENNIAL, 1962

Women stitched fancy, lace-trimmed long dresses and men grew beards and donned top hats as Madison County got ready for a look back to pioneer days set for a week in the fall of 1962. That year was the 150th anniversary of the founding of the county, and sesquicentennial fever gripped county citizens, especially those in Edwardsville, where many of the commemorative events were held.

The centerpiece of the celebration was a pageant, "Our 150 Years," which involved hundreds of local people and was presented on six nights during the weeklong sesquicentennial, September 9-15, 1962. The pageant, and other events, were held on the abandoned Kettle River industrial site, which was just south of Center Grove Road and a quarter mile or so west of Illinois Route 159. The location was flat, treeless and cindery, ideal for crowds of thousands.

The show was 90 minute long and was divided into 20 episodes, starting with the moundbuilders at Cahokia, and going through many famous visitors. The last episode before the finale being "The Atomic Age." Fireworks produced a loud bang and a mushroom cloud.

Roles by the hundreds went to women, children and men. There were square dancers, pioneer men and women, pupils in school, a brass band, can-can dancers and bathing beauties. There were people on horses and people in churches, a Gay Nineties cop, a bootlegger and Legionnaires to fire rifle salutes.

All of this was held together by a professional pageant director, Carl Hawley, of the

This Shaving Permit Button was standard during the Sesquicentennial, when normally clean-shaven townsmen allowed themselves to grow beards. People who wore beards regularly were seen as somehow suspect, perhaps dirty and disorderly.

John B. Rogers Company, of Fostoria, Ohio. Mayor Straube and Albert Pauli gathered a small committee of R. Louise Travous, Ella Tunnell, and Jessie Springer, plus others, according to Edward A. Kane Sr., who wrote about how the pageant had been organized a month after it was over.

This committee brought in people from all over the county—mayors, representatives of historical societies and county officials—to make plans for what came to be commonly known as the "Sesqui."

As more and more citizens joined the various committees, the planners found themselves perennially short of money. One fund-raiser was the sale of shares of souvenir stock in the Sesqui, at $1 per share. Purchasing stock got you a fancy souvenir certificate.

But a lot of what made the event such a success was the efforts of hundreds, maybe thousands, of volunteers.

On the final day of the Sesqui, a "Giant Parade" through Edwardsville was held starting at 1 p.m. at the Rohrkaste Dairy parking lot, in the 1000 block of North Main Street. The parade—like many in Edwardsville—proceeded south on Main to Vandalia, then west on Vandalia and St. Louis streets to Hadley House and the High School. There were some 90 parade units in five divisions, each division with its own color guard. The Edwardsville Municipal Band and the St. Boniface Band were two of the musical units taking part. In charge of the parade was Legion Post 199.

The general chairman of the Sesqui was Lesley M. Marks, an Edwardsville mortician. Irene Timmermiere, of Alton, who was active in the Madison County Historical Society, was secretary, and Leo

A group of Edwardsville "pioneers" ready for Sesqui pageant. Left to right, they are: Dora Bohm, Mrs. G. H. Bollman, Mrs. Oscar Ochs, Director Carl Hawley, Hugh Head.

Junior high kids raise money for the Madison County Historical Museum, in 1963.

Dustmann, president of the Bank of Edwardsville, was treasurer.

In 1963, amid the hullabaloo of the Sesquicentennial, Madison County acquired an historic building, the John Weir House at 715 North Main, as the new site for the Madison County Historical Society and Museum. For many years previously, the County Museum had been housed on the third floor of the Courthouse. Several history-minded local citizens were responsible for acquiring the Weir House for use as a museum. The committee included Stephen and Sheila Stimson, Mary Blixen, John Abbott and Eleanor Boeschenstein Godfrey, all of Edwardsville and Maitland and Irene Timmermiere, of Alton. "We raised the $12,500 purchase price of the house and turned the money over to the (Madison County) Historical Society so they could buy the house," Sheila Stimson recalled in 1996. Added to this amount was $7,500, representing the profit from the county Sesquicentennial celebration of 1962. Organizers of the

Sesqui had pledged any profits to the historical society. The extra money paid for making the Weir House ready for opening to the public, including structural steel bracing throughout the old three-story building. The new museum opened on November 1, 1964.

A sign directs visitors to the Madison County Museum on the third floor of the courthouse.

Volunteers get ready to move Museum collections to the new Madison County Historical Society (MCHS) building in 1963. Left to right are Carrie Wolf, curator of the museum, 1946-1959, Louise Ahrens, curator from October 1961 to March 1963, Mrs. Austin Lewis, a director of the MCHS, and Mrs. Harris Blixen, also a director.

Restored bedroom displays antique furniture at John Weir House, 1963.

Lesley Marks, who chaired the Sesquicentennial celebration, drives antique car to advertise MCHS fund-raising ball, 1963.

Watershed Nature Center with visitors center shown, is located off Tower Avenue next to Hoppe Park. Most of the WNC occupies the site of the city's former sewer lagoon. The Nature Preserve Foundation, a not-for-profit corporation chartered by the City of Edwardsville, is dedicated to the restoration and preservation of this area as a 66-acre wetland and natural park for city residents and visitors. The visitors center, designed by local architect, Jamie Henderson, was completed in 1995.

The historic Wesley Chapel A.M.E. Church at 414 Aldrup, built in 1881, modernized inside, is one of the city's earliest churches still in use.

The Travous House, at 824 St. Louis Street, shown here in a photograph taken in the 1920s, forms part of the St. Louis Street neighborhood, which has been placed on the National Historic Register.

Stahly Cartage occupies what was formerly Illinois Bell's building. In 1984, Stahly received a commercial preservation award from the Goshen Preservation Alliance.

THE COMING OF SOUTHERN ILLINOIS UNIVERSITY AT EDWARDSVILLE

Southern Illinois University at Edwardsville, with its dozens of buildings, its acres of parking lots and a four-square-mile campus made up of rolling fields, river bottomland and dense woods, owes its existence, basically, to one man: Dr. Delyte W. Morris, president of Southern Illinois University at Carbondale.

Yes, there were many others involved in making a university in this area a reality: people like George T. Wilkins, of Edwardsville, Madison County Superintendent of Schools and later Illinois Superintendent of Public Instruction, who believed that the state's second largest metropolitan area, after Chicago, ought to have its own state university. The area was growing and new businesses and industries were demanding employees with college educations. Worthy colleges like Shurtleff, Monticello, Blackburn, Greenville and McKendree, plus a community college at Belleville weren't adequate to train the masses of students expected in the coming decades.

Furthermore, many of these students would come from families of limited means, which meant they'd have to live at home while getting an education in order to be able to pay even the low tuition of a state school. Many of them were expected to be first-generation college students.

Early in 1955, the Edwardsville Chamber of Commerce established a College Planning Committee with George L. Moorman Sr. as chairman. This group quickly evolved into a larger body, the Southwestern Illinois Council for Higher Education, with Dr. Robert B. Lynn, an Alton surgeon, as president. In the fall of 1956, the council met jointly with the Board of Trustees of Southern Illinois University, Carbondale, and plans for an Edwardsville campus gained momentum.

In 1957, SIUE began classes in two new centers, both of them in older school buildings, one in Alton (Shurtleff College) and the other in East St. Louis (the old high school building downtown). But far more students enrolled at both centers than anticipated; two years later enrollment had doubled.

It was time for a permanent solution to the problem of providing higher education opportunities for what had come to be known as the Metro East area. The planners, who wanted a campus of more than 2,000 acres in size, considered several sites, but settled on the present campus site of some 2,600 acres of rolling farmland on top of the ancient bluffs of the Mississippi River, with some athletic fields spilling down onto the American Bottom below the bluff. There were areas ideal for buildings and parking, plus woods and fields for wildlife sanctuaries, and areas that could be developed into lakes, both for recreation and to provide water for the university's heating and cooling plant. Also, the Edwardsville site was within convenient traveling distance from Metro East cities like Alton, East St. Louis, Granite City and Belleville. As the Interstate highway system developed, the new university also became accessible throughout the region, especially to residents of north St. Louis county and St. Louis, Missouri.

There was, of course, some opposition to the purchase of land for the university from some of the owners of the more than 80 parcels of land involved. Some of the landowners objected bitterly to the takeover of what were ancestral farms. One farmer opened fire with a shotgun at a helicopter which he said was bothering his horses. The chopper had been engaged to fly visitors over the new SIUE site during a state bond issue rally in 1960. But many people realized that a major university was sorely needed in metro East, and that a brand new college campus would be good for the area.

With Delyte Morris leading the way, there were studies and conferences and planning sessions to design the new campus. Finally, in May 1963, Morris took silver shovel in hand and turned the first bit of earth in the first campus groundbreaking. Six buildings were planned initially, starting with the Peck Classroom Building on the northeast of what was to become the campus core. Then followed the Lovejoy Library, a Science/Laboratory building, the Communications Building, the University Center and, finally, the Rendleman Building, for administration, named for John S. Rendleman, the first chancellor, and later president, of SIUE.

SIU President Delyte W. Morris turns the first shovel of dirt on May 2, 1963, to start construction of the Edwardsville campus of the university.

The campus core was on a slight rise above the surrounding terrain, on what was a grand old farm, with its own horse track and a fine, two-story home with tall white columns, all belonging to the Freund family. The house was sold at auction, for a pittance, and was dismantled and moved off campus to a site on the east side of Route 157 not far south of Interstate 270. It was rebuilt to something like its former glory. Many of the trees around the Freund house were saved, on orders of Morris, who loved trees, so that the new campus would have a head start on a shady central mall.

The original intention had been to make SIUE a commuter campus, with minimum on-campus housing. However, the initial apartment buildings at Tower lake, north of the campus core, proved popular with families and even groups of single students, and more apartments had to be added. Finally, in 1994, the university opened its first real student dormitory—called a residence hall in the parlance of the era—immediately south of the core campus.

SIUE soccer coach Bob Guelker is hoisted onto the shoulders of his players. Guelker is holding the NCAA Division 1 championship trophy, after SIUE defeated Clemson 3-2 for the soccer title on December 11, 1979.

The Mississippi River Festival, held at SIUE in the 1970s in a grassy natural amphitheater with an enormous tent at the bottom, attracted big crowds to hear music by the St. Louis Symphony Orchestra and by pop and rock groups. A few of these events drew as many as 30,000 people.

Other major campus buildings constructed since the completion of the six core buildings have been: Religious Center, 1971; Classroom Buildings 2 and 3, 1976; Vadalabene Center (gymnasium, swimming pool, fitness), 1984; James F. Metcalf Student Experimental Theater, 1984; Student Fitness Center, 1993; Art and Design Building, 1993.

On January 1, 1991, University Park opened along a new, curving drive in the east-central sector of the campus, between the core and Route 157. The purpose of the park is to build the university by attracting businesses and agencies which could benefit from the school's expertise while fostering economic development and the creation of high-tech jobs in the area.

SIUE in 1996 offered 41 baccalaureate degrees, 30 master's degrees, and four specialty programs. Since the early years the university has maintained an enrollment of around 12,000 on the main campus and at the dental school, on the old Shurtleff College campus, in Alton.

This aerial view, taken in 1964, shows the campus core of SIUE, looking west, with the pedestrian oval, now landscaped, in the foreground. The Peck classroom building, the first to be built, is at right center; across from it are the beginnings of the Rendleman building, for administration, the last core building to be constructed.

The central SIUE campus in 1996, looking northwest across the fan-shaped main parking lots. The new student dormitory building is the cross-shaped structure at left; the growing University Park, a business-university development, is at lower right.

SPORTS HIGHLIGHTS by Joe Meyer

The roots of Edwardsville's rich sports tradition can be traced to the early 1920s, when Edwardsville High School became a charter member of the prestigious Southwestern Conference which, in the beginning, also featured teams from East St. Louis, Alton, Granite City, Belleville and Collinsville.

For many long-time followers of Edwardsville High School sports, the high-watermark occurred in the 1950s, when three basketball teams advanced to the state tournament in a span of six years under the guidance of Coach Joe Lucco, later named to the Illinois Coaches Hall of Fame. The 1956 team came the closest of any EHS basketball team to a state championship, though EHS has sent teams to the State Tournament on five other occasions: 1951, 1954, 1976, 1993 and 1995. In 1965, the district honored Coach Lucco's leadership by naming Edwardsville High School's new gymnasium for him.

Jack Butler, long-time owner of Butler Chevrolet, was the 6-3 center on the 1951 team that lost in the first round to eventual champion Freeport. Don Ohl and Bob Gregor formed the one-two punch of the 1954 team that placed fourth. Ohl became a five-time national Basketball Association all-star during his career, playing with the Detroit Pistons, Baltimore (now Washington)

Bullets, and the St. Louis and Atlanta Hawks. He retired from professional basketball in 1970. Gregor went on to become a teacher and basketball coach at EHS. His most successful teams were those of 1968 and 1969. The 1969 team finished 14-4.

The 1956 team, led by all-staters Mannie Jackson and Governor Vaughn, finished second in the state, losing a two-point battle to West Rockford. The title game is still considered one of the classic confrontations in the long, storied history of the state tournament. The 1956 team remains the measuring stick by which all EHS basketball teams are judged. Its record that year was 28-7, and its starting five all went on to successful careers: Jackson became an executive and the owner of the Harlem Globetrotters, and Vaughn became a corporate executive in Detroit. The others in the top five were Harold Patton, Jim Chandler and Kenneth "Buzz" Shaw. The last became a university executive, and for a time was president of southern Illinois University at Edwardsville.

Edwardsville's first state high school team championship came in 1978, when a girls field hockey team ended up first in Illinois. The girls' sports program had begun in 1972, with federal law providing the impetus. Coach Sharon Petty started field hockey at the school in 1974 as part of an expanding girls sports program, which

Coach Joe Lucco smiles with three Edwardsville players who moved on to play with the University of Illinois. These three, Mannie Jackson, Govoner Vaughn, and Don Ohl, may be the only three players from the same high school to be on the starting five at the same time at a Big 10 school.

The 1978 Illinois State Champion Girls Field Hockey Team was Edwardsville's first. In the front row, left to right, are: Barb Smith, Fullback-Sr., Deb Ludwig, Goalie-Sr., Karen Berry, Fullback-Sr.; middle row: Nancy Meyer, Mgr., Sandy Gerstenecker, Halfback-Soph., Tina Greer, Halfback-Jr., Becky Kolesa, Halfback-Jr., Melinda Bort, Right Wing-Jr., Karen Weber, Mgr.; back row: Sharon Petty, Coach, Pat O'Laughlin, Right Wing-Sr., Lisa Henderson, Right Forward-Jr., Amy Armstrong, Center Forward-Soph., Julie Foehrkolb, Left Forward-Sr., Deb Seybert, Left Wing-Sr.]

included volleyball, track, softball, tennis and basketball. Today, the EHS program is one of the most comprehensive in downstate Illinois. The EHS field hockey team made local and state history when it also became the first non-Chicago-area team to win the title. Deb Seybert led the scoring in the championship victory over previously unbeaten Chicago University High. Defensively, the 13-1 Tigers were led by goalie Deb Ludwig and backs Karen Berry and Barb Smith.

The first boys team title for EHS came in 1990, when coach Tom Pile led the baseball squad to a championship. Playing key roles were pitcher Tom Price, outfielder Mark Little, shortstop Tim Funkhouser and first baseman Greg Morrison. Price would later pitch and star for Notre Dame, before turning pro with the Los Angeles Dodgers. Little currently is a top outfield prospect with the Texas Rangers organization. Funkhouser coaches high school baseball at Triad. Edwardsville has been ranked No. 1 nationally twice in the early 1990s.

The 1991 Tigers came within a whisker of repeating as state champs, but lost the title game. In doing so, they established a state winning-streak record of 64 games, counted over two seasons.

Edwardsville's first individual state championship belongs to sprinter Russell "Buck" Southard, in 1919. Southard won both the 50-yard and 100-yard dashes at the state track tournament. Nine years later, Bert Young was an individual gold medalist in the 1928 state meet, winning the 440-yard dash in 51.2 seconds, becoming the second Edwardsville sportsman to win a state championship.

Swimming teams from Sunset Hills Country Club, opened as a golf course in 1925, and Montclaire Pool compete each summer in the Southwestern Illinois Swim Association, and from that program have come all-Big-Eight swimmer Darcy Gregor, AAU swimmer Bobby Stille and all-American and Olympic swimmer Bill Stapleton. Stapleton earned All-American honors at Texas before qualifying for the 1988 Olympics in Seoul, South Korea, in the 200-meter individual medley.

Young golfers from Sunset Hills, the American Legion public course, and Oak Brook, another public course northeast of town, have provided talent for coach Dick Gerber's highly successful EHS teams. Tiger golfers brought home second-place state trophies in 1985 (boys), 1986 (girls) and 1988 (boys). Individually, Joe Malench, in 1977, and Barb Anderson, in 1978, earned silver medals at their respective state meets.

Recreational sports have been sponsored both by the city and by the YMCA. The `Y' has taken the lead in

Tigers joyfully display state baseball championship trophy in 1990.

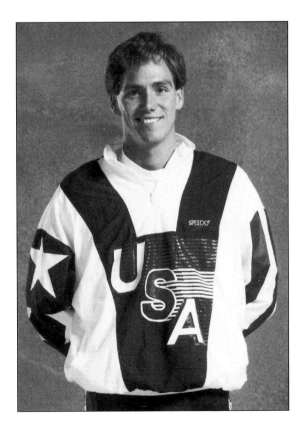

Bill Stapleton, 200-meter individual competitor, wears the official uniform of United States participants in the 1988 Olympic Games in Seoul, South Korea.

sponsoring youth swimming, basketball and soccer programs. The beginning of the EHS soccer program can be traced back to the early 1970s when 'Y' director Dale Trinka introduced youth soccer. The 1995 high school team was the first at EHS to reach the state quarterfinals.

City-sponsored softball and basketball programs continue to be popular. Olin Pence and Joe Giardina provided the respective leadership during the 1960s and 1970s. In the adult city basketball league, the Saints have been the most talented and colorful team in recent years, with Bobby White, Otis Vaughn, Mickey Moore and Harry Penelton at the core of the team.

In men's softball, Coleman Painting, the American Legion and Sievers Auto Body have been dominant. The city softball program formed back in the 1940s, using Leclaire Field at first, according to Olin Clawson, the veteran Coleman shortstop. Games in recent decades have been played at Vadalabene Park, site of the old Voge coal mine, and at newer diamonds at Hoppe Park.

As this is written, EHS is enjoying much success in football, and may well be close to its very first Southwestern Conference championship. The heroes of today will join such notables as Cliff Hoppe, Bob Hoskins, Houston Lowry, Tony Penelton, Len Menoni, Morris Bradshaw, "Wib" Volz, Clarence Ax, Mark Helle, Steve Carpenter, Gus Hydron and a host of others. Years ago, one former area coach described Edwardsville's football this way: Edwardsville's best players were as good as any in the Southwestern Conference; Edwardsville just lacked numbers and often was regarded more for its strong basketball teams than its football team.

Bradshaw, Hoskins, Carpenter and Volz played pro football, and Bradshaw was fortunate in his eight-plus National Football League seasons to play on two Super Bowl teams with the Oakland Raiders. Volz spent time with the AFL Buffalo Bills, Hoskins played with the San Francisco 49ers and Carpenter split time in the NFL and Canadian Football League. Hydron turned down a draft from the Detroit Lions for a career in the Air Force. Until the 1995 football team finished with an 11-1 record, reaching the quarterfinals of the 5A state playoffs, the two most successful teams were the 7-0-1 1940 team that shared the conference title with East St. Louis after tying the EStL Flyers 0-0, and the 1975 conference

Bob and Carolyn Hoskins greet crowds in a parade.

Morris Bradshaw, one of Edwardsville High School's most outstanding athletes, at left, takes first place in the 100-yard dash in a county meet in 1970.

E.H.S. new facility under construction on Center Grove Road 1996.

co-champion team that became Edwardsville's play-off team with an overall record of 8-2.

Edwardsville High School has fielded strong individuals in track and field through much of the 20th century, but never has had enough depth for a team title. From the early days of sprinter Russell "Buck" Southard (1919), and the 1920s and 30s, featuring Bert Young, Clarence Bohm, Teno Tenor, Gus Hydron and Paul Burrus, EHS has made its mark in each succeeding decade. Many remember Jim Marks only as a superb basketball player in the mid-1940s, but Marks also excelled as a long- and high-jumper. Many outstanding high-jumpers would follow in his footsteps. Kevin Mosby won a state title in the triple jump in 1982, and Darren McDonough, back-to-back state pole vault titles in 1991-92. McDonough's vault of 17 feet 1/2 inch is the current state record.

In the 1980s, Christina Perozzi became the most celebrated girls track and field standout for EHS. During her career, which ended in 1990, she captured five state medals, including back-to-back golds in the 300-meter hurdles, in 1989-90. She held the state record for six years in that event. She currently holds five individual EHS records and was part of a record-setting 4x200 relay team. Mary Kay Hyten, Teresa Johnson, Terri Ahart and Esta Saverson also own state meet medals and continue to rank among the all-time Tiger track and field elite.

The mention of wrestling at EHS brings to mind the school's biggest athlete ever—Louie Hartman, a sectional champion and state qualifier at 6-feet-6, 387 pounds in the 1960s. Coach Mel Kuethe had to have his wife, Carolyn, make a special uniform to fit Hartman's massive waist. The Tigers are still looking for their first state champion in wrestling. However, down through the years, four individuals have placed at the state tourney; the first was Herbert Simons, who placed third at 155 pounds, in 1937.

Warren "Babe" Stahlhut, who followed Kuethe as wrestling coach, collected 420 dual-meet victories and saw three of his individuals place at the state championships. Steve Hagstrom, at 167 pounds, was a silver medalist in 1974, finishing with a 33-1 record. Two years later, Steve Wopat, at 167 pounds, placed fifth, and Derek Baugh, 171 pounds, was fourth in 1991.

Founded by high school students Ken Evers, Jr. and Joe Schrage, the "bleacher bums" epitomized school spirit during the early 1970s. Wearing handpainted hard hats, they are shown here giving the victory sign.

The 1970 E.H.S. cheerleaders. "GO TEAM GO!"

A MAYOR RECOLLECTS

Edwardsville's mayors over the years look like a patrician lot, judging from their formal portraits, hanging there on the city council chamber wall. The earlier mayors sport beards, sideburns, magnificent moustaches. The more recent mayors, by and large, appear pleased with themselves, and the city's progress, optimistic about the future and, above all, wise.

Many Edwardsville mayors have come from among the city's upper-class movers and shakers—from the law and business. One who came from the blue-collar ranks was Clyde L. Hartung, born in Edwardsville in 1917 and mayor for one term in the mid-1970s. Before that, he was an alderman for 14 years, and before that, a member of the Edwardsville School Board for three years.

Hartung graduated from Edwardsville High School in 1935, so he was just the right age to serve in World War II, and serve he did—in the Army Field Artillery. He ended up a sergeant-major and a participant in the Battle of the Bulge.

When Hartung returned to Edwardsville after the war he decided he wanted to do something to serve his hometown. He counseled with his father, Louis H. Hartung, an alderman and an assistant postmaster here for 35 years, and it was decided young Clyde would seek a seat on the School Board. The trouble was, the election back in 1947 was to fill two seats on the board, and there were already two powerful candidates, well-known businessmen Harry Butler, an auto dealer, and Les Brockmeier, a banker. These two, said Hartung, were running as a pair, and would be hard to beat.

Louis and Clyde worked out an ingenious strategy. Clyde—the young, unmarried, "uneducated" candidate, as he puts it—deliberately ran as an underdog, a loner. He went door-to-door to sell himself, and he sent out 600 postcards to drum up votes. His message: Don't vote for two; vote for just one—me. That way, voters inclined to vote for Hartung and one of the other men would vote only for Hartung—which robbed one of the others of a vote. The outcome was that Hartung and Brockmeier got elected—not Butler and Brockmeier—and lots of people were mad at Hartung. In fact, some threatened to block Hartung from being seated at his inaugural board meeting at Columbus School. The "vote-for-one" strategy was illegal, they said. Also, Hartung added, "They crucified me in the Intelligencer."

Alderman Clyde Hartung, center, seen in profile at a meeting of the City Council.

Hartung went to a family friend and neighbor, Wilbur A. Trares, a highly respected county judge, and asked him to go with him to the school board meeting and, in effect, run interference. Trares walked into the meeting room with Hartung and there were gasps and murmurs of recognition. Superintendent E. L. Alexander asked the judge why he was there, and Trares said he was there to see his friend get the School Board seat he had won and therefore deserved. From then on, Hartung recalls, opposition melted and things went smoothly for him on the board.

One action stands out for Hartung as a member of the board: school integration. The year was 1950 and school districts were being ordered to admit black students to all schools. "Some cities were stalling around" about integration, said Hartung. "But we OK'd it. We had a big meeting down there in the Lincoln School gym, and there were six of them going to graduate from Lincoln, and I never will forget it—I never will forget it. They played that song, or sang that song, 'Now Is the Hour.' It just brought tears to your eyes because they finally got free to go to school out here. This was the best thing that happened to me when I was on the school board," Hartung said. Yes, there was opposition: "Some people were very bitter. You'd think they were still in the South."

Hartung went to work for Clark Oil Company and stayed there more than 30 years. he was a special tester in a laboratory and a member of the Operating Engineers. He was mayor for only one four-year term, but counts several proud accomplishments from that time.

He put the city's muscle behind an effort in 1973 to open a center for senior citizens in the old Rohrkaste Dairy building at 1006 North Main Street. The building had been acquired by Eden United Church of Christ, which was nearby and which wanted the area to expand parking. Hartung and other backers of the center negotiated with Eden's Pastor Wesley Bornemann and found him an eager supporter. The church agreed not to tear down the Rohrkaste building, but to lease it for a token amount. Thanks to people like Kay Kendall, Helen King and Dr. William Tudor of SIUE, the center became a reality and the original Rohrkaste building has been expanded and remodeled to serve more and more elderly people.

DOWNTOWN BECOMES AN ADMINISTRATIVE CENTER

A series of remodelings, demolitions and rebuildings changed the face of downtown. In 1964, the watertower, behind the city hall and fire station on North Main, a structure which had provided many a photographer with bird-seye views of North Main Street, had been razed. In March 1973, Rohrkaste Dairy, 1003 North Main, closed its doors, ending a family business which had started with a milk route after World War I. Remodeled in 1973, the Rohrkaste business became the Senior Citizens Center within the year. In November 1973, the last remnant of the Leland Hotel, most of which had been torn down before World War I to build the Edwardsville National Bank, was taken down. The Leland Barbershop, which had been operating under various owners since the 1880s, was no more. In 1978, another reminder of Edwardsville's fading connection with agricultural business, the Dippold Brothers grain elevator complex at West High and North Second Streets, came down. The elevator's site would soon be occupied by the new Madison County Jail, under construction the same year.

St. Louis Street at the corner of North Main, showing Leland Hotel and Vanzo's Tap Room in 1960.

This undated aerial photo, probably from the 1950s, shows a North Main with buildings now gone and tree-covered areas now asphalted.

The transformation of North Main Street continued during the 1980s, beginning in March of that year with the leveling of the 109-year-old Gerber Building, which had recently housed a Woolworth store and, between 1970 and 1980, Jessie's Cafe, run by Jessie Brown. The Gerber Building was razed to make way for Cassens and Sons' expanded auto sales lot. The end of the Gerber building was followed in April 1982, by the demolition of the old county jail and sheriff's residence, which had been built in 1869. The County's action aroused bitter but unheeded protests by citizens who wanted to preserve the sheriff's residence as an historic monument.

The new Madison County Jail was completed in 1979.

Crowds visit and look for bargains at the "Hexabuckle" Sidewalk sale of July 1963.

Edwardsville Motor Service, one of the last farm implement-repair places in town, stood on Randle Street, where the county jail is now. The business was run by Joyce and Dave Bardelmeier. It is seen in 1965, the courthouse is in the background.

This building served as the residence for the Madison County sheriff. It was built between 1869 and 1871. The structure was one of the few examples of Second Empire architecture in the city. It was razed in 1982.

KEEPING COUNTY GOVERNMENT DOWNTOWN

The final attempt to take the seat of county government out of Edwardsville—or at least downtown Edwardsville—came in the mid-1970s when the county board faced the need for a new jail. As in the past, the attempt was thwarted by local businessmen who took action.

Lloyd Schwarz took over as executive vice-president of the Edwardsville Area Chamber of commerce in 1971 and spent time in those early years hanging around the courthouse, which was just across St. Louis Street from the chamber office. Schwarz says he learned a lot from those visits to the courthouse. County employees had begun to resent the complaints of downtown merchants that the county people were hogging the best parking places and thereby discouraging shoppers. The county workers, after all, were bringing a certain amount of business to downtown Edwardsville. But there was bad feeling and a decision on where to locate the new county jail loomed. Although the courthouse and most of the county offices were downtown, there was no land available for a jail. There was, however, plenty of land, already owned by the county, on the south end of town, around the Madison County Nursing Home. Yes, it would be mighty inconvenient to have the jail two miles from the courthouse. On the other hand, there was room enough down there to build a brand new courthouse, plus a county administration building as well. If that happened, downtown Edwardsville would wither and die.

Schwarz made use of SIUE urban studies students to do a downtown survey as a class project. The survey found that, yes, there were parking problems and resulting bad feeling. But it also found that, despite the bad feeling, the courthouse meant a very great deal to the merchants of Edwardsville; by an overwhelming majority, they wanted the seat of county government to remain where it was. As Schwarz put it, "We found that the courthouse was worth a nice chunk of money to the merchants."

Schwarz went to Clyde Hartung, then mayor of Edwardsville (1973-1977) and got his help in rounding up a small group of downtown movers and shakers to see what could be done to keep the county happy. A committee was formed under co-chairmen Albert Cassens, of Cassens & Sons Inc., the auto dealer, and Arthur Boeker, chairman of the board of the Edwardsville National Bank & Trust Co. Under these two powerful men, the committee raised $200,000 to put together a land package just west of downtown. This amount included the $40,000 appraised value of the Knights of Columbus hall, a former residence, on Center Street. Parts of Center and Benton streets were obliterated in the deal. The jail would face Randle Street on the south. The committee turned their money over to the county board and county government stayed downtown.

In 1980, the new jail opened and, two years later, after efforts by preservationists to save it, the 1870s sheriff's residence on North Main Street and the jail behind it, were demolished. The county allowed the iron fencing at the sidewalk line to stand, and constructed a small park where the old buildings had been.

—Dick Norrish

In 1983, Cassens & Sons opened its new lot adjacent ot the dealership to celebrate 50 years in business.

Albert Cassens, a leading businessman in the community. Lloyd Schwarz of the Edwardsville Chamber of Commerce noted in 1988 that "most major things in the community have had his blessing and that guarantees they will be successful."

BETTY MALONEY AND HISTORIC EDWARDSVILLE

Betty Maloney arrived in Edwardsville in 1969. She devoted many of her talents to community service. Although she moved away in 1989, she left a mark that will endure. Appointed to the Human Relations Commission by Mayor Clyde Hartung in the 1970s, she helped to revitalize it and, while serving, complied a study of housing in Edwardsville that showed a clear pattern of racial discrimination since the 19th century. She assisted in the development of a successful application for federal money to set up the Edwardsville Township Community Improvements Corporation, a not-for-profit group providing new roofs, repairs to foundations, insulation, and minor repairs for poorer individuals living in sub-standard housing. Maloney also joined Elaine Burrus, John Celuch, Ed Kane Sr. and Carl Lossau in drafting an ordinance establishing the city's Historic Preservation Commission. In addition, she became intensely interested in Edwardsville's history and compiled thousands of pages of information and an archive of photographs and data on most of the town's buildings. Her studies of housing patterns, town history and buildings now form part of the collections of the Madison County Historical Society. According to Maloney, membership in the League of Women Voters inspired many of her interests. In 1978, she received the Jefferson Award for Distinguished Public Service at the Local Community Level, a competition sponsored by KSD-TV in St. Louis, one of only 6 winners chosen from 600 nominees within a 50-county service area. Maloney counted the months of her years in Edwardsville with bricks from demolished buildings. "Oh dear," she would say, "this was a three brick month!"

During the 1980s, the owners of several well-known, long-established businesses on North Main Street retired. Helen Auerbach, who had come to Edwardsville from Ashley, North Dakota, with her husband, Nate, in 1937, to found Auerbach's clothing store, sold her store in 1981, after 45 years. In 1984, the Shupack sisters, Ester and Celia, who had sold shoes for 40 years in a family business that dated back to 1906, also retired. Celia Shupak had taken over the store in 1943, when their father, Abe Shupak, the founder, died, and while three of four brothers were overseas in service. Sister Ester joined her in 1947. By the end of the 1980s, these businesses, which had kept their names under new owners, were closed, ending an era in the history of downtown Edwardsville.

The first block of West Vandalia Street during a blizzard of 1978 looks hemmed-in by buildings, the elevators on the left and Wells Tire on the right. The elevators were demolished; Wells moved.

In April of 1982 a tornado struck Edwardsville, causing considerable damage to area homes and businesses.

Jack Minner's Phillips 66 has survived the demolitions since the 1950s.

HELEN AUERBACH RECALLS COMING TO EDWARDSVILLE IN 1937

"We left Ashley [North Dakota] on the fourth of November, 1936. We went to the polls and voted for Roosevelt, and then we left. . . . as we passed Edwardsville, I said, 'Here's a town I'd like to live in.' Those were my exact words. We had a salesman with us, and he said there was a store for sale here. The owner was Julia Hoffmeir. The whole family came back to Edwardsville that Sunday, and we bought the store later and named it Auerbach's. It was a small store, a very small store, and you know what we paid for it? We bought that store for $2,700. And we got 600 dresses with it. We thought we made a pretty good buy. . . . My prediction when I came here turned out to be right: We found nothing but fine people in Edwardsville and the surrounding area."

Interview with Dick Norrish, 1981

TOM EAKER, BARBER, ON CHANGES DOWNTOWN, AUGUST 1996

"Hundreds of people lived downtown. . . . You don't have that anymore. When 5:30 rolls around, you don't have anything. The perimeter changed as businesses moved out to A & W. This is a major factor why businesses are not here anymore."

FRANK VANZO RECALLS ORIGINS OF THE MINE RUN UNIVERSITY

"You can't say that MRU was formed, created or was organized—nothing like that. It just sort of evolutionized—that's a word?

You see, during the depression when there was no air-conditioning, the out-of-work coal miners used to lie around the courthouse yard. When they'd see a beer salesman come in the saloon, they'd all come over here. They knew he'd be good for at least four or five nickel beers apiece.

And then they'd talk. My goodness, how they would talk—about religion, philosophy—you name it, they talked about it. But mostly they talked about people, people who lived right here in Edwardsville. They got to cataloguing everybody, like 'he's stuck-uppish' or 'he's livin' over his head.' But for those they liked, there was a special phrase: 'He's mine run.' That meant, 'he's average—just like us—like mine run coal.'

Well, some of the professional people and others around town heard about the wonderful kind of educational conversations going on here and began dropping in. And pretty soon people would say to each other, 'Let's go down to the university for a beer—you know, Mine Run University.' And I guess that's how it all got started."

St. Louis Post-Dispatch *September 8, 1966*

MARYANN PAPROTH, ANTIQUE DEALER, ON CHANGES DOWNTOWN, JUNE 1996

"There were houses, new houses, and apartments on Main Street. It used to be we knew everyone by their first name. Now, it's a rare occasion when you see someone you know. . . . On Main Street, you can't buy a sheet, pillowcase, towel, a dress or a pair of shoes. Remember Mode O'Day, Libson Shop, Auerbachs, and Shupacks? Schwartz's is there—Ballweg's always had such a nice soda fountain. . . . It was a large drugstore. I can't get over the change in the Library. I appreciate it."

A culminating sign of changing times downtown was the closing and demolition in 1988 of a town center for more than 50 years, Vanzo's Tavern, home of the legendary Mine Run University, at 110 St. Louis Street, across from the Courthouse. Louis Vanzo, the family patriarch, came to Edwardsville from Livingston in 1925 and took over Pfeiffer's Hotel at 323 St. Louis Street. In 1933, when Prohibition ended, Louis Vanzo opened a bar at the hotel. His sons, Frank and Jim bought the taproom in 1954 when Louis became ill. Frank Vanzo died in 1973, leaving brother Jim in charge. The Mine Run University moved to its St. Louis Street location in 1940. Filled with Americana, such as Franklin Roosevelt campaign posters and pre-prohibition beer labels, donated by customers over the years, Vanzo's rivaled many museums. "All kinds of people come here," said Jim Vanzo in 1980, "Lawyers, judges, farmers, businessmen, gamblers, drunks. It's never mattered who. Everybody's got their own worth. We called the place a Mine Run University. Famous for sending all regular customers a birthday card, Vanzo's bartenders also kept an encyclopedia, dic-

Jim Vanzo, philosopher behind the bar.

tionaries, and books of record behind the bar to settle disputes between customers. Jim Vanzo remembered "the changing of the guard" downtown, early in the morning. As he was leaving his tavern, Jack Minner would be opening his Phillips 66 station on West Vandalia, lawyer Harry Armstrong would be arriving at his office, and Bob Schwartz would be unlocking his drug store. What did Vanzo's do for the city of Edwardsville? Jim Vanzo summed it up: "We kept the lights on downtown."

During the last 40 years, a series of buildings have been constructed in the downtown area which provide the city with a legacy of modern architecture. The new county office building, completed in 1993, while complimenting the courthouse, dwarfs older structures on Main Street. What was once a more harmonious mixture of two-to-five-story buildings on Main Street has given way to an eclectic and random blending of the historic with the recent. The feeling of a small town, once conveyed by the blocks of varied stores on Main Street, has been replaced by the ambience of an urban administrative center. A gem among downtown structures, a building which, in scale and openness keeps the atmosphere of a small city, is the new City Hall at 118 Hillsboro, created by remodeling and refacing a building which had most recently housed a Sears catalogue store.

Florists' Mutual Insurance headquarters, at 500 St. Louis Street, opened in 1959, with its simple lines and pale marble overlay is a handsome near-downtown building. Actually, it's two buildings: the one-story structure dates from 1959; the three-story building behind, from 1973. Florists' does business nationwide.

This Madison County Administration Building was designed to complement the 1915 courthouse next door. The steps in this photo mark where Purcell Street used to be.

Richards Brick built a small administration building in 1964–of brick, of course–and installed a display patio with this elegant serpentine wall. As the housing boom continues in the area, Richards continues to be a major employer.

The First Federal Savings and Loan building, constructed in 1966 at 300 St. Louis Street, features attractive landscaping plus an unusual tubular glassed-in elevator in the two-story windowed section at left. While the elevator does move customers between the parking lot and the main business floor, its purpose is as much for fun as function.

Workmen in the process of creating Edwardsville's new City Hall put a new facade on the old Sears building at 118 Hillsboro.

The new City Hall, opened in 1995.

THINKING ABOUT CHANGE AND CONTINUITY

Edwardsville in the last half of the twentieth century remains a fine, comfortable place to live, but it has changed notably in the last 50 years. From a mecca for European immigrants and African-American migrants from the South, it has evolved into a small suburban city, a bedroom community in America's heartland. Its large employers are no longer industrial. Downtown, once filled with factory workers and farmers on Saturday night, now hosts crowds of jurors and government employees during weekdays only. The U.S. Radiator plant on East Vandalia Street and Wagner Electric, on the grounds of the old N. O. Nelson Company, both closed in the 1950s. Richards Brick is the only manufacturer left. Farmers go elsewhere to buy machinery and get it repaired. Southern Illinois University and the Madison County Courthouse now provide the largest number of jobs. Many residents commute to work in other communities. The population exceeds 18,000. Yet, despite these transformations, the Public Library in City Park, the Senior Citizens Center, the YMCA, the new Watershed Nature Center, the Edwardsville *Intelligencer* and certain communal events like the Halloween Parade and Thursday evening City Band concerts in the summer still provide places and occasions for townspeople of diverse origins to mingle.

Churches and clubs, local sporting events, high school graduation, and the friendly smiles of local residents, continue to nourish in those who settle here a sense of place. Highway 157 winds down the ridge of Tanyard Hill, past the high school and into the town, perhaps reminding drivers of the Indian trail it once was. Main Street still straddles a ridge of Cahokia Creek's watershed. In 2008, the Courthouse will have occupied the same ground for 150 years. Many residents, old and new, maintain their awareness of Edwardsville as an historic community.

E'VILLE

Sometimes, Edwardsville can be a mouthful. It's got 12 letters and three syllables. It's longer than, say, Troy or Alton or Hamel. In recent years, as many of us have become obsesses with speed, our city's name has often gotten truncated, chopped up, squeezed, shortened.

In the 1980s, the misnomer Eddersville came into use—but only for native Edwardsvillians. The use of Eddersville by newcomers was considered, well, inappropriate, for some reason. Newcomers were allowed to say Edardsville. Or something like that.

Some of the young athletic teams began using E'ville on their uniforms despite the obvious connotation of something we prayerfully beg to be delivered from. Well, young people are eternally optimistic, by and large, and E'ville fits nicely on a sports uniform. Cheerleaders, who have to fit the city's name into cheers shouted intelligibly above the din of fans in a gymnasium have come up with Eds-ville.

So you can take your choice. The postmaster, however, would prefer Edwardsville, spelled correctly, followed by all nine Zip Code numbers.

Dick Norrish, 1996

The Leclaire Centennial Committee, civic-minded neighbors, pose for a formal portrait taken by Jerry Thirion in 1990. Front row: Karen Hangsleben (Chairman), Diane Jacober, Bob Blain. Second row: Bill Freymuth, Bennett Dickmann, Kenny Krumeich, Delores Story Kaufmann, Janet Foehrkolb, Helen Buford, Bonnie Wherned. Third row: Mary Blain, Lisa Kenney, Debby Niebur. Fourth row: Carl Lossau, John Abbott, Betty McKinnon, Donna Simons, Laurie Kocur, Jim Fralinger, Jean Hughes, Cindy Cassens.

In 1996, Leclaire Lake got a cleaning and a new fountain, the latter paid for by hundreds of community donations.

Supported by Edwardsville's taxpayers, the City Library was remodeled in 1990. In 1991, the expansion and renovation, which added 12,000 square feet to the 8,000 square foot building, won the top award in a contest sponsored by the Southern Illinois Chapter of the American Institute of Architects.

Viuda True, Lillian Chrissman, Clara Barth, and Ruth Bartels quilting at the Senior Citizens Center in the remodeled Rohrkaste Dairy building at 1003 North Main. The Center opened in 1973 and doubled its space in 1984. Ed Kane, Sr. designed the addition.

POSTSCRIPT

Were the ghost of Edwardsville's namesake to come to town, he would be lost. Coming from Kaskaskia, Ninian Edwards would take the Bluff Road along the American Bottoms, come up by Judy Creek to high land and enter Edwardsville on what is now Highway 159. Going down Troy Road, would he recognize the home of his close friend, Benjamin Stephenson, now painted white, stripped of its fields and orchards, and occupied by a college fraternity? As a classically educated man, he might recognize the Greek letters on the Stephenson House. Riding on, he might remember City Park, on land he donated to the town, a place now the site of several public monuments and a library beyond the wildest dreams of Edwardsville's founders. Looking for the many trees that marked the landscape of Upper Town and seeing the gleaming white marble courthouse with its now modest vegetation, he might think, "at last a building worthy of a county that stretches to the border of Canada." In Lower Town, location of his original activities, he would discover a modest city neighborhood devoid of public buildings. Pogue's store has been transformed into a upscale restaurant. Our founder's 1805 cabin hides under an unassuming residential facade. Cahokia Creek, made straighter in 1911, is now bridged by a four-lane road. Fort Russell's location has been lost to history. Yet, Ninian Edwards might recognize the pride that residents of the late 20th century feel in their old town, still alive and vibrant after almost 200 years.

EDWARDSVILLE TODAY

Children's playground at Township Park built by the Rotary Club with all labor provided by Edwardsville citizens.

Couple enjoying a daily issue of the *Edwardsville Intelligencer*.

Officers of the Women's Federated Club, an African-American women's service club active since 1929, were photographed in 1962 for the Sesquicentennial edition of the "I". From the left, front row: Alberta Isom, treasurer, Blanche Lewis, chaplain. Back row, Roberta Shaw Spiller, secretary, Ethel Aitch Shaw, president, Alma Aitch Jackson, assistant secretary.

Modern sports phenomenon shown at the YMCA soccer field.

Marvin "Preach" Webb, an Edwardsville "Goodwill Ambassador."

Flags line Sunset Cemetery on Memorial Day.

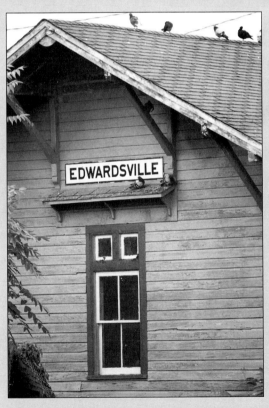

Edwardsville Leclaire Depot awaits its place in Edwardsville's future.

Edwardsville High School Tiger Marching Band awaits the beginning of the Little League Parade.

211

ACKNOWLEDGEMENTS

We thank the following people and institutions for special assistance, encouragement, and inspiration: Dr. John Abbott, historian, archivist, and citizen, who took the necessary steps to launch the project; Marian Sperling, Librarian, MCHS, who offered invaluable help in research as well as critical comment on chapters; Anna Symanski, Director, MCHS, who facilitated our use of the rich MCHS collections; Martha Hansen and Maxine Hogue, MCHS Staff, who frequently lent their expertise and knowledge of local history; Angela Farrell and Staff, Edwardsville Public Library, who facilitated research by loaning microforms and by unfailing courtesy; Louisa Bowen, Director, and Steve Kerber, Staff, SIUE Archives; the Bank of Edwardsville, who subsidized the publication; Joe Meyer, who allowed his unchallenged mastery of Edwardsville sports history to flow into these pages; Nola Jones, Edwin Gerling and Betty Maloney, who generously shared results of their own research; David Werner, Provost of SIUE, who granted one member of the team a sabbatical during spring 1996; Steven Hughes, for displaying with good will his understanding of N. O. Nelson's Leclaire; our families and friends, who loved us through piles of notes and photos and innumerable phone calls and meetings.

CONTRIBUTORS

Myrtle Ahart
Grady Ambuehl
Marylynn Armstrong
Fred and Clara Autenrieb
Evelyn Ballweg
Dave Bardelmeier
Hugh Barnett
Edward Bauer
Errol Berlemann
Prof. Robert Blain
Mary Blixen
Clarence Bohm
Louisa Bowen, SIUE Archives
Karen Brengard
Herb Brockmeier
Warren Brown

Winston Brown
Mary Barnsback Byron
Cassens Transport, Inc.
Fred Carpenter
Mary Carpenter
Dorothy Catalano
Charles Caulk
Susy Wilson Close
Bob Coultas
Louise "Jetty" Deitz
Helen Delicate
Kathy Dickmann
Suzanne Dietrich
Kay Ballweg Dudacek
Tom Eaker
Edwardsville Public Library Staff

Margarite Eickhoff
Shawn Etzkorn
Ken Evers, Jr.
Angela Farrell
Bonnie Mottar Farrington
Dorothy Fink
Carol Fruit
Carol Genteman
Ed Gerling
Fred Gillham
Jim and Linda Ginalick
Joe Gregor
Phoebe Hamlin
Loni Hansel
Donna Brockmeier Hart

Cay Hartnagel
Clyde Hartung
Gladys Barraclough Hayter
Olga Herberer
J. Ray Hessel
Clarence and Frances Hoppe
Evelyn Ireland
Judy Isselhardt
Pastor Steve Jackson
Malweda Jason
Jessi Jumper Johnson
Nola Jones
Jody Keating
Steve Kerber
George Key
Prof. Stanley Kimball

Jeff Lantz
Jerry Legow
Gary and Dodie Levi
Freida Lewis
Joe Lucco
Susan Lucco
Madison County Historical Museum
Joe Meyer
Mary Michaels, IL State Library
Chester Michel
Jack Minner
Frank Novak
Jean Oates
Meg Oberlag
Sam OVerbeck

Mary Ann Paproth
Jane Ponder
Prof. Shirley Portwood
Ray Rathert
Norman Rosenthal
Joe Rotter
Freg Schwager
Lloyd Schwarz
Kenneth Shaw
Leigh Sills
Roberta Spiller
Carol Sporrer
Anna St. Pierre
Brooke Stapleton
Dolly and Cliffort Stolte
Fred Stone
Nancy Giacomelli Suhre

Dr. Wayne Temple, IL State Archives
TheBANK of Edwardsville
Ernie Tosovsky
Mickey Van Hooser
Jim and Sandy Vanzo
Earl Vaugniaux
Thad Vaugniaux
Roger Weber
Prof. Joseph Weber
Nancy Weeks
Peggy Wehlint
Rev. Warren Wider
Betty Willard
Prof. Rudolph Wilson
Edna Wolfe
Helen Zahradka

PHOTO CREDITS

CHAPTER 1. Illustrations, p. 1, courtesy of Lovejoy Library, Louisa Bowen Archives, SIUE. Maps, p. 11, were drawn by Steven Hughes. Plat map, p. 14, is from Madison County Clerk's Records.

Unless otherwise acknowledged in captions, other photos and illustrations in this chapter come from collections of the Madison County Historical Society (hereafter MCHS).

CHAPTER 2. Photographs and illustrations in this chapter come from the collections of MCHS, with five exceptions: on p. 25, farmer with steel plow, courtesy Karen Mateyka; "Smiling Lincoln," p. 38, courtesy of Southern Illinois University at Edwardsville (SIUE); regimental flags, p. 41, courtesy of Ed Gerling from his book, *THE ONE HUNDRED SEVENTEENTH ILLINOIS INFANTRY VOLUNTEERS, 1862-1865* (Privately published, 1992); the quilt, from the MCHS collections, p. 42, photographed by Debbie Caulk (hereafter DC).

CHAPTER 3. With the following exceptions, photographs and illustrations in this chapter come from the collections of the MCHS. The following photographs are reproduced courtesy of the Illinois State Historical Library: p. 44, St. Boniface Church; p. 48, the interurban; p. 50 Madison No. 3; p. 68, the St. James Hotel; p, 70, the Palace Store; p. 77 Wolf's Lake. On p. 71, the Bohm fireplace, is courtesy of Clarence Bohm. On p. 75, the first fire "engine" was taken by Richard Norrish (hereafter RN). On p. 84, Charles Boeschenstein's home, is reproduced courtesy of Gary and Dodi Levi.

CHAPTER 4. With the following exceptions, photographs and illustrations in this chapter come from the collections of the MCHS. St. Mary's confirmation class, p. 92, comes from St. Mary's Parish 150th Anniversary book; residence at 314 Clay and residence on Union Street, p. 93, by DC; women stirring applebutter and Olga Heberer, p. 94, courtesy of Olga Heberer. Turner Hall, p. 98, by DC. Photos of Czechs, pp. 99-100, courtesy of Louisa Bowen Archives, SIUE. Columbus School, p. 108, and the Post Office, p. 125, appear courtesy of the Illinois State Historical Library. On p.109, the Scott family and Mt. Joy Baptist Church appear courtesy of Fern Stone. Lincoln School belles is reproduced courtesy of Nola Jones (hereafter NJ).

CHAPTER 5. With the following exceptions, photographs and illustrations in this chapter come from the collections of the MCHS: Catalano's truck, p. 140, private collection (hereafter PC); First Presbyterian, 1924, and windows, 1983, p. 144, DC; St. John's Methodist, 1924, p. 145, DC; Intelligencer building, p. 147, DN; bungalows and Griffin house, p. 148, DC; Ed Ballweg, Jr., and Ballweg's Drugs, p. 155, PC; WPA sidewalk, p. 155, DC; Hi-Way Tavern, p. 156, PC; Mottars and Mottar's Drugs, p. 158, PC; Lincoln School team, p. 160, NJ; Cathcart's, p. 161, PC; St. Boniface class, p. 162, PC; Weeks and dirt racing, p. 163, PC; Waldo Vuagniaux, p. 164, PC; Birdseye and snowy view, p. 165, PC; Jones family, p. 165, NJ; Ernest Tosovsky, p. 165, DN; Queen candidates, p. 169, PC; John Gemoules, p. 170, PC.

CHAPTER 6. The following are from collections of the MCHS: Steinmeyer home, p. 175, N.O Nelson School and 1908 Class Reunion, p. 181, Inglis Fletcher portrait and home, p. 183, postwar paraders, p. 184, Lions Club and Moose, p. 187, Terry House, p. 189, "pioneers" and fundraisers, p. 190, Lesley Marks and MCHS, p. 191, Travous House, p. 192, Tiger baseball, p. 197, Coach Lucco, p. 196, Bob and Carolyn Hoskins and Morris Bradshaw, p. 198, St. Louis Street and aerial photo, p. 201, sidewalk sale, p. 202, and Leclaire Committee, p. 208. These pictures are by DC: Stolte House, cottages, p. 176; "Glory Be," p. 177; original Montclaire, p. 179; Pinebrook home, p. 181; Frozen Foods, Kriege, p. 182; YMCA, p. 189; Nature Center, Wesley Chapel, Stahly Cartage, p. 192; Jail, Sheriff's residence, p. 202; Tornado, Minner's, p. 204; County Administration, p. 206; Richards Brick, First Federal, City Hall, p. 207; Leclaire fountain, p. 208; Library, p. 209. The following belong to PCs: Site, p. 174; A & W, Dog'n Suds, p. 175; Max Autenrieb, p. 177; Workmen, p. 179; Little League, pp. 184-186; League, p. 188; Swimmers, p. 189; Hockey team, p. 196; Stapleton, p. 197; EHS, p. 198; Bums, Cheerleaders, p. 199; Motor Service, p. 202; Cassens, p. 203; and Vanzo, p. 205. The following were taken by RN: Aerials, p. 176, 178, 180, and early SIUE, 195; Schoolbus, p. 180; Farm sale, p. 182; Straube, p. 183; Hoppe Park, p. 187; Morris, p. 198; Festival, p. 194; Hartung, p. 200; Blizzard, p. 204; Quilters, p. 209. University News Service, SIUE, supplied: R. Wilson, p. 178; B. Guelker, p. 194; Aerial (recent SIUE), p. 195.

BIBLIOGRAPHY

Circuit Court, Chancery, and Naturalization Records of Madison County before 1900. Southern Illinois University at Edwardsville Archives. Lovejoy Library.

COURT RECORDS OF MADISON COUNTY, ILLINOIS, 1818-1821. Complete with Index by Bob Johnston. 1983. Records copied from a typed transcription completed by Edna Feldner in April 1939, for the Works Progress Administration. Edwardsville Public Library.

Caulk Collection. Photographs and slides of buildings, streets and historic events in City of Edwardsville by Debbie Caulk. City of Edwardsville Historic Preservation Commission.

EDWARDSVILLE INTELLIGENCER. 1862 - present. Available on microfilm at the Edwardsville Public Library.

EDWARDSVILLE INTELLIGENCER INDUSTRIAL ISSUE. December 17, 1895.

EDWARDSVILLE INTELLIGENCER CENTENNIAL EDITION. August 31, 1912.

EDWARDSVILLE INTELLIGENCER 75TH ANNIVERSARY ISSUE. November 14, 1937.

EDWARDSVILLE INTELLIGENCER SESQUICENTENNIAL EDITION. September 4, 1962.

EDWARDSVILLE INTELLIGENCER "Panorama '86: An A-to-Z Guide To Central Madison County. September 19, 1986.

EDWARDSVILLE INTELLIGENCER 125TH ANNIVERSARY EDITION. October 2, 1987.

EDWARDSVILLE SPECTATOR. May 29, 1819 - October 20, 1826. Available on microfilm at the Edwardsville Public Library, at the Madison County Historical Society, and at SIUE's Lovejoy Library.

Federal Census (Manuscript). Madison County. Selected years available on microfilm at Edwardsville Public Library.

Flagg Family Papers. Southern Illinois University at Edwardsville Archives. Lovejoy Library.

Fletcher, Inglis. PAY, PACK, AND FOLLOW: THE STORY OF MY LIFE. New York: Henry Holt and Company, 1959.

Ford, Thomas. A HISTORY OF ILLINOIS: FROM ITS COMMENCEMENT AS A STATE IN 1818 TO 1847. Rodney O. Davis, ed. Urbana: University of Illinois Press, 1995.

Johnston, Bob, ed. RECORDS AND INDENTURES MADISON COUNTY, ILLINOIS: 1813-1815, VOL. I, WITH INDEX. 1982. Typescript in Madison County Historical Society.

Lawrence, Barbara and Branz, Nedra. THE FLAGG CORRESPONDENCE: SELECTED LETTERS, 1816-1854. Carbondale and Edwardsville: Southern Illinois University Press, 1986.

League of Women Voters, Papers. Southern Illinois University at Edwardsville Archives. Lovejoy Library.

Madison County Historical Society. Photographic Files.

_____. Vertical File: Edwardsville. Files in the Society's Library contain information on most of the topics in this book.

MADISON COUNTY POOR FARM DEATH RECORDS INDEXES INCLUDING BURIALS IN POTTER'S FIELD. Edwardsville: Madison County Historical Society, 1986.

Norrish Collection. Photographs and interviews related to the history of Edwardsville primarily after 1962. Privately held by Dick Norrish.

Polk & Company, R. L. EDWARDSVILLE CITY DIRECTORY. Taylor, Michigan: R. L. Polk & Company [Various years]

Powell, Paul, comp. COUNTIES OF ILLINOIS: THEIR ORIGINS AND EVOLUTION. Springfield, n.d. Maps.

Public School Statistics of Madison County, Illinois. Edwardsville: EDWARDSVILLE INTELLIGENCER, 1886.

Records of the County Clerk, Madison County, Illinois, 1818-1996. Office of the County Clerk, Madison County Administration Building, Edwardsville, Illinois.

Revised and Consolidated Ordinances of the City of Edwardsville, Madison county, Illinois. Edwardsville: EDWARDSVILLE INTELLIGENCER, 1927.

Reynolds, John. REYNOLD'S HISTORY OF ILLINOIS. MY OWN TIMES: EMBRACING ALSO THE HISTORY OF MY LIFE. Chicago: Chicago Historical Society, 1879.

Robinson, Benaiah. ILLINOIS FARMER'S ALMANAC, FOR THE YEAR OF OUR LORD, 1832, BEING BISSEXTILE ON LEAP YEAR. AND (AFTER JULY 4) THE 57TH OF AMERICAN INDEPENDENCE. Number 1. Edwardsville: Sawyer & Angervine, 1832. Copy in Madison County Historical Society.

Royce, Charles C., comp. INDIAN LAND CESSIONS IN THE UNITED STATES. Bureau of American Ethnology Annual Report, No. 18, Part 2 (Washington, D.C.: GPO, 1899): 662-67.

THE KICKAPOO, 1927-1928. Newspaper edited by Louise Travous. Available in Madison County Historical Society.

Waters (Watters), Joel E. Correspondence, June 1, 1856-January 13, 1865.Typescript in Madison County Historical Society.

WORKS PROGRESS ADMINISTRATION, NEWSPAPER FILES FOR EDWARDSVILLE, ILLINOIS. Madison County Historical Society.

Wolf Family Civil War Letters. Typescript in Madison County Historical Society.

Secondary Works

A CENTURY OF PROGRESS AND A PROMISE OF TOMORROW: EDEN UNITED CHURCH OF CHRIST, EDWARDSVILLE, ILLINOIS, 1868-1968. Privately printed, 1968.

Ades, John Irvine. THE CHURCH ON NORTH KANSAS STREET, BEING A FAMILIAR HISTORY OF THE FIRST PRESBYTERIAN CHURCH OF EDWARDSVILE ON THE OCCASION OF THE 175TH ANNIVERSARY OF ITS FOUNDING IN 1819. St. Louis: Mills Graphic Productions, Inc., 1993.

Brink, W. R. HISTORY OF MADISON COUNTY WITH BIOGRAPHICAL SKETCHES. Edwardsville: n.p., 1882.

_____. ILLUSTRATED ENCYCLOPEDIA AND ATLAS MAP OF MADISON COUNTY, ILLINOIS. St. Louis: Brink, McCormick, 1873.

Blain, Robert R. THE HISTORIC COOPERATIVE VILLAGE OF LECLAIRE, EDWARDSVILLE, ILLINOIS: A CENTENNIAL COLLECTION. Edwardsville: Leclaire Centennial Committee, 1990.

Broadway, James M. JAMES R. BROWN AND THE EDWARDSVILLE ILLINOIS INTELLIGENCER: 1862-1882. Southern Illinois University at Edwardsville: M.S. Thesis, 1978.

Buck, Solon Justus. ILLINOIS IN 1818. Springfield: Illinois Centennial Commission, 1917.

Cassens, Albert and Rami, Tom. HUMBLE BEGINNINGS: THE HISTORY OF CASSENS TRANSPORT, 1933-1935. Dallas: Heritage Press, 1995.

Gerling, Edwin G. THE ONE HUNDRED SEVENTEENTH ILLINOIS INFANTRY VOLUNTEERS (THE MCKENDREE REGIMENT): 1862-1865. Privately Published by the Author, 1992.

GAZETTEER OF MADISON COUNTY. Alton: James T. Hair, 1866.

Hammes, Raymond H. "Land Transactions in Illinois Prior to the Sale of Public Domain," JOURNAL OF THE ILLINOIS STATE HISTORICAL SOCIETY 77 (1984): 101-14.

Hermsmeyer, Rex. AN ANALYSIS OF HOUSING FOR BLACKS IN EDWARDSVILLE, ILLINOIS. Southern Illinois University at Edwardsville: M.S. Thesis, 1972.

Kane, Edward. DRAWINGS: AN ADDRESS BOOK. Edwardsville: Goshen Preservation Alliance, American Printing, 1989.

League of Women Voters. KNOW YOUR TOWN:

EDWARDSVILLE ILLINOIS. Privately published, 1976.

_____. STUDY OF EQUALITY OF HOUSING OPPORTUNITY IN EDWARDSVILLE. Privately published, 1968.

_____. Papers on Edwardsville Architecture. Typescripts in Madison County Historical Society.

Madison County Genealogical Society. MADISON COUNTY, ILLINOIS: HANDBOOK FOR GENEALOGICAL RESEARCHERS. Privately published, 1991.

Maloney, Betty. EDWARDSVILLE MINI-HISTORIES, 2 Vols. Privately Published, 1982.

_____. MISCELLANEOUS COLLECTIONS ON EDWARDSVILLE HISTORY, 2 Vols. n.d. City of Edwardsville Historic Preservation Commission.

_____. HOUSING PATTERNS IN THE CITY OF EDWARDSVILLE. Unpublished MS. Madison County Historical Society.

Matousek, Ladislaw. "The Beginning of Illinois Surveys," ILLINOIS LIBRARIES 53 (1971): 23-44.

Meyer, Pauline. KEEP YOUR FACE TO THE SUNSHINE: A LOST CHAPTER IN THE HISTORY OF WOMAN SUFFRAGE. Edwardsville: Alcott Press, 1980.

Norrish, Dick. BRICK IN THE LAND OF GOSHEN. Edwardsville: Goshen Preservation Alliance, 1988.

_____. CHURCH ARCHITECTURE IN EDWARDSVILLE. 1986. Goshen Preservation Alliance, 1986.

_____. A PICTORIAL HISTORY OF EDWARDSVILLE AND GLEN CARBON, 1800-1991. Edwardsville: EDWARDSVILLE INTELLIGENCER, 1991.

Norton, Wilbur Theodore, with associate editors, N. G. Flagg and J. S. Hoerner. CENTENNIAL HISTORY OF MADISON COUNTY, ILLINOIS, AND ITS PEOPLE: 1812-1912. Chicago and New York: The Lewis Publishing Company, 1912.

Nygard, Paul D. JUDGE JOSEPH GILLESPIE OF ILLINOIS: WHIG, KNOW NOTHING, REPUBLICAN. Southern Illinois University at Edwardsville: M.A. Thesis, 1992.

ONE HUNDRED YEARS OF ST. BONIFACE, 1868-1968. Privately published, 1968.

OUR 150 YEARS, 1812-1962: IN COMMEMORATION OF THE MADISON COUNTY SESQUICENTENNIAL. East 10 Publishing Co. Inc., 1962.

Raffaelle, Vivian Virginia. A HISTORY OF NINE MADISON COUNTY, ILLINOIS PUBLIC HIGH SCHOOL BANDS. Southern Illinois University at Edwardsville: M.S. Thesis, 1970.

Rathert, Ray C. FOR GOD AND COUNTRY: A HISTORY OF AMERICAN LEGION POST 199 AND AUXILIARY UNIT 199 EDWARDSVILLE, ILLINOIS, 1919-1979. Privately published, 1979.

Richardson, Betty and Henson, Dennis. SERVING TOGETHER: 150 YEARS OF FIREFIGHTING IN MADISON COUNTY, ILLINOIS. Collinsville, Illinois: Madison County Firefighters' Association, 1984.

Sesquicentennial Committee, St. Mary's Parish. SESQUICENTENNIAL HISTORY: ST. MARY'S CHURCH, 1842-1992. Privately Printed, 1992.

Williams, Nola Jones. LINCOLN SCHOOL MEMORIES: A HISTORY OF BLACKS IN EDWARDSVILLE, ILLINOIS. [Includes History of Mount Joy Baptist Church, 1869-1986, and Historical Sketch of Wesley Chapel A.M.E. Church, 1871-1985.] Privately published, 1986.

Thomas, Elizabeth. THE GOLDEN AGE OF EDWARDSVILLE THROUGH THE EYES OF THE RESIDENTS AT 744 ST. LOUIS STREET. Southern Illinois University at Edwardsville: M.A. Thesis, 1995.

Woods, William I., ed. PREHISTORIC AGRICULTURE: OBSERVATIONS FROM THE MIDWEST. Studies in Illinois Archeology, no. 8. Springfield: Illinois Historic Preservation Agency, 1992.

Zochert, Donald. "Illinois Water Mills, 1790-1818." JOURNAL OF THE ILLINOIS STATE HISTORICAL SOCIETY 65 (1972): 173-201.

INDEX

Pictured is the Madison County Historical Museum staff. Standing in the back are Anna Symanski (left), Museum Director, and Martha Hansen. Seated in front are Marion Sperling (left) and Maxine Hogue.

TheBANK of Edwardsville History

Edwardsville became a city in 1812. However, the town did not have a stable banking institution until Edward M. West and his son-in-law, Major William R. Prickett, founded "West & Prickett," later renamed "TheBANK of Edwardsville," on January 1, 1868. When it opened on the corner of Main and Purcell streets, TheBANK's original capital was only $10,000. Even with a growing population, most early Edwardsville banks failed due to faulty banking practices. In 1899, TheBANK began a period of growth by consolidating with the Madison County State Bank.

In the early 1900s, TheBANK grew even larger by absorbing the First National Bank and by constructing a new building on its original site, the corner of Main and Purcell. Customer accounts were protected by F.D.I.C. insurance for the first time in 1933. TheBANK installed an innovative new sign and became known as the bank at "The Time and Temperature Corner" in 1960. One year later, a sidewalk teller window was added for greater customer convenience. By the late 1960s, TheBANK experienced severe space shortages, and plans began for a more spacious facility at 330 West Vandalia.

In January 1972, the new facility opened with assets of $27 million. TheBANK took an innovative step by introducing its Magic Touch Automatic Teller Machine (ATM) Banking in 1977. (Today, TheBANK has

a total of 15 Magic Touch ATMs.) The following year, TheBANK moved forward again by installing its own computer processing department, one of the first banks in the area to do so. Magic Phone Banking was introduced in 1988 to service the surrounding region.

February 1990 marked the completion of TheBANK's next expansion program. The Main Office was enhanced with the construction of a two-story addition and six new drive-up lanes. This doubled the size of the Main Office to just under 40,000 square feet. In May of 1990, TheBANK acquired the Collinsville and Troy offices of the Madison County Federal Savings and Loan. The purchase was a natural extension of TheBANK's growing customer base in Madison County. TheBANK acquired the Alton office of the Olympic Federal Savings and Loan in March 1992 and opened a new banking center in Highland in January 1995. Today, TheBANK has 8 banking centers, serving Edwardsville, Madison County, and the surrounding metro-east.

Today, TheBANK remains the leading independent, locally-owned bank in Madison County with current assets exceeding half a billion dollars and a staff of over 230 employees. TheBANK of Edwardsville is proud of its tradition of service and its history of commitment to community involvement and participation.

TheBANK of Edwardsville Board of Directors

Front row (left to right): Olin A. Wetzel, Clinton H. Rogier, John A. Hunter, Jr., William S. Alexander. Back row (left to right): Mark S. Shashek, Robert L. Plummer, Robert A. Wetzel – President/CEO, Albert D. Cassens – Chairman of the Board, Kay Sharon Cassens, Allen Cassens, Donald L. Metzger.